PRODIGAL SONS

❦ *David Wyatt*

PRODIGAL SONS

A Study in Authorship and Authority

The Johns Hopkins University Press
Baltimore and London

Copyright © 1980 by The Johns Hopkins University Press

Manufactured in the United States of America

The Johns Hopkins University Press, Baltimore, Maryland 21218
The Johns Hopkins Press Ltd., London

Library of Congress Catalog Number 79-22930

ISBN 0-8018-2325-0

Library of Congress Cataloging in Publication data
will be found on the last printed page of this book.

For Libby

A certain man had two sons:

12. And the younger of them said to *his* father, Father, give me the portion of goods that falleth *to me*. And he divided unto them *his* living.

13. And not many days after the younger son gathered all together, and took his journey into a far country, and there wasted his substance with riotous living.

14. And when he had spent all, there arose a mighty famine in that land; and he began to be in want.

15. And he went and joined himself to a citizen of that country; and he sent him into his fields to feed swine.

16. And he would fain have filled his belly with the husks that the swine did eat: and no man gave unto him.

17. And when he came to himself, he said, How many hired servants of my father's have bread enough and to spare, and I perish with hunger!

18. I will arise and go to my father, and will say unto him, Father, I have sinned against heaven, and before thee,

19. And am no more worthy to be called thy son: make me as one of thy hired servants.

20. And he arose, and came to his father. But when he was yet a great way off, his father saw him, and had compassion and ran, and fell on his neck, and kissed him.

21. And the son said unto him, Father, I have sinned against heaven, and in thy sight, and am no more worthy to be called thy son.

22. But the father said to his servants, Bring forth the best robe, and put *it* on him; and put a ring on his hand, and shoes on *his* feet:

23. And bring hither the fatted calf, and kill *it;* and let us eat, and be merry:

24. For this my son was dead, and is alive again; he was lost, and is found. And they began to be merry.

25. Now his elder son was in the field: and as he came and drew nigh to the house, he heard musick and dancing.

26. And he called one of the servants, and asked what these things meant.

27. And he said unto him, Thy brother is come; and thy father hath killed the fatted calf, because he hath received him safe and sound.

28. And he was angry, and would not go in: therefore came his father out, and intreated him.

29. And he answering said to *his* father, Lo, these many years do I serve thee, neither transgressed I at any time thy commandment: and yet

thou never gavest me a kid, that I might make merry with my friends:

30. But as soon as this thy son was come, which hath devoured thy living with harlots, thou has killed for him the fatted calf.

31. And he said unto him, Son, thou art ever with me, and all that I have is thine.

32. It was meet that we should make merry, and be glad: for this thy brother was dead, and is alive again; and was lost, and is found.—Luke 15: 11-32

Contents

ᴥᶴ Acknowledgments

I owe a debt to my teachers and friends at Berkeley. Especially helpful were Gordon Taylor, who gave one of my chapters its first critical reading, and Andrew Griffin, who set me in the direction of my theme.

My colleagues at Virginia assisted in many ways. Daniel Albright, Paul Armstrong, William Kerrigan, Austin Quigley, and Stephen Railton each gave my early chapters the benefit of his intelligent scrutiny. Leo Damrosch supplied me with an invaluable anecdote. J. C. Levenson and David Levin offered welcome encouragement along the way.

John T. Irwin's faith in my project always took the form of finding ways to publish it. He deserves special thanks.

David McWhirter contributed with his imaginative research, and Eileen Zimmer smoothed the way to a conclusion with her peerless typing.

Chapter 3, "Hemingway's Uncanny Beginnings," originally appeared in the *Georgia Review*. Chapter 6, "Robert Penn Warren: The Critic as Artist," originally appeared in the *Virginia Quarterly Review*. Permission to reprint both articles here is gratefully acknowledged. I also wish to thank Mrs. Paul D. Summers, Jr., for giving permission to quote from the manuscripts of the William Faulkner Collections in the Manuscripts Department at the University of Virginia Library.

The Rembrandt painting used as the frontispiece to this volume is reprinted courtesy of the Hermitage, Leningrad.

My wife, always my most generous and critical reader, deserves more acknowledgment than a simple mention can bring.

✍ Introduction

THE MOMENT OF RETURN

One of William Blake's favorite Biblical passages was the parable of the Prodigal Son. His reading of it to Samuel Palmer proved unforgettable:

> I can yet recal it when, on one occasion, dwelling upon the exquisite beauty of the parable of the Prodigal, he began to repeat a part of it; but at the words, "When he was yet a great way off, his father saw him," could go no further; his voice faltered, and he was in tears.

At the crucial moment in the story, Blake is halted in his steps. Father and son are left stranded in the middle of the road. Perhaps it was the poignance of the completed verse that caused Blake to falter: ". . . and had compassion and ran, and fell on his neck, and kissed him." Whatever the reasons for Blake's inability to go on, his experience of the parable can be taken as emblematic of the careers discussed in this book. Each acts out its unique version of the parable, and each turns upon the moment of return Blake found so difficult to traverse.

Everything in the parable looks forward to this moment, yet the moment acquires value only by virtue of the story it completes. The frontispiece arrests the parable at the point of reconciliation. The father's hands rest upon the shoulders of the penitent son. All passion is spent. Whatever power the story had to move Blake has here been dispelled. Is this the truth of the parable, this moment of extreme quietude? In his many renderings of the story, Rembrandt places it almost always at the entrance to the father's house. He was moved most by the image of return. But whatever moment in the parable he had chosen to isolate, would the moment have become the parable? Dürer engraved the son in the fields with swine. Brancusi sculpted the son alone. In the failure of any one of these images to capture the full force of the parable, we are reminded that paintings or statues lack beginnings, middles, and ends.

xiii

They find themselves committed by their very nature to the truth of a moment. Only a story could capture this experience of falling, wandering, and returning. The parable embodies the very pattern of story itself; in our identification with the prodigal son, we discover that the possibility of transport depends upon a resolution separated from a departure by a suspenseful middle. In many ways, the parable is about the psychological conflict that generates narrative time.

The parable as told by Christ is uncanny. The plot is familiar—it is, we sense, the story of our own growing up. But the moral Christ draws is not one we usually celebrate in the light. The erring son is forgiven and valued above the obedient son. The elder brother protests against this injustice, but the audience is clearly expected to judge his complaint superfluous. If we think of the parable as a fantasy about psychological options, it seems to be one in which Christ himself wanders a moment from filial piety. All sympathy flows toward the brother who falls rather than the brother who stands firm. But in God's heaven, as Milton's account suggests, an older brother falls, a younger brother stands firm, and the father above all cherishes the ever-faithful son. Christ, as a storyteller at least, seems to entertain here the possibility of a reversal of roles between himself and Satan. His parable acknowledges an acute sense of division between filial options, even as he identifies himself, through the logic of the story, with the forbidden choice. The older son remains not only divided from his younger brother but, by virtue of having repressed the alternative he represents, separated as well from the possibility of authoring his own story. In having passed through both fall and return, the younger brother's story actually includes the older's: he simply takes it as his ending. The older brother's identity is framed by the father: "Son, thou art ever with me." Because the obedient son has always been only himself, there is no possibility of his coming upon himself. Moments of self-recognition entail the assertion of a fundamental doubleness ("he came to himself") that the obedient son rules out in his perpetually maintained piety. Christ's parable expresses his utter alienation from his dark double, since the cost of his obedience is to remain innocent of the very waywardness he has been sent to judge and redeem.

For the New Testament to occur, however, Christ must appear to imitate Satan's departure from his father's house. Christ's story of descent and wandering in the world is, in a sense, a divine parody of Satan's fall. Satan's story has priority over Christ's: without waywardness, obedience would have nothing to redeem. Satan may be doomed to perpetual fall, but without him, Christ is doomed to perpetual return. For his story to mean anything, he must seem at least to be tempted to incorporate his Satan, however clear it eventually becomes that there was no real chance of his ever doing so. It is only Adam's story that incorporates both Christ and Satan. His career, though ultimately resolved, remains truly at risk. He falls *and* wanders *and* returns. The story of the prodigal son is finally the parable of human story, of the simple fact that if a true middle requires a new departure from everything that is received, it can only resolve itself in an acknowledgment of what has gone before.

The story of the prodigal son is above all the story of a career, what happens on the road home. My interest here is less in the occurrence of the paradigm *within* individual works than *across* a developing body of them. In each essay I search for a decisive turn in a career, the moment when an author makes his accommodation with authority and ceases wrestling with his role as a son. For some, the moment insures future strength; for others, a waning of energy. If every son experiences an Oedipal conflict, these prodigal sons find themselves especially engaged in defining themselves within the terms of this conflict. The point is not to show that each of these authors undergoes such an experience, but rather to retrace the unique ways in which each is able to transform it into the drama of a career.

If I seem to isolate a moment, however, it is only to emphasize it as significant within a continuing process. As Warren says in *All the King's Men:* "Meaning is never in the event but in the motion through event. Otherwise we could isolate an instant in the event and say this is the event itself. The meaning. But we cannot do that. For it is the motion which is important." I try to trace, then, the eventuation of authorship. "Development" is perhaps the best word to describe this ingathering of force. The psychology I assume is developmental in that it conceives of the activity of writing as carrying an author *toward* a destination but also *through* stages which, as they are experienced, each carry with them their own sense of arrival.

My book has a plot of its own in which each chapter extends or resolves previous discussions. I begin with Henry James, whose father was a theorist of sonship.

Henry James senior held to a theology of perpetual reclamation in which the creating father could offer his creation nothing more cruel than independent being. His second son borrowed the trope of an author's relation to his work as that of a father to his offspring, and so tried to become the father in his art that he was wise enough to know he would never become in his life. The issue of filial piety became transformed for Henry James into the question of the right relation of an author to the often erring language of his works. Revision became the necessary corollary of creation. The tension between the freedom of the work to wander from its origin and the authority of the father to reclaim it surfaces most dramatically in the prefaces to the New York Edition. In the preface to *The Golden Bowl,* an older fatherly self forgives (proposes to rewrite), without omitting to chastise, the productions of a younger one. From the vantage point afforded by the preface, James seems to acquire authority in two broad and discontinuous movements, in a wayward creation and a curtailing self-criticism. The pattern would seem to serve a simple chronology: James's quest for authority begins with the career proper but is only completed with the work of the revising New York Edition. Yet these apparently successive stages prove increasingly simultaneous as one becomes aware of the interplay between "precipitation" and "reflexion" that informs James's work from the beginning. Since *The American* suffered the greatest expenditure of belated parental charity, I have tried to show how the themes and strategies of the novel anticipate and even partially resolve the question of what a creator owes to his creation. If James achieves authority by self-consciously repossessing what he has created, these activities so continuously interpenetrate one another as to afford no dramatic moment in which he finally assumes a father's authority.

With Yeats the case is almost the reverse. He has left us an embarrassing abundance of those moments on which a career can be said to turn. Biography here helps to isolate those episodes in the life and work (he never really chose between them) that mark Yeats's struggle for authoritative voice. In his Family Romance with John Synge, Yeats reversed those roles he seemed fated to play out with John Butler Yeats. As the story of the Playboy undoes the story of Cuchulain, so Yeats's friendship with Synge allowed him to assume more than a son's part. Yeats's defense of Synge on the Abbey stage involved sponsorship of a man and a play that stood for a renovating rebelliousness. As he stood before the howling pit, it was through life, not art, that Yeats was transformed. I take the measure of this change to be the beautiful expression of a father's resentful love, an ambivalence that might forever have seemed beyond him, on the birth of his son.

Hemingway intensifies Yeats's sense of the fated by imagining beginnings which foreclose the possibility of an open middle. With Hemingway the challenge has been to clear biography away from the novels without forgetting that they take as their most compelling subject the trauma of birth. *His* birth? With no evidence either way, we are left to appreciate Hemingway's terror of origins as a potentially universal anxiety which he converts into a fascination with ends. The challenge becomes to create a novel that will sustain a sense of unpredictable life. Once Hemingway finds a style which liberates duration from repetition and foreshadowing, he can create a fiction in which every moment is experienced as present. The author's descent into time entails an acceptance of generation. He finds himself placed in a line of descent in which natural traumas can no longer be repressed as uncanny (birth) or worshipped as inevitable (death). As the son forgives the father for having brought him into a world in which he can only die, beginnings and endings cease to overshadow what happens in between. This is a generosity his reader should also extend to Hemingway. What has been taken as the central episode of Hemingway's career—his taking his own life —should cease to dominate our appreciation of its heroic middle.

The chapter on Faulkner is the climax of my narrative line. Faulkner also works toward the possibility of forgiveness. Unlike Hemingway, he always keeps his true subject (the burden of the past) directly in view, and unlike Hemingway, he makes it clear from the start that the challenge is to forgive oneself one's place in time. The challenge to Faulkner criticism is not, therefore, to reveal a hidden theme, but to locate the source of his obsession with it. While his "revenge against time" is certainly overdetermined, we are more likely to gain insight into Faulkner's genius by treating the theme as a personal rather than a universal legacy. The biography reveals a pattern of repetition and revenge which Faulkner had reason to claim as his unique inheritance, one which he sought to resist, understand, and undo. The years between 1928 and 1938 are dedicated to establishing an heir's authority over the plots established by a family history. The act of retelling becomes the essentially redemptive act, but it is not until Faulkner completes *The Unvanquished* that a son succeeds in rewriting the story of his ancestors without resorting to violent repudiation or passive identification.

In my Agee essay I examine a truncated development in which the mid-career turning point marks its end point as well. James Agee confounded the authority of the father with that of the word. "Writing seemed to him," in the words of a recent biographer, "like a dreaded maturity." Success in print threatened to confer upon him the very authority against which he spent nearly a lifetime in rebellion. He always preferred conversation to authorship; the voice ought not become imprisoned in the text. His inveterate reluctance to publish made it inevitable that his most mature achievement would be posthumous. *A Death in the Family* had to be finished by others. Unlike Freud on the Acropolis, Agee never had the chance to analyze his lifelong fear of success. But he had outlived his father, and in the act of recreating that trauma he found that documentary, the illusion of notation, would not serve. This was a fact that could only be redeemed by a word; there were truths here it was impossible ever to have seen. The visible world could no longer act as the criterion of the word; the measure of a man finally became for Agee his power to generate a voice which could embody in fiction the invisible and previously unutterable life of a family.

In the face of Robert Penn Warren's career, development might appear to proceed along three lines at once. In which role has he truly risked the self-discovery which proves the goal of each of his fictional characters—as a novelist, a poet, or a critic? Warren makes no apology for criticism and it remains a fundamental activity of authorship; he understands that consciousness falls into a world and inhabits a self that demand interpretation. While he typically regards his work as an object of understanding, his most untrammeled development occurs in those works which he enters as vehicles for experience. As a novelist, Warren writes with a critical self-consciousness which distances him from the very experience he tries to present. He begins in possession of the insight that each of these other authors works toward. As the heir of Faulkner and Hemingway, he understands what they do but he cannot do it. Through the manipulation of narrative time and the aid of overt commentary, Warren keeps his reader so constantly aware of the necessity and probability of return that falling and wandering (and hence the activity of reading itself) have difficulty becoming truly suspenseful alternatives. Home haunts these novels like the threat of death—it will get you in the end. It is as a poet that Warren's development toward authority takes place; the very forces in response to which the poetry is produced ensure that this will be so. In writing his poetry as the personal record of a life, Warren submits in his poems to a story whose ending he cannot foresee. The drama of the poems is in watching Warren acquire personal voice by virtue of becoming a father. *Or Else* marks the perfection of Warren's unique poetic rhythm, one indebted to an experience which only time, not understanding, could bring.

The accession of authority occupies, for those authors fortunate enough not to exhaust their energies in acquiring it, only the first half of a career. Robertson Davies takes the second as his implicit subject. The conflict of interpretations in his work reduces to the question of whether to understand development in terms of antecedent facts or final meanings. In the Deptford Trilogy, Davies's characters act in response to determining motives even as their behavior pays tribute to the shaping power of emerging aspirations. His deceptively reticent style "misdirects" attention away from the hegemony of origins while creating at the same time the suspicion that they constantly shape our careers. As a critic, Davies argues for the other half of the journey, from maturity to death, as the time of promise. The shape of his own career, with its late access of sudden genius, makes perhaps the best case (a case never resolved in his resolutely double-minded fiction) for an author as developing toward the future rather than out of the past. My speculations on Davies thus act at once as a coda and a new departure. In playing Jung (life as *telos*) against Freud (life as *arche*), Davies suggests that the shape of any career may be a function of the interpretative strategies we bring to bear upon it. Autobiography emerges as the definitively human act insofar as it preserves the sense of every moment as at once a reaction and a promise. As anxiety over sonship dissolves in the play of interpretations he generates, the metaphor of the prodigal son is resolved in Davies's apotheosis of the potentialities of middle age.

The fruitfulness of the process of wandering and return confirms its importance for the understanding of a literary career. Each of these authors eventually gathers an initial prodigality into an inclusive paternity and so acquires the authority against which the act of writing was originally conceived as a defense. The straight line of flight curves into the arc of homecoming. There is nothing unique in this closing of the circle; one need not be an author in order to repeat the experience of the parable. Authorship sees no wisdom in any recapitulation of what might be called the First Story; it takes possession of the story as though enacting it for the first time. Repetition is above all what these authors come to redeem. They will have nothing of the world of *again*. Criticism knows better, and insists that these careers are exceptional not for being original but for finding within the limitations of creaturehood the possibility of creation. Wallace Stevens, who had exhausted by the time he wrote these lines any easy pretensions to being first, offers to all returned prodigals this consoling "perhaps":

> Perhaps,
> The man-hero is not the exceptional monster,
> But he that of repetition is most master.

PRODIGAL SONS

One

MODERNITY AND PATERNITY

James's *The American*

How have I then with whom to hold converse
Save with the Creatures which I made—Milton, *Paradise Lost*

The Son of His Father

James's last great act of self-criticism adopts a fatherly tone. In the preface to *The Golden Bowl* he retraces the lines of connection to his "uncanny brood" with a demanding but forgiving hand. While his earlier offspring fairly plead for understanding—"Actively believe in us and then you'll see"—James finds himself unable to suppress in their presence an uncharacteristic embarrassment. We can almost see his face redden as he asks us to view (we are his "visitors") "the reappearance of the first-born of my progeny . . . as a descent of awkward infants from the nursery to the drawing-room." One prodigal son in particular is singled out. James's paternal discomfiture reaches "its maximum, no doubt, over many of the sorry businesses of 'The American.'" While reacquainting himself with his third novel he is struck by "the long-stored grievance of the subject bristling with a sense of over-prolonged exposure in a garment misfitted." His yearnings to rewrite become acute. "A certain audible splash of soap-and-water" may eventually compensate for *The American*'s prolonged display of bad "literary manners." James proposes to reclaim the wayward child, but not before giving it a bath.

The preface tests the limits of a creator's responsibility for his creatures. James beings by remarking his tendency to impose a mediator—a Strether —between himself and his fictions. This "deputy or delegate" acts as "a convenient substitute or apologist for the creative power otherwise so veiled and disembodied." His intent had been to *share* responsibility for his creation with "some more or less detached" observer whose presence

1

would protect James himself from displaying "the mere muffled majesty of irresponsible 'authorship.'" Authorship is apparently "irresponsible" when it reigns alone. It ought to risk embodiment in a character who can "breathe and rub shoulders and converse with the persons engaged in the struggle that provides for the others in the circling tiers the entertainment of the great game." This is a nostalgia rather than an achievement. James admits of *The Golden Bowl* that "it's not that the muffled majesty of authorship doesn't here *ostensibly* reign; but I catch myself again shaking it off and disavowing the pretence of it." This is a residual attempt to escape culpability; James has already begun to embrace "the point of view that . . . will give me most instead of least to answer for." Disavow as he still may, James begins here to accept his responsibility as that not of the involved participant but of the lonely creator.

The preface contrasts James's early uneasiness over total authority with his late celebration of it. The majesty of authorship is now seen to guarantee a continuity based upon dependence. Unlike our incomplete and living children (of whom else does James speak when he admits that "we give them up even when we wouldn't—it is not a question of choice"?) his collected works have no power to repudiate him. James above all retains this power: they "leave us indeed all licence of disconnexion and disavowal, but positively impose on us no such necessity." The lines of connection between James and his creatures prove subject to the vicissitudes of no temperament save his own. So it is with relief that James after all discovers himself not entirely committed to the trope of his works as children. "Our literary deeds enjoy this marked advantage over many of our acts, that, though they go forth into the world and stray even in the desert, they don't to the same extent lose themselves; their attachment and reference to us, however strained, needn't necessarily lapse—while of the tie that binds us to *them* we may make almost anything we like." In a great hymn to James's choice of one sort of reproduction over another, and to the apparently one-sided degree of attachment it fosters, the preface concludes:

> Our relation to them is essentially traceable, and in that fact abides, we feel, the incomparable luxury of the artist. It rests altogether with himself not to break with his values, not to "give away" his importances. Not to *be* disconnected, for the tradition of behaviour, he has but to feel that he is not; by his lightest touch the whole chain of relation and responsibility is reconstituted.

It is difficult to imagine a more eloquent and roundabout plea that the stability of a line of descent might become wholly subject to the authority of the imagination. James approaches the admission that he can afford to be a loving father to his works because he has not suffered separation from any natural children of his own.

The elder Henry James would have appreciated his son's solicitude as a revising creator. Henry senior saw creation without reclamation as the ultimate irresponsibility. His theology divided Creation into three stages: (1) the Creator is whole; (2) He creates a separate "creature"; (3) the Creator reunites with his creature. Given the "abject want or destitution" of the separate creature, the accent naturally falls upon the necessity of return:

> how very discreditable a thing creation would be to the creator, and how very injurious to the creature, if it stopped short in itself, — that is, contented itself with simply giving the creature natural selfhood, or antagonizing him with the creator. Nothing could be more hideous to conceive of than a creation which should end by exhibiting the subjective antagonism of its two factors, without providing for their subsequent objective reconciliation.

Henry junior accomplishes such a reconciliation when he welcomes his "awkward infants" back into the fold.

With Emerson and Blake, Henry senior identifies Creation and the Fall. The product of these simultaneous events is self-consciousness. "The discovery that we exist" leads to a conviction of the reality of our own being so strong as to deny the priority of any other:

> the only hindrance to men's believing in God as a creator is their inability to believe in *themselves* as created. Self-consciousness, the sentiment of personality, the feeling I have of life in myself, absolute and underived from any other save in a natural way, is so subtly and powerfully atheistic, that, no matter how loyally I may be taught to insist upon creation as a mere traditional or legendary fact, I never feel inclined to believe in it, save as the fruit of some profound intellectual humiliation or hopeless inward vexation of spirit.

Henry senior was rescued from selfhood by his *"vastation,"* a conversion experience William was to duplicate. He too "became a mass of quivering fear" in face of an hallucinated, horrible shape, and he too found the universe a different place ever afterward. But his aggressive identification with his father made it difficult for the first son to accept Henry senior's pretensions to mere "spiritual sonship." William's introduction to the *Literary Remains* salvages some originality for the father by claiming that apart from the dependent role thrust upon him by his theology, the theology itself remains original. After explicating its major phases, William adds: "I should say that in no such successive shape as this did the scheme have *authority* over Mr. James' own mind." Thus the very scheme through which the father had sought escape from selfhood the son values for its having arisen from a "voice within him."

Henry junior typically identified with his father's physical weakness. He suffered his "obscure hurt" while fighting a fire; his father had lost his leg while stamping out a flaming balloon. His father's theology, on the other hand, provided him with a model for spiritual strength. He did not try, like William, to convert a theology of filial dependency into evidence of psychological originality. He simply spent a lifetime appropriating the spiritual authority his father had relinquished to the Creator. "We ourselves can modify existence almost at pleasure," the father asserts, "we can change the form of existing things,—that is, can convert natural forms into artificial ones. But we cannot confer life; cannot make these artificial forms self-conscious or living." The son agrees that true creation is of the spirit, but dismisses the priority of natural to artificial forms. He not only celebrates his power to confer life upon artifice, he goes further: "Art *makes* life."

From a natural perspective, Henry junior was thus bound to lead a lonely life. "The port from which I set out was," he writes in 1900, "that of *the essential loneliness of my life.*" But in his avoidance of any natural paternity he was again acting upon his father's principles. The father displayed a theoretical and the son a practical ingratitude toward the institution that made them Jameses. Henry senior's lecture "Socialism and Civilization" husbands its most passionate language for an attack on "the tie of the insulated family." As a family member "I am a natural partisan, and . . . if I should practically disown the obligation, that blissful home which furnishes the theme of so much sincere as well as dishonest sentimentality, would become on the instant a very hell incapable of pacification." Here the case against the family expresses itself as an anxiety over the strength of the passions which bind it together. This passage verges upon the fantasy of rebellion and its reward—rejection—which continually informs the elder James's sense of family life. Rejection or separation is the frightening possibility his reforms would prevent. "You know by experience that you cannot set your life's happiness upon any outward possession, be it wife or child, or riches, without an incessant and shuddering dread of betrayal." Could we but begin with loosened ties, we would effectively deny the risk of becoming a prodigal son.

Or perhaps Henry senior was trying to deny an immense indebtedness: he was, after all, busily spending his inheritance from *his* father. The will which he succeeded in breaking had left him with but one-eighth of his eventual settlement; it had above all meant to "discourage prodigality." The other convention Henry senior's lecture attacks is "property." Only the heir of an immense earthly fortune could be so cavalier in redefining the term. Property becomes, as in Emerson's *Nature*, a kind of visionary possession which one owes to one's spiritual father. We enjoy with him relations more cordial than those with "every person bound to us by any other tenure than his own spontaneous affection." Intimacy with a spiritual father apparently depends upon dismissal of a debt to a natural one.

In his *Autobiography* Henry senior dismisses the Oedipal family, in all of its volatility, as the perversion of an original harmony.

> The truth is, that the family tie,—the tie of reciprocal ownership which binds together parent and child, brother and sister,—was when it existed in its integrity a purely legal, formal, typical tie, intended merely to *represent* or symbolize to men's imagination the universal family, or household of faith, eventually to appear upon the earth.

James immediately admits this aboriginal family to be a fantasy: "But it never had the least suspicion of its own spiritual mission." Based upon the elder James's own experience, the family appears in fact to be evolving rather than deteriorating. He has already surmised that the reason his habitual thefts of silver from his father's dressing table

> did not spiritually degrade me in my own esteem was, I suppose, that they were at worst offences committed against my parents; and no child as it seems to me with the heart of a child, or who has not been utterly moralized out of his natural innocency and turned into a precocious prig, can help secretly feeling a property in his parents so absolute or unconditional as to make him *a priori* sure, do what he will, of preserving their affection. It would not have seemed so in ancient days, I grant. The parental bond was then predominantly paternal, whereas of late years it is becoming predominantly maternal. At that period it was very nearly altogether authoritative and even tyrannous with respect to the child; while in our own day it is fast growing to be one of the utmost relaxation, indulgence, and even servility. My father was weakly, nay painfully, sensitive to his children's claims upon his sympathy; and I myself, when I became a father in my turn, felt that I could freely sacrifice property and life to save my children from unhappiness.

Taken together, Henry senior's theories and reported experience of family life contribute to a deeply felt wish to abdicate paternal authority while reinvesting it in a transcendent substitute. This was a resolve he successfully carried out, and its effect on Henry junior was incalculable. Near the end of his career, the novelist was even to celebrate his father's "living superiority to all greed of authority." If the "paternal bond" chose to withdraw its influence upon the life of the second son, the "maternal" found ways to fill the vacuum. *That* relation largely conditioned the circumstances surrounding the writing of *The American*, but it is the measure of how fully the work of a lifetime was capable of transforming the legacy of the mother that the son who had wandered so far from home returns, in the preface to his last great fiction, to the charitable spirit of the father.

Precipitation and Reflection

What in particular about *The American* tempts James to disown it? Its having come too close, I believe, to admitting the virtue of the necessity

—marriage and fatherhood—it eventually shuns. Since James had no intention of ever permitting such a compromise to occur, the question arose, in rereading the novel, as to how he could have permitted us to become, in the words of one reviewer, such "conscious victims of misplaced confidence" in the chances of Newman's success. The preface of 1907 explains how little of the novel's original power proceeds from a conscious intention. James had written it in the service of "unchallenged instinct." He simply admits to having been, while inventing the story, largely out of control. His original novel became "romantic," he suggests, insofar as it had been created by an unconscious will toward an "effect" perceivable only "after the fact" of composition rather than in light of "conscious design." Resumption of control becomes the task of revision. In rewriting the novel James subordinates "precipitation" to "reflexion" so as to reclaim for critical knowledge what he had ceded, as a young man, to creative power.

The preface endorses a way of reading whose consequences, however, James may not have fully anticipated. It projects a reader who might assume the task of converting latent into manifest content. In issuing this invitation, James encourages a kind of attention much more free than his own to fathom that "instinct" which had deflected his imagination toward romance:

> the cause of the deflexion, in one pronounced sense or the other, must lie deep, however, so that for the most part we recognise the character of our interest only after the particular magic, as I say, has thoroughly operated—and then in truth but if we be a bit critically minded, if we find our pleasure, that is, in these intimate appreciations (for which, as I am well aware, ninety-nine readers in a hundred have no use whatever). The determining condition would at any rate seem so latent that one may well doubt if the full artistic consciousness ever reaches it; leaving the matter thus a case, ever, not of an author's plotting and planning and calculating, but just of his feeling and seeing, of his conceiving, in a word, and of his thereby inevitably expressing himself, under the influence of one value or the other.

Halting syntax and inconclusive reference here feint with matters James cautiously approaches. The bathos of his conclusion—what a drop there is in "under the influence of one value or the other"—distances James from the particulars of unconscious processes even as it tantalizes us with the general question. The preface thus poses a challenge to the "critically minded": can we, after the particular "magic" of the novel's romance has operated upon us, return to appreciate its "determining condition"?

Among James's novels *The American* creates perhaps the most acute gap between an experience and an understanding of it. While reading we share the generous but limited consciousness of a hero whose fate we are made to wish, with a vengeance, to share. In reconsidering this fate, we discover our complicity in an action so fully in the service of "unchallenged instinct" as to make us approach, with Newman, a wonder bordering on shame. As a fall away from the experience of unreflective creative power, criticism substitutes for it the belated consolations of knowledge. We necessarily purchase such knowledge with a loss of power. Yet James himself has set the precedent for such an exchange. In his revisionary attempts to credit Newman with reflective consciousness, he registers his uneasiness over leaving intact a novel, however powerful, which he had all too instinctively made.

Revision in the New York Edition consistently sacrifices perceived effect to conscious design. Newman declares at one point in the 1877 text that "I am a highly civilised man." When he is made to say, in the 1907 version, "I have the instincts—have them deeply—if I haven't the forms of a high old civilisation," he voices an insight as appropriate to a critic of the novel as to a character in it. For it is just these surprising instincts which the original story masks and which it is the task of criticism, as it is the intended failure of reading, to discern. *The American* asks us to share unwittingly the experience of a "modern" man somehow in the possession of traditional instincts acquired without his having had any experience of "history." It is essential to this original effect that Newman lack historical consciousness but possess historical instincts. In the tension between Newman's apparent modernity (upon which we are made to believe his actions based) and his actual historicity (of which we become only belatedly aware) the reader is caught up in a dialectic between modes of being—and their determining "latent" conditions— whose authentic embodiment the original novel repeatedly calls into question.

Modernity and history are the two terms central not only to the opposition of forces in the novel, but to the opposition between its two versions. They surface for the first time in two crucial passages in the revised edition. In doing so these terms register James's desire to convert the emotionally latent into the intellectually abstract, to make explicit the burden of the originally implicit. In the 1877 text we are not aware, for instance, that "history" specifically underlies Valentin's assessment of Claire's emotional state:

> "Is she unhappy?"
> "I won't say that, for unhappiness is according as one takes things, and Claire takes them according to some receipt communicated to her by the Blessed Virgin in a vision. To be unhappy is to be disagreeable, which, for her, is out of the question. So she has arranged her circumstances so as to be happy in them."

In response to essentially the same question, Valentin gives in the 1907 text a much more telling answer:

Newman wondered. "Then she has troubles?"

"My dear man, she has what we all have—even you, strange to say. She has a history."

This is the definitive statement about Claire. That it also takes in Newman will be worth pondering in a moment; for the present, we should note that having a "history" has everything to do with one's chances for happiness, that its effects in the revised text displace the original notion that one can arrange one's circumstances.

The concept of modernity provokes James into an even more striking revision. The Marquise Urbain, in one of her repeated efforts to make up to Newman, initially asserts their commonality through political affinities:

> Besides, you and I belong to the same camp. I am a ferocious democrat. By birth I am *vielle roche;* a good little bit of the history of France is the history of my family. . . . But I don't care a pin for my pedigree; I want to belong to my time. I'm a revolutionist, a radical, a child of the age! I am sure I go beyond you.

James sharply revises this into

> Besides, you and I belong to the same camp. I'm a ferocious modern. I'm more modern than you, you know—because I've been *through* this and come out, very far out; which you haven't. . . . I only want to belong to my time. So, being a reactionary—from the reaction—I'm sure I go beyond you. That's what you look, you know—that you're not reactionary enough.

To Newman's credit, the revised Marquise talks herself out of his camp by means of an irony of whose full force she is unaware. Going *through* his experience in Paris will put to the test the true depth of Newman's modernity. A revisionary James here forsakes a political definition of modernity for one which specifies it as a complex of attitudes toward life in time. If the 1907 revisions explicitly question Newman's modernity, it is only because the 1877 version had seemed to affirm while implicitly undermining it.

The original affirmations are numerous indeed. In the phrase with which Valentin reacts to the news of his friend's hasty courtship he seems to sum up the essence of Newman's modernity: "Time is money!" Throughout the opening of the novel we are led to believe that Newman confronts time, and its creations, as a quantity which might be purchased. The first word he utters in the book is *"Combien?"* Newman's commercialism is usually taken by critics as the primary obstacle to his appreciation of all those historical values embodied in Paris. Yet his attempts to buy life—to acquire its products without undergoing its processes—only superficially evidence his modernity. Newman himself is allowed early on to gauge the cost of such behavior: "He had spent his years in the unremitting effort to add thousands to thousands, and, now that he stood well outside of it, the business of money-getting appeared extremely dry and sterile." This should be enough to warn us that *The American* will not merely chronicle Newman's inability to transcend his "specialty" of making the "largest possible fortune in the shortest possible time." Yet James comes to feel that it is not enough, and so revises Newman's self-judgment into an unambiguous repudiation of commercial life: "He had spent his years in the unremitting effort to add thousands to thousands, and now that he stood so well outside of it the business of mere money-getting showed only, in its ugliness, as vast and vague and dark, a pirate-ship with lights turned inward." This may be the most striking simile in the final version. An intrusive display of authorial artifice, it asks figure to express what is, in the original, left more to action to demonstrate. We are led by this action to discover that for all his reliance upon commercial talk, Newman's response to experience increasingly belies the limitations of his conceptual apparatus.

If Newman's modernity only apparently inheres in his commercialism, of what is it essentially constituted? Minister Babcock gets at the gist of it: "You appear to care," he writes to Newman, "only for the pleasure of the hour, and you give yourself up to it with a violence which I confess I am not able to emulate. . . . You seem to hold that if a thing amuses you for the moment, that it is all you need ask for it." Newman apparently lives in the present tense. "The fact is," Newman admits, "I have never had time to feel things. I have had to *do* them." He naturally acts with extreme speed. "Reflexion" is the last power he has had time to cultivate. His life, conceived as it proceeds, knows no precedents. The only work he acknowledges is the task of "resembling oneself." As his own origin, Newman creates himself from himself. A man "doesn't have to be born with certain faculties on purpose; he needs only to be a man." That Newman's identity superficially exists in the present apart from all its appurtenances James emphasizes in revising this declaration. The hero of 1907 claims that "He doesn't have to be born with certain faculties on purpose; he needs only to be—well, whatever he really *is*." As a modern man, Newman simply *is*.

James thus seems to have meant by "history" and "modernity" much what Emerson meant:

> It is one of the *feelings* of modern philosophy, that it is wrong to regard ourselves so much in a *historical* light as we do, putting Time between God & us; and that it were fitter to account every moment of the existence of the Universe as a new Creation, and *all* as a revelation proceeding each moment from the Divinity to the mind of the observer.

The "modern" expresses itself as an urge toward an everlasting now and thus defines itself in opposition to the "historical." Historical man knows himself as part of a temporal sequence which confirms his place in an irrevocable line of descent. Emerson here abolishes the distance between himself and the Creator by abolishing time. But to deny this interval is to deny the distance that is generation. If his creative power is timed perfectly with the Divine the difference between the two evaporates. This is the deepest impulse modernity expresses: the unwillingness to acknowledge the limiting priority of origins. Paul de Man speaks of modernity as composed of "moments at which all anteriority vanishes, annihilated by the power of an absolute forgetting." In just such a mood Emerson refuses to "build the sepulchres of the fathers." De Man remarks the dependence of literary modernity upon "parricidal imagery." The attack on history and tradition inevitably leads to an assault on the authority of the father.

The terms "modernity" and "history" thus help to clarify James's attitudes toward the language of *The American*. In the 1877 text he had been, on his own testimony, the immediate agent of his language; in the 1907 version he strives to become its reflective critic. De Man argues that an author of fictions can never escape either function:

> The historian, in his function as historian, can remain quite remote from the collective acts he records; his language and the events that the language denotes are clearly distinct entities. But the writer's language is to some degree the product of his own action; he is both the historian and the agent of his own language. The ambivalence of writing is such that it can be considered both an act and an interpretative process that follows after an act with which it cannot coincide.

James claims to have written *The American* as a modern—"under too immediate an impression—the impression that prevents standing off and allows neither space nor time for perspective." He rewrites it as a historian —in response to "the critical sense which the exercise of one's *whole* faculty has, with time, so inevitably and so thoroughly waked up." These widely separated compositional efforts create the impression that James experiences his ambivalence toward the language of *The American* in two successive phases. Yet the conflicting claims of modernity and history operate simultaneously on James, as I will show, from the start of the project. The act of revision converts this implicit tension into an explicit theme without alleviating the tension. Newman's original experience is to live as a modern man even while discovering himself to be a man of historical instincts. James wrote the book as an unreflective modern even while building into it a critique of spontaneous self-expression. Yet this implicit critique was not enough: what James could not get round was the way in which the book came to him. It originated in a moment of creative forgetfulness which allows us to perceive a curious symmetry between the birth of the hero in the book and the birth of the book in the author.

The Hack

"Are you going to write a book?" It is in Newman's response to Tristram's question that James comes closest to revealing his concern over the nature of the novel's origin. Newman answers with the following story, the only episode from the past he tells in his own voice. "One day, a couple of months ago," Newman tells us, he began plotting revenge against a business party who had played him a "very mean trick." He vows that he will, "figuratively speaking, put his nose out of joint." In the "immortal, historical hack" carrying him to the showdown

> "I felt the want of sleep. At all events I woke up suddenly, from a sleep or from a kind of reverie, with the most extraordinary feeling in the world—a mortal disgust for the thing I was going to do. It came upon me like *that!*"—and he snapped his fingers—"as abruptly as an old wound that begins to ache."

The resulting sense of renewed life sends Newman in search of a "new world." And so he travels to Europe.

Newman marvels that "all this took place quite independently of my will, and I sat watching it as if it were a play at the theatre." This turning point in his history has apparently been authored by a force beyond conscious volition. The experience brings him to the conclusion that a man can act in the service of instincts of which he is unaware: "there are things going on inside of us that we understand mighty little about." Newman has made the discovery of nothing other than the unconscious.

The episode acquires greater force once we learn, in the preface to *The American*, its origin in the life of its author. In just such a hack, the germ of Newman's history came to James:

> I recall sharply the felicity of the first glimpse, though I forget the accident of thought that produced it. I recall that I was seated in an American "horse-car" when I found myself, of a sudden, considering with enthusiasm, as the theme of a "story", the situation, in another country and an aristocratic society, of some robust but insidiously beguiled and betrayed, some cruelly wronged, compatriot: the point being in especial that he should suffer at the hands of persons pretending to represent the highest possible civilisation and to be of an order in every way superior to his own. What would he "do" in that predicament, how would he right himself, or how, failing a remedy, would he conduct himself under his wrong? This would be the question involved, and I remember well how, having entered the horse-car without a dream of it, I was presently to leave the vehicle in full possession of my answer. He would behave in the most interesting manner—it would all depend on that: stricken, smarting, sore, he would arrive at his just vindication and then would fail of all triumphantly and all vulgarly enjoying it.

In both episodes the unconscious suddenly fathers. A moment of self-forgetfulness leads to a creative act. The moment of a book's birth was certainly anxious for James; at such a moment he could best establish his rights of paternity. James here purchases creative power at the cost of willful authority. His concern that such a way of creating may be irresponsible passes into the novel, where Newman not only rehearses his own moment of inception but expresses the resultant uncertainty over motivation which must have been James's.

But does not the end here justify the means? This "accident of thought" leads, does it not, to an end "most interesting"—a forsaking of revenge. Newman will be spared the aggressive pursuit of his own interests with the Bellegardes, as he himself gives up revenge against the business party. The accident which brought the book to birth also creates its marvelously selfless but completely frustrating logic, of which so many readers have complained. The anonymous reviewer of 1877 protests that "up to the time of Valentin's death, we had gained such faith in his stability and in his straightforward determination . . . that it would have seemed the most natural thing in the world for him not only to marry Madame de Cintré, but to become the guiding head of the whole house of Bellegarde." While this last may exceed any reasonable expectation, the reviewer does provide for the recognition that Newman's second renunciation of revenge is as unmotivated as his first. Certainly nothing in the novel succeeds in explaining Newman's final passivity. Apparently free from the pressure of any more compelling motive, he simply decides that "to talk to anyone whomsoever about the Bellegardes would be extremely disagreeable." He then simply turns away. Newman does not engage in further speculation because he cannot; the motivations precipitating his withdrawal lie not in him, but, as I hope to show, in his author.

James thus leaves Newman's moral responsibility in question at the very moment he had hoped to assert it. His is an unmotivated renunciation. Apparently it is possible to act creatively and irresponsibly. James failed to perceive the unlikelihood of Newman's withdrawal because of his deeper investment in making it inevitable. His inability to distance himself from the plight of his hero from the first moment he conceives him makes James as much the immediate agent as the reflective historian of the novel's language. The two prefaces address this tension: the first reveals the novel's birth as spontaneous creation, while the second announces James's resumption of conscious control. Revision might not succeed in clearing up the question of motivation, but it certainly could restore the author's sense of responsibility for even the unlikeliest of events. Revision was the best available means whereby James could assure himself that birth in a hack could be fully legitimized.

The American thus plays a central role in the drama of authorship and authority which is the New York Edition. Whereas James had exercised a minimum of authority in conceiving his third novel, he was to enjoy that power to the maximum in revising it. James rewrote the book on every single page. The consistently felt need to revise reveals that for James authority is something only fully achieved afterwards—then, not now. Authorship is established at a remove in time. James was "a passionate corrector." Like Dencombe in "The Middle Years," his "ideal would have been to publish secretly, and then, on the published text, treat himself to the terrified revise, sacrificing always a first edition and beginning for posterity and even for the collectors, poor dears, with a second." James stubbornly resists the inherent modernity of literary language, its "constitutive affinity with action, with the unmediated, free act that knows no past." An act of forgetting can never complete—it can only precipitate —an act of creation. For creation to be complete, an author must acknowledge it through an act of reflection. What originates in a spontaneous modernity must be reclaimed by a responsible paternity.

The House of Atreus

The crisis of paternity dramatized in the prefaces is also a crisis of modernity. Can *The American* effectively renounce its author by claiming to have been born by accident? Has its father been so irresponsible as to have lost all rights in paternity? The author's embarrassment in the face of his self-begotten and "misfitted" creation betrays what might be called the "anxiety of influencing." It is as if the author were unable to claim any effective influence over the work which originates from him. Since the action of the novel turns upon the absence of powerful fathers, the issues surrounding the creation of the novel are also the most compelling *in* the novel. No father in the book is any more successful than James had originally been in asserting his authority. Threats to the father abound. The family possessed of the most "fabulous antiquity" proves guilty of the novel's most vicious "modern" attack on fatherhood. In Chapter 22 James reveals the story of Henri-Urbain de Bellegarde's murder by his wife and son. We cannot fully appreciate the modernity of *The American* until we discover that its core story, from which the action flows, turns on an act of parricide.

Mrs. Bread relates this "decent narrative." She has been kept alive all these years in order to tell it. She is the novel's true historian. Until speaking to Newman, however, she has lived as its actual Cassandra, without an audience able to hear the truth she has to tell. How do we become this audience? Why does James make her the bearer of this tale, and why do we believe her?

John A. Clair believes that Mrs. Bread is an unreliable narrator. In an ingenious hypothesis he argues that she is actually Madame de Cintré's

natural mother, that with this knowledge she has blackmailed the
Bellegardes in order to stay with them, as she uses it, once Newman
appears, to force his marriage to Claire. Under this pressure the actually
honorable Marquise tells Claire of her true origins and Mrs. Bread's plan
backfires. "Claire de Cintré, the tragic heroine, refuses to marry Newman
because of her illegitimate birth." Such a reading deprives every main
character of authentic motivation except Mrs. Bread. Valentin's apology
for his family would be pathetically mistaken, Claire's refusal of Newman
primarily self-protective, the Bellegardes' exaggerated hauteur gratuitous
given their actual sense of virtue, and Newman would be, finally, every-
one's dupe. Worst of all, this reading presents the novel as a kind of
roman à clef which James—against all compositional evidence—writes
from the beginning with a consciously hidden intention.

Yet unless we posit some such hypothesis, Mrs. Bread's motivations
appear inexplicable. Why has she kept silent for so many years, in a
house where she is hated, with the accusing note unread? She remains
incredible, I think, because she fulfills two incompatible functions. The
first is a narrative function. The plot demands that someone preserve and
eventually reveal, to a suitable interloper, the Bellegarde family history.
A history so awful makes it impossible that this narrator be both willing
to tell it and remain a member of the family. Yet she must maintain ties
with the family strong enough to prevent her from publishing the truth
until the plot's rising action turns toward crisis. So for the purposes of the
plot what she has to tell and when she tells it are more important than her
motivations for doing so. At the appropriate moment—and no sooner
—James must simply make her talk. She even accuses Newman, in words
just as applicable to James, of manipulating her: "I see you have your
idea, and I have no will of my own." She functions as the intruding
messenger—a messenger who has, strangely enough, never left home.

For what then must have appeared to him structural rather than
psychological reasons, James does not grant Mrs. Bread a will of her
own. We might be able to accept this did she not fulfill a psychological
function at odds with her narrative one. All of the imaginative energy
which James does not expend upon his other female characters he invests
in Mrs. Bread. Since this energy is both considerable and positive, it
invests her with a presence unique in the novel. She is its one nurturant
woman. Mrs. Bread has been, as much as anyone, a mother to Claire: "I
received her in my arms when she came into the world." In the choice of
her name James very likely responds to Mrs. Bread's function in the novel
as a daily, dependable source of sustenance. Yet, as we have seen, James
discovers a narrative rationale for divesting this woman of real power.
Did she possess it, there would be no explaining her failure to exercise it
earlier to free Claire. If she helps to sustain life, James must also make it

clear that she does not have the power to generate and order it. She lacks the aggressive, mature sexual force of the lady she serves. The absence of powerful fathers in *The American* complements the absence, as Mrs. Bread's presence emphasizes, of powerful and nurturant mothers.

The Nioche subplot pits a powerless father against the daughter of a betraying wife and unloving mother. The first entrance in the novel—by M. Nioche—completes the essential triad of romantic comedy with an irony which we will not be long in detecting. Nioche quickly emerges as anything but the *senex difficilis*, the blocking father, whose opposition to the lover's attachment only stimulates our interest in it. No more does Noémie fulfill the role of a romantic heroine. The Nioche connivings to cheat Newman soon discredit them as characters capable of responding to his innocence. The impatience with which we endure this subplot's clearly introductory maneuvers (these cannot be the people with whom such a hero will realize his fate) obscures the ways in which it does prepare us for the experience of the main one. As a product of James's ironic self-consciousness rather than his romantic unconscious, the Nioches allow James to present a case study of the very paradigm which Newman will more fatefully encounter in the Bellegardes.

"The old man will not do what Virginius did": so Valentin sums up M. Nioche's fate. Acting rather as a Pandarus, he attempts to convert his daughter's talents into "specie." If Mrs. Bread attracts James's positive feeling for nurturant maternity, M. Nioche focuses his ambivalent feelings toward ineffectual paternity. Are we meant to scorn or pity this father? He does fail, after all, at the task represented by the novel as most perilous—raising a child. Noémie, rather, cynically raises him. Her injunction—"Remember what you are—what you have been!"—provokes his admission that his time has passed: "Much more formerly and much less to-day!" As his authority has waned, so has his voice. James thus claims the privilege of mediating it for us. "The result, in the form in which he in all humility presented it, would be scarcely comprehensible to the reader, so that I have ventured to trim and sift it." Noémie's sufficiency as a modern woman of the world James directly credits to her upbringing, in which her father failed to restrain a wayward mother. Because M. Nioche was unable to assert himself, Noémie repeats in the second generation the abuses practiced by her mother in the first. The fact of her mother's influence Nioche cannot accept. Newman puts the question to him:

> "Her influence on your daughter, then," said Newman encouragingly, "is not to be feared."
> "She cared no more for her daughter than for the sole of her shoe! But Noémie has no need of influence. She is sufficient to herself. She is stronger than I."

Noémie's completely successful assertion of her modernity registers a lack of that chastening influence whose pressure might have made her capable of valuing human bonds rather than mere freedom. She defines freedom, in response to Newman's request for a definition, as the lack of these bonds: "You have nothing to bother you—no family, no wife, no *fiancée.*" In the course of the novel's action, the unrepentant Noémie thoroughly exposes the poverty of her unencumbered existence. Yet James's hesitation over resolving the question of how to suffer or assert parental authority lingers until the end. The first serious question his novel raises—will M. Nioche remember who he is?—is also its last. We are left in suspense, in an English park, as to just how, if ever, M. Nioche will "stop her!"

Since Newman has no romantic interest in Noémie, it is not incompatible with his emotional quest that he be, even more than M. Nioche himself, solicitous of his honor as a father. Even if M. Nioche is not, Newman feels "rather disgusted at the smooth operation of the old man's philosophy." But with the woman he loves the case is different. We naturally expect Newman to compete against the father for the affections of the daughter. Yet the plot denies him this invigorating and perilous rivalry. In her first report about Claire, Mrs. Tristram reveals that "her father is dead, and since her widowhood she has lived with her mother and a married brother." Her omission of Valentin from this inner circle hints at his accessibility to us, and it is eventually through this "wild" younger brother that we gain admission to the Bellegarde family. Once again we find ourselves confronting a mother-dominated home. Its crucial members quickly pair off into open and closed characters. The mother and Urbain confront Newman with arrogance and power. Her signature is a most "especial" detail, her mouth: a "conservative orifice, a little pair of lips at once plump and pinched, that looked, when closed as if they could not open wider than to swallow a gooseberry or to emit an 'Oh dear, no!'" Newman correctly surmises that "Madame de Bellegarde had paired with her eldest-born." But Urbain strikes him less as her partner than a poor imitation: "He is the old woman at second-hand." As an "incarnation of the art of taking oneself seriously," Urbain lives under the compulsion of his personal vanity. Yet his stature proves wholly derivative; if Urbain appears puffed up, it is his mother who has discreetly supplied the hot air.

Their mother's effect upon Valentin and Claire has been, on the other hand, deflating. Valentin lives, he admits "with a sigh, 'beneath the eyes of my admirable mother.'" But she exiles him from any truly supportive contact. Her feelings toward Valentin are, at best, ambivalent. She dryly apologizes for him to Newman: "You must see my other son. . . . He is much better than this one." The consequence of such treatment Valentin can imply, but not admit:

"I have done nothing—I can do nothing!"

"Why not?"

"It's a long story. Some day I will tell you."

Only on his deathbed does Valentin tell his story, thereby forging the crucial link between his mother's behavior—especially as he suspects her of a crime—and his own demoralized existence. She has left him "'alone and palely loitering.'" Thus Mrs. Tristram's question—"Did you ever read Keats' 'Belle Dame sans Merci'?"— is gratuitous. Valentin has actually suffered the effects of that ambivalence which Keats, himself the victim of a similar fate, displaces into the poem.

Claire's sense of blocked life emerges as no less extreme than her brother's. Anything but a "statue which had failed as stone," her fate is to freeze rather than to flow. She momentarily comes to life only to die, during her one kiss, her first and last. "He kissed her white face; for an instant she resisted and for a moment she submitted; then, with force, she disengaged herself and hurried away over the long shining floor." The poverty of her fate can also be directly traced to her mother. For commercial reasons she sacrifices Claire's bloom to an aging, impotent spouse. James, in speaking for Newman, adumbrates the chilling effect which life in her family is to have on Claire: "in observing Madame de Cintré he seemed to see the vague circle which sometimes accompanies the partly-filled disc of the moon." Their mutual sense of frustration has, not surprisingly, made Valentin and Claire "very good friends." Surprising, rather, is Valentin's choice of a myth to express the quality of their intimacy: "we are such a brother and sister as have not been seen since Orestes and Electra."

Valentin and Claire suffer the fate of their mythical counterparts except in their failure to perpetrate, against their mother and her accomplice, a brutal revenge. We are made to feel, as with Agamemnon, that however much Henri-Urbain de Bellegarde has deservedly provoked his wife's resentment, the crime of the story is her murder of him. Clytemnestra is then "paired with" an Aegisthus, a man clearly unequal to her in power, less a paramour than a son. Electra has been, as in the myth, forced by the demands of family policy to marry a man incapable of consummating their union. And Orestes, effectively exiled from his ancestral home, returns to seek vengeance upon his mother and her accomplice for the slaying of his father. In James's adaptation of the myth, however, Valentin's assumption of this project coincides with his death. The self-wounding which Orestes inflicts upon himself *after* killing his mother, Valentin suffers *before* he has begun the attempt. The duel, which he purposely loses, provides an escape from the burden of his fate. Although Valentin does claim that the "honour of the name" of Bellegarde is "safer in his hands than in those of some of its other members," he admits, on his deathbed, that he has not displayed the cruel courage of an Orestes.

"I have been ashamed—afraid to know." All he can do is "apologise for
my family. For my mother. For my brother." No more is Claire an Electra
capable of plotting revenge. She senses a grievance she cannot face.
"There's a curse upon the house; I don't know what—I don't know why
—don't ask me." So terrified is she of confronting this curse that her
mother, it appears, can manipulate her merely by threatening to make
her face it. The House of Atreus appears to lack a second generation that
can redress the crimes of the first.

Only Newman seems competent to assume both the burden of this
knowledge and this revenge. Does he not appear to be free of those
family bonds which account for the younger Bellegardes' paralyzing fear
and guilt? In Newman's seeming independence of such pressure lies much
of his romantic appeal. In the preface James's *"general"* definition of
romance evokes the experience of a man alone, "disencumbered" from
"all our vulgar communities." He announces his hero as the perfectly
disencumbered man. Newman never mentions his father; his mother, he
tells us, died when he was young; she is survived by his two sisters. He
lacks a family history, we assume, which might have conditioned him
either to succeed or fail in the paternal role. Madame Bellegarde responds
to just this impression: "It is not your disposition that we object to, it is
your antecedents." More precisely, they object to his *lack* of antecedents.
Does not his history suggest an absence of contact with antecedents, an
innocence of the generational conflict which she has exploited to control
her own children?

Given all this, the quiet irony with which James undermines such
appearances takes, with the reader, almost unconscious effect. The preface
again points the way. James responds there to his sense that he has, if his
"hocus-pocus" has been successful, encumbered Newman after all. In
romance the "greatest intensity may so be arrived at evidently—when the
sacrifice of community, of the 'related' sides of situations, has not been
too rash." While discourse tends to enforce a sense of Newman's disen-
cumbered modernity, his actions betray in him, as they stimulate in us,
those "historical" instincts which acknowledge generational claims. Of
all the men in the novel, only Newman emerges as responsive to the
demands and responsibilities of fatherhood. James balances Newman's
apparent innocence of relations against an emerging desire for them and
the community they create. He stands as the one male capable of en-
countering the women in the novel not as an aggrieved or subordinate
son, but as a mature, even paternal man. We have already seen that
Newman takes greater offense at Noémie's abuses of her father than
does M. Nioche himself. As Valentin's self-proclaimed "elder brother,"
Newman comes to the defense not of his vain honor but of his actual life.
He concludes, too late, that "I ought to have treated you as a small boy."

Even with Claire, Newman assumes a role as nurturant as it is romantic. This culminates in his second proposal to her:

> "With me," he went on, "you shall be as safe—as safe"—and even in his ardour he hesitated a moment for a comparison—"as safe," he said, with a kind of simple solemnity, "as in your father's arms."

The care with which this sentiment is expressed, as much as the sentiment itself, testifies to Newman's almost fatherly concern. And this "comparison" reduces Claire to utter tears and eventual assent. That she never had such a protecting father, will prove, however, the final obstacle to her enjoyment of Newman's fatherly love. But a crueler irony awaits him, one that reveals even Urbain and his mother as sensitive to the depth of Newman's respect for fathers. In his final offer to him, Urbain extends Newman the chance to defend Urbain's own father! "What we offer you is a chance—a chance that a gentleman should appreciate. A chance to abstain from inflicting a terrible blot upon the memory of a man who certainly had his faults, but who, personally, had done you no wrong." Newman reacts to this as "great nonsense!" but his identification throughout with paternal interests shows it as not wholly misdirected. Whether or not Newman instinctively responds to the motivation to withdraw that Urbain here provides, he does, after having shown himself willing to compete for the favors of a daughter, withdraw. After shaping his hero into the novel's one possible founder of a true community, why does James subject Newman to what he himself calls the "outrage" of denial?

The Cause of the Deflection

At the center of this action lies an Oedipal crime: after disposing of the father, a mother and son pair off together. While James had exploited such a theme in tales like "Master Eustace," we can scarcely discern the myth operating in *The American*. The traumatized hero of that story makes explicit his repetition of an archetype: "I am like Hamlet—I don't approve of mothers consoling themselves." The novel does not focus itself through the guilty consciousness of Urbain or his mother. Their crime is not the subject but the object of the action. We see it not from the point of view of an Oedipus but of an Orestes. Valentin's consciousness, and that of his eventual second, Newman, becomes the stage upon which the drama is played out. In these terms, the novel does not dramatize the guilt of an Oedipal past but the passion for an Oresteian revenge.

If Orestes fails to act he becomes Oedipus. Hamlet discovers himself in the situation of the former but uncovers in himself the consciousness of the latter. His delay breeds doubt, and doubt arises from the unconscious guilt that he, too, has wished to supplant the father in order to possess the mother. The *Oresteia* is a myth of reverence for fathers; Oedipus is a myth of competition with them. Orestes acts out a social tragedy of passion for which the final retribution is justice. Oedipus suffers a psychological tragedy of innocence for which the final retribution is knowledge. When Freud begins to formulate a modern psychology, he turns to Oedipus, not to Orestes. Is not the former acting in the service of unconscious drives, while the latter embodies changing social values? Oedipus's motivations are well known; what motivates Orestes? Robert Graves summarizes the traditional view: as a myth the story of the House of Atreus seeks "to invalidate the religious axiom that motherhood is more divine than fatherhood." In what had been a strongly matriarchal culture, Graves explains, Orestes succeeds in the revolutionary act of avenging his father upon his mother. The myth appears to celebrate the successful violation of a taboo, not the psychological cost of violating one. Why then did so resolutely psychological a novelist as James, starting from a core story promising Oedipal guilt, subordinate it to the action of an Oresteian social revenge?

The Orestes myth recommended itself to James's imagination, I think, precisely because it dramatized unconscious feelings unavailable to his introspection. Philip Slater, in a thoroughly Jamesian fashion, has "gone behind" this myth to reveal the limitation of any view which reduces it to a "politico-religious allegory." In *The Glory of Hera* he presents convincing evidence that the Orestes myth (and those cognate with it) expresses a complex of unresolved psychosexual feelings as formative as Oedipal ones. The myth derives, he argues, from an ambivalence in the Greek mother-son relationship which results not in genital but in oral conflicts. This ambivalence results from a social and family structure which the myths both reflect and attempt to justify. Slater describes the Greek family structure as characterized by an absent (or seemingly weak) father free to enhance his ego publicly, and a mother without social power or consistent marital fulfillment, her influence confined to the home. This influence cannot help but be, for the male child left with the mother, considerable. From his earliest years the son becomes the recipient of his mother's ambivalent feelings. She alternatively smothers him with unfulfilled love and rejects him as inadequate to provide such fulfillment. The inconsistency of her emotions, as much as the emotions themselves, can produce in the child a profound sense of insecurity on the one hand and vanity upon the other. As a result he experiences a lasting anxiety over the preservation of his own boundaries which Slater has called the "'oral-narcissistic dilemma.' It originates in a failure to negotiate successfully the transition from the infantile state of total narcissism and total dependence to one involving an awareness of the separate existence of others. As this awareness grows, one's sense of narcissistic integrity and one's dependency needs are simultaneously violated." The child's psychology becomes dominated less by a genital conflict between sexual initiative or guilt, than by an oral conflict between total fusion or total separation.

What effect does such a family structure have upon the child's view of sex roles? Either because of his real absence or perceived weakness, "the father did not compete with his son within the family." The son can respond to the father's absence with "idealization" or, in response to the mother's explicit or implied derogation of him, can view him as "capricious and irresponsible." In neither case does the mature male emerge as realistically capable of competing with, or satisfying, the mother. Since the father does not effectively interpose between mother and son, she can be felt as strong, self-willed, and, finally, threatening to the developing male ego. He lives in "danger of being gobbled up" by her unsatisfied drives, of being dominated by her seeming imperiousness. The mature woman can even be perceived by the son, in extreme periods of anxiety, as a threat to his life itself. Thus in Greek "tragedies it is young women and virginal goddesses who are helpful and benign, while the mature ones tend to be jealous, vindictive, and destructive." The one kind of woman such a son can safely approach is chaste, remote, coolly passive—a kind of statue.

> At some stage the thought came to him that men derive strength from the women they marry and that conversely women can deprive men of their strength and life. Mothers—women—apparently were expected to give themselves wholly, submerge themselves . . . in their family. Men used women, were propped by them and sometimes could not go on living after the woman was dead. This meant that women could control the lives of men and this he believed was what happened to his father. . . .
> This led to further considerations. What happens to anyone who gives himself to another? . . . Would the man collapse and become weak . . . if he ever allowed himself to love a woman? might it not mean collapse into a stultifying dependency—and one in which love and death seemed to be coupled? In the James family annals there seemed to be answers: women were strong and survived their men, or if they did not, then somehow the men could not continue to live. In either case the man seemed doomed. . . . On all sides strong-minded firm-handed women swallowing up their men.

With these words Leon Edel climaxes his most daring speculations on the tortured thinking that led James into celibacy. Edel makes it very clear that James's view of the sexes originates in an experience of maternal ambivalence complemented by a reversal of parental roles:

> Before the little boy's observant eyes there was this ever-present picture of ambiguity and reversal of relation: a father strong, robust, manly, yet weak and feminine, soft and yielding, indulging his children at every turn; and a mother, strong, firm, but irrational and contradictory.

Edel gives examples enough. The James children are in the habit, for instance, of purposely embracing their mother while mocking their father. On one of the many occasions when the elder Henry is working on a manuscript at home, William designs for it his notorious frontispiece: a picture of a man beating a dead horse. The younger Henry, in his most profound act of identification with his crippled father's "apparent ineffectuality," suffers an accident the effects of which, he soon prophesies, are to be of long "duration." It is the back injury that appears to have confirmed his unsuitability for the pursuit and capture of mature women. Memory after childhood memory testifies to an upbringing in which, as James blithely admits, "we wholesomely breathed inconsistency and ate and drank contradictions."

We can multiply examples of parental inconsistency and role reversal from James's life; it is in his work that their effects most powerfully manifest themselves. *The American* serves James as a crucial defense against the dilemmas he had inherited from childhood. The cause of its deflection into romance, into what must have seemed to James upon reflection to be the shockingly Gothic myth of Orestes, certainly did "lie deep." Why did this particular myth, which James's experience had rendered inevitably compelling, suggest itself to him at this particular time? R. W. Butterfield advances the standard explanation that the novel results from James's guilt over expatriation. The Bellegardes "are creations who in their odiousness bear witness to the intense guilt felt by the expatriate novice. For it is surely the very intensity of this guilt that necessitates the stereotyped character of the conflict and the allegorical polarization. Europe must be as vicious as possible, the American as decent as possible, for James to punish himself sufficiently for his cultural treason." America was certainly alienating, but it was not his homeland alone that conferred upon James the role of the prodigal son.

It is less leaving home than the sense of having lost it long ago that James expresses in *The American*. A yearning for exile pervades his experience of family from the beginning. His "first assured conception of true richness" had been "that we should be sent separately off among cold or even cruel aliens in order to be there thrillingly homesick. Homesickness was a luxury I remember craving from the tenderest age." It was to become the sweet deprivation of his maturity. On the evidence of *Notes of a Son and Brother*, James required deliverance from a presence far more pervasive than his native country: "she *was* he, *was* each of us, was our pride and our humility, our possibility of *any* relation." Mary James simply swallows up here, in her son's recollection, all these relations which it had been her task to nourish and define. She so thoroughly mediated Henry's relation to his father that the son even left it to her to express his filial misgivings:

> How can I better express what she seemed to do for her second son in especial than by saying that even with her deepest delicacy of attention present I could still feel, while my father read, why it was that I most of all seemed to wish we might have either been much less religious or much more so?

It was finally impossible to imagine his father apart from his mother:

> To have attempted any projection of our father's aspect without an immediate reference to her sovereign care for him and for all of us as the so widely open, yet so softly enclosing, lap of all his liberties and all our securities, all our variety and withal our harmony, the harmony that was for nine-tenths of it our sense of her gathered life in us, and of her having no other—to have so proceeded has been but to defer by instinct and by scruple to the kind of truth and of beauty before which the direct report breaks down. I may well have stopped short with what there would be to say, and yet what account of us all can pretend to have gone the least bit deep without coming to our mother at every penetration?

Through an interrogative James attempts to distance himself from the unarguable ubiquity of his mother's "lap," yet he nevertheless admits it to lie at the bottom of any account we may give of him. In such a passage, James is betrayed by his determination to be discreet. No "direct report" could locate more dramatically the source of James's anxiety over wide openness and soft enclosure. This is a kind of love that would foil all but the most extreme attempts at fusion or separation. If James is here mystified by his own discourse—he diagnoses where he means to praise —he compels us to recognize a maternal bond that left the son feeling neither entirely liberated nor wholly secure.

At a crucial turning point in his development, *The American* allows James to assume the full burden of his past in an attempt to transform it into a workable future. In imagining the House of Bellegarde, James defends against a maternal image more threatening than any fear of cultural treason. We have already seen Madame Bellegarde as the ambivalent mother who rejects and also threatens to swallow up her son as she has, with a single stare, killed his father. We have seen Urbain as the pompous but ultimately dependent Aegisthus, the figure whose "role" in the core myth "is analogous to that of the son used by the mother to destroy the father." Valentin and Claire, as Orestes and Electra, enlist our sympathies on the side of fathers and their aggrieved children. But they fail of achieving their seemingly deserved revenge. Having invented the essential dramatis personae, James cannot deliver them up to their promised end. The full force of the myth is vitiated, and the maternal threat remains undispelled.

But then the maternal figures in the novel had never been merely threatening. That James does not carry out the revenge to its conclusion suggests, on its positive side, that his identification with Valentin as

Orestes is incomplete. The characters of Mrs. Bread and Newman focus just those positive aspects of James's own experience which rescue him from the severity of an Oresteian fate. Having confronted his "oral-narcissistic dilemma" in the Valentin plot, does he not oppose it with those constructive drives toward intimacy and generativity which these two characters embody? *"Soundless, selfless, sleepless"*: in these words, with which the James family summed up the hovering attentiveness of Mary James, we find Mrs. Bread adumbrated. She becomes the one woman in the novel under whose care a man *might* be enabled to venture safely and confidently out into the world of women. And Newman appears to be the man to do it. He does not perceive women as a threat. Upon hearing Valentin's ominous claim that with respect to women he is an *"idealist,"* Newman "mentally" repudiates "the idea of a Frenchman having discovered any merit in the amiable sex which he himself did not suspect." Of such a disposition the reader is early made aware. Once his hero has met Mrs. Tristram, James declares that "Newman was fond, under all circumstances, of the society of women." This promises that nothing will, that nothing can, stand in the way of Newman's attempt to enjoy such society.

No more than Valentin does Newman embody for James, however, a successful wish fulfillment. He serves rather as a much more subtle defense than simple identification with a matricide against the threat women embody. Through this hero he reverses his unacceptably negative attitudes toward women. If he experiences inadmissible anxiety over sharing his life with a woman as a husband and father, cannot his fiction convert this fear into a desire? If he desires the unacceptable sacrifice of community consistent with a self-generating modernity, cannot he invent a hero who displays instead those historical instincts which promote social union and family continuity? We call this act of saying one thing and meaning another "irony." Through revision James attempts to take full control of this irony by making it explicit. He believes that he has written a novel in which the irony takes in the reader, but the deepest irony takes in James. James *says* that Newman is a modern but *means* that he has historical instincts. But the novel, finally, says the opposite about James. The conscious irony with which he rewrites the novel is still resisted by its unconscious origin, which continues to write him. James proves incapable of carrying out the ironic project—which he typically deems until the end a mere problem of technique—of defending against unconscious anxiety by transforming it into a fulfilled drive. The fatherhood which Newman ironically reveals himself best qualified to embody is not ultimately granted to him. Claire remains, after all, a "statue." Events conspire to leave Newman unrequited in love. His decision not to pursue revenge, to renounce the project which might ensure the consummation of his marriage, is made to appear as an act of character, not as a consequence of unconscious conflict. It is not the hero who is unready, James would have himself believe, but the world. But James is the truly unready one. He can imagine a more than modern hero, but not a more than modern fate. Faced with the crisis of maturity in his early thirties, James invents a "strong man" willing to receive the world, but cannot imagine a community—especially a woman—with whom he can truly share his life.

Thus begins the sacrifice of community which awaits the fate of so many strong Jamesian characters. James's response to the perils of fatherhood may have been extreme, accomplished some will say at the cost of life itself. He conceived a relation to his works that would forever protect him against the crime—betrayal—which threatens any of his characters worth trial. His children may have no power to rebel, but then he has no real freedom to reject. If he gave them life, they give him identity. In realizing himself through his imaginative offspring, James attains to his father's definition of God: "a being who is without selfhood save in His creatures." As the demanding but forgiving author of his creations, James simply absorbs both parental roles.

Perhaps the very experience of family which fostered James's anxieties over establishing a household of his own also helped to liberate his vision of what a total parent might be. If James's maternal bond had worked to limit the appeal of natural paternity, it became all the more necessary to assert his literary paternity, and with a mothering tenderness. James's indulgence of "the first-born" among his progeny is a repetition with a difference, a wholly internalized revision of a fructifying family tradition. The New York Edition remains James's most affectionate performance; revision became a labor of love. No other author has more carefully exercised his authority, however belatedly, on behalf of the potential maturity of his work. His having kept open the possibility of return, even to the most prodigal of his "awkward infants," still stands as an unexampled display of paternal piety.

✍§ Two

YEATS AND SYNGE
The Cuchulain Complex

Answering the Sphinx

"Go to the Arran Islands." Yeats's prophetic advice to Synge was to be confirmed by a second oracle. Near the end of his first stay on Inishmore, Synge's aged blind guide asked him the following riddle:

> Did ever you hear what it is goes on four legs when it is young, and on two legs after that, and on three legs when it does be old?

This is a crucial moment of election. Synge is here divined to be a potential Oedipus. Yeats had sent Synge on a journey, but only the uncanny recognition of the sphinx could reveal it as an errand. His is a riddle against riddles, a question whose answer is simply "man." Oedipus was capable of giving the answer because he already *was* the answer. Synge's way of answering reveals that he too knows that answers are not outside but inside, not distant and occult but hidden within the familiar. His reply is even more authoritative than the guess of Oedipus, expressive of the superfluity—so self-evident should be his command of the riddle —of any response: "I gave him the answer."

Oedipus Redux

Yeats's Oedipus prefers to spell answers out: "But I will start afresh and make the dark things plain" (*King Oedipus*, Yeats translation, 1928). Yeats's work, from his meeting with Synge until his death, can be read as an attempt to acquire the nonchalance which allowed Synge to pay the riddle so little heed. His struggle to speak more as a usurping Oedipus depends upon his speaking less in the accents of a lifelong son. Yeats came to see all history as presided over by two of its most famous:

What if Christ and Oedipus . . . are the two scales of a balance, the two-butt
ends of a seesaw? What if every two thousand and odd years something
happens in the world to make one sacred, the other secular; one wise, the other
foolish; one fair, the other foul; one divine, the other devilish? What if there is
an arithmetic or geometry that can exactly measure the slope of a balance, the
dip of a scale, and so date the coming of that something?

Christ's is a myth of obedience, "self-sacrifice," and reward; the myth of
Oedipus one of rebellion, "self-realization," and guilt. As the prevailing
myth of his culture, the example of Christ was one Yeats worked diligently
to overthrow. He repeatedly emphasizes Christianity's sacrificial rather
than its redemptive aspect, Christ on the cross rather than Christ
resurrected. Those who "copy Christ" are victims, Yeats argues in *Auto-
biographies*, yet he wonders whether or not one is fated to such emulation:
"All my proof that mind flows into mind, and that we cannot separate
mind and body, drives me to accept the thought of victimage in many
complex forms." The Imitation of Christ remained a key piece of evidence
for Yeats's belief that our lives are lived on behalf of a script.

While not a designation he would accept, "victimage" sums up the
conditions Yeats imposes on himself in his typological universe. Yeats
saw life as a struggle between mental archetypes ("mind flows into mind")
rather than within a psychological field ("mind and body"). No less
deterministic than Freud's, his view of behavior simply externalizes the
problem of motivation. The recognition and embracing of an archetype
—usually experienced as a contrary (a "Daimon" or "mask")—amounts
to the taking on of one's identity. Yeats's system faces its greatest difficulty
when it attempts to account for the phenomenon of change. For the
question of how to resolve a conflict, Yeats substitutes the problem of
how to escape the repetition of an archetype. While not a problem Yeats
himself need confront (he finds for himself a congenial script within the
system), it remains a problem. Can we freely become, rather than compul-
sively repeat? The elasticity in Freud's system derives from the belief that
any failure to undo a neurosis is a *"willful* failure"; the flaw in Yeats's
scheme is that it deprives us from the outset of any responsibility for the
domination of our Daimon. It chooses us.

Yet Yeats's enthusiasm for a fixed fate has been exaggerated, especially
when it involves anything like copying Christ. If the stories of Christ and
Oedipus are both about fathers and sons, Yeats was bound, for much of
his life, to find himself adumbrated by the former. A sacrifice of the son's
life to the will and power of the father, however redeemed by the paradox
that the Son *is* the Father, could serve as one script for the filial drama
being played out in Yeats's life. The elaboration of a typological de-
terminism served many purposes, but it certainly allowed Yeats to displace
responsibility for this particular kind of "victimage" onto an external
apparatus, even as the apparatus was a system within which Yeats could

complete a revision of his sense of self. Certainly Yeats's belief in fate
preceded his systematization of it, one which at once codified and allowed
him to transcend fate. By the time *A Vision* came to articulate the conflict
as between Oedipus and Christ, Yeats's romance with fated repetition
had already served its most paradoxical purpose: it had called into being
those defenses—prophecy and revision—with which Yeats warred so
creatively against one sort of victimage and on behalf of another.

Yeats's prophetic theory of history, developed between 1910 and 1920,
played a crucial role in his psychic economy. It promises an apocalypse
in which the forces which liberate are about to supersede those which
repress. Even as the theory continues to assert our subordination to
cycles and avatars, it discovers by a lucky chance that its author lives in a
historical vortex. Hence the tragic dignity of embracing one's fate can be
preserved even while discovering in an inhumanly determined pattern a
breach which promises a second chance. Perhaps it is just this possibility
of divining an imminent break within the pattern that encourages Yeats
to call the pattern into being. Chiliasts frequent only the nick of time.
Thus when *A Vision* proclaims the emergence of the "new divinity" that
Freud had already converted into secular scripture, it at once confirms
the hegemony of historical cones and offers a rebirth to those fortunate
enough to be living through the time of troubles. In sinking "down soul
and body into the earth," Oedipus will "balance Christ who, crucified
standing up, went into the abstract sky soul and body." This rebalancing
is happening now: by the luck of his location in time, Yeats can enjoy the
freshness of discontinuity within a universe of repetition.

Revision served Yeats as his final imaginative defense against the drive
to copy Christ. In "Vacillation" he still speaks as if emulation of the self-
sacrificer were an option, albeit an option he refuses:

> I—though heart might find relief
> Did I become a Christian man and choose for my belief
> What seems most welcome in the tomb—play a predestined part.

Yeats here distorts the conflict; it had been less a question of choosing
between conscious beliefs than one of an inescapable drive to imitation.
Certainly by 1932 Yeats had succeeded in changing parts, and so may be
content to label his recasting as a version of Oedipus "predestined." But
he had also been helped to achieve reversal by conversion to the insight
that the Christian story was itself a misreading of a more fundamental
one. The apostate Ribh here denounces the obedient Patrick:

> An abstract Greek absurdity has crazed the man—
> Recall that masculine Trinity. Man, woman, child (a daughter or a son),
> That's how all natural or supernatural stories run.

The Christian Trinity derives from the Oedipal triangle. Whereas Christ is put forward in *A Vision* as the true contrary of Oedipus, in "Supernatural Songs" he is seen to be his inauthentic negation. Oedipus no longer need supersede Christ in historical time; in this synchronic view, all stories simply "run" in place, within the three walls of the aboriginal triangle.

Yeats had come to see the Christ story as a latter-day corruption of Oedipus once he had recognized it as a truncated version of its original, one which conferred upon its "victims" the potentially crippling role of the perpetual son. He came to such a position after having successfully revised his own "part" into one in which the son had assumed the power and priority of a father. The imaginative defenses deployed against the architecture of fate confirmed the end of a process of recasting largely carried out through life. Yeats had learned through direct experience that such a transformation was possible, even as he had come to accept the struggle for ascendancy as necessary. This reversal of roles certainly had everything to do with becoming a father himself, but it was furthered, just as surely, by Yeats's experience of the work and friendship of John Synge.

Synge's plays promise the reversal of generations; Yeats's, their fatal hegemony. Both depart from Sophocles. But while Synge embraces the myth of Oedipus as a comedy, Yeats rejects it as a tragic nostalgia. The Playboy of the Western World "kills" his father on impulse and confirms his deed through repetition. In *On Baile's Strand* the son proves fatally unsuccessful in carrying out a mission of revenge against the father. What is easeful for Synge is impossible for Yeats. It was in the Family Romance which they lived out together that both began to accomplish an escape from the paternal humiliations and filial losses of which they wrote. The drama of fathers and sons within their works sought and found resolution in their lives.

On Baile's Strand

When Yeats speculates that "there is some one myth for every man, which, if we but knew it, would make us understand all he did and thought," we answer "Yes, and for you, it is the myth of Cuchulain." The Cuchulain story serves Yeats for over forty-five years as his most durable myth. Peter Ure argues that "the Cuchulain theme is perhaps the most 'permanent image' of all the images that Yeats took from the Irish sagas." After writing "The Death of Cuchulain" in 1892 (renamed "Cuchulain's Fight with the Sea"), Yeats is to return to his hero six times in five plays and in the late and beautifully antiheroic "Cuchulain Comforted." Yeats singled out one of these dramatic works for special praise; he called *On Baile's Strand* his "best play." And when in "The Circus Animals' Desertion" he passed a last judgment on his career (though there were still more Cuchulain plays to come), his enumeration of "old themes" culminates in a tribute to his hero's dramatic debut:

> And when the Fool and Blind Man stole the bread
> Cuchulain fought the ungovernable sea;
> Heart-mysteries there, and yet when all is said
> It was the dream itself enchanted me

"Heart-mysteries there": at the age of sixty-three, Yeats acknowledges that the riddle of the play is in the heart of the riddler. The play's origins are at once evoked and obscured; while the turn into exclamatory reverie admits that more can be said, the line ends by telling us that nothing more will be said. "Heart-mysteries" thus becomes a token of repression, an admission of unplumbed inwardness which really acts as a defense against further introspection. So Yeats leaves the play the enchanting "dream" he first found it: "The first shape of it came to me in a dream, but it changed much in the making, foreshadowing, it may be, a change that may bring a less dream-burdened will into my verses." "Dream-burdened will" suggests a poet overborne by involuntary mental processes. But this dream comes to relieve the poet of dreaming. The play appears to be at once a symptom and a cure: it originates from unwilled fantasies, but results, Yeats hopes, in a poetry freed from determination by the unconscious mind.

Yeats was as willing to admit that a friend's art might function as a "compensating dream" as he was reluctant to apply such reductions to himself. In *Per Amica Silentia Lunae* (1918) he entertains the view of art as motivated wish-fulfillment, and turns to Synge as an example:

> There are indeed certain men whose art is less an opposing virtue than a compensation from some accident of health or circumstance. During the riots over the first production of *The Playboy of the Western World* Synge was confused, without clear thought, and was soon ill—indeed the strain of that week may perhaps have hastened his death—and he was, as is usual with gentle and silent men, scrupulously accurate in all his statements. In his art he made, to delight his ear and his mind's eye, voluble daredevils who "go romancing through a romping lifetime . . . to the dawning of the Judgment Day."

The point here is that a man who imagines "voluble daredevils" cannot raise a whisper in his own defense. The ironic contrast between Synge's wishes and his deeds leads Yeats to posit a theory of art as compensation. While Synge is pursued by an "accident" within, Yeats pursues an "opposing virtue" from without. It is the Daimon, and not internal "circumstance," which determines his creation: "I think of life as a struggle with the Daimon who would ever set us to the hardest work among those not impossible." It requires only a little suspicion before one recognizes such a scheme as a projection of the entire activity known as *conflict*. "Man and Daimon feed the hunger in one another's hearts": such a symbiosis results in an art every bit as compensatory as Synge's. What is Yeats's talk of the Daimon but a highly metaphoric musing on the insistent return of the repressed: "We meet always in the deep of the mind, whatever our work, wherever our reverie carries us, that other Will." To meditate the mask is to allegorize into an extrapsychic conflict the internal struggle between the censor and the forbidden.

We are compelled to interpret not our Daimon, but our dreams. Yeats admits the possibility of *Traumdeutung* a few pages after positing the ubiquity of the Daimon:

> The doctors of medicine have discovered that certain dreams of the night, for I do not grant them all, are the day's unfulfilled desire, and that our terror of desires condemned by the conscience has distorted and disturbed our dreams. They have only studied the breaking into dream of elements that have remained unsatisfied without purifying discouragement. We can satisfy in life a few of our passions and each passion but a little, and our characters indeed but differ because no two men bargain alike. The bargain, the compromise, is always threatened, and when it is broken we become mad or hysterical or are in some way deluded; and so when a starved or banished passion shows in a dream we, before awaking, break the logic that had given it the capacity of action and throw it into chaos again.

What we would call "identity" results for Yeats, as it does for Freud, in the bargain each makes with universal desire. They differ as to which class of productions ought to be (or can be) the interpreter's legitimate domain. The psychoanalyst studies only the dream work; should he not extend his researches to those wishes that have undergone the "purifying discouragement" of successfully sublimated art?

On Yeats's own testimony, *On Baile's Strand* stands on the borderline between a dream and an accomplished work of art. If Yeats's conscious will chose Cuchulain as a heroic mask, it was in part because his story expressed an unconscious complex of passions still resisted and distorted by the censoring power of dream. The appeal of the myth lay in its power to at once excite and forbid "the day's unfulfilled desire." If, as Yeats hopes, the play has accomplished the "purifying discouragement" of these desires, he will be liberated from a dream-burdened will into a style less enervated by fantasy.

On Baile's Strand turns upon the conflict between father and son. But it does not begin there. Against all the dictates of the Cuchulain myth,

Yeats centers the play upon a longing for a partnership between the generations. The heart of the play is Cuchulain's temporary fantasy of an alliance with his unrecognized son. In the face of a challenge he cannot finally reject, Cuchulain begins by rejecting heroism:

> Put up your sword; I am not mocking you.
> I'd have you for my friend.

The Young Man hesitates; Cuchulain pleads, and the boy gives way:

> We'll stand by one another from this out.

But as Cuchulain begins to offer his son the cloak received from his father, a sudden reversal occurs:

> *First Old King.* Some witch has worked upon your mind, Cuchulain.
>   The head of that young man seemed like a woman's
>   You'd had a fancy for. Then of a sudden
>   You laid your hands on the High King himself!
> *Cuchulain.* And laid my hands on the High King himself?
> *Conchubar.* Some witch is floating in the air above us.
> *Cuchulain.* Yes, witchcraft, witchcraft! Witches of the air!
>   [To Young Man.] Why did you? Who was it set you to this
>   work?
>   Out, out! I say, for now it's sword on sword!
> *Young Man.* But . . . but I did not.
> *Cuchulain.*   Out, I say, out, out!

At a loss for credible motivation, Yeats turns to the occult. Cuchulain is tricked by the *illusion* of witchcraft back into his fatal role. For an author to whom such presences were in fact anything but an illusion, the depiction of witchcraft as mere paranoia risks a considerable degree of self-irony. Yeats proves willing to belittle one of his cherished fascinations in order to convey Cuchulain's half-crazed state. As the weakest point in the play's dramatic action, Cuchulain's change of heart thus raises questions about Yeats's commitment to the very myth within which he has chosen to operate. An alternative ending has been glimpsed and approached, but the longing for reconciliation must be subdued to the severity of the myth. Its tragic ending ends the play, and the father kills the son. The logic of a story beyond Yeats's authorship insists upon censoring nostalgias central to the play Yeats is authoring.

The real drama of *On Baile's Strand* takes place not so much *in* the play as *between* the author and the play. It is curious that Yeats would have made so obvious the conflict between mythic inevitability and his own interest in free play. He risks implausibility at the one moment his play demands total assent, as if to prefer the tension of working within these materials to the proven appeal of the materials themselves. There surfaces here a dissatisfaction with the direction Yeats knows his play must take, and it perhaps comes as no surprise that *On Baile's Strand* is the last of the Cuchulain works in which Yeats represents his hero in the role of the slaying father.

Yeats deploys an even more successful defense against the promised end through the Conchubar plot. Most critics read the play as turning upon the debate between Cuchulain and Conchubar. Ellmann, while he begins by holding that *On Baile's Strand* "was written on the theme of father against son," proceeds to claim that "the real struggle is between the warrior Cuchulain, instinctively loving and hating, and the crafty king Conchubar who forces Cuchulain to slay unwittingly his own son." But the play no more resolves itself within this struggle than *Oedipus* does between Oedipus and Creon. Why then does Yeats displace attention toward it? Perhaps to shift emphasis from the theme of priority (fatherhood) to the theme of authority (kingship). Both relationships are hierarchical. But while authority is an acquisition, priority is a fact. The fact that fathers come before sons is at the heart of this tragedy, and no amount of effort can actually reverse it. Kingly authority does not come before, it stands above, and so is subject to reversal. If *On Baile's Strand* can be read as a struggle between two kinds of authority, the tragedy appears to flow less from an unalterable natural fact than from an institutional fact subject to alteration by the will.

Since kingly authority depends upon conscious assent, the climax of its career in the play turns upon the taking of an oath. Cuchulain's promise to obey Conchubar seems to come out of nowhere:

> You've wives and children now
> And for that reason cannot follow one
> That lives like a bird's flight from tree to tree. —
> It's time the years put water in my blood
> And drowned the wildness of it, for all's changed,
> But that unchanged. — I'll take what oath you will.

This is the play's first unmotivated change of heart. It makes inevitable what could have remained a matter of choice. Since we cannot answer the question "Why does Cuchulain swear?" we may wish to ask another: "Why does his author imagine such a deed?"

This oath-taking raises for the first time the question of whether these characters have a dramatic existence apart from an unresolved authorial intention. Is Cuchulain's assumption of the role of juggernaut a projection of Yeats's desire to overcome the father? Or is it a reflection of his relationship with a father "who was affectionate but intellectually dominating," one in which Yeats for many years fought a holding action? Certainly it provided an imaginary resolution to unresolved episodes from Yeats's own past:

The poet had first broken away from his father by taking up occult science, and now their conflicts of opinion were frequent. One night at Bedford Park W. B. expressed an appreciation of Ruskin's *Unto This Last*. He was put out of the room so violently that he broke the glass of a picture with the back of his head. Another night when they had been in some similar argument, J. B. Y. squared up and wanted to box, and, when Willie said that he could not fight his own father, replied, "I don't see why you should not."

It was not as a man of power, however, that John Butler was likely to intimidate William. Yeats doubtless thought himself a practical success burdened by a charming failure. He was to write, in 1919, of his father's hopelessness as a breadwinner, and of the stimulus this had given to his own worldly achievement:

> It is this infirmity of will which has prevented him from finishing his pictures and ruined his career. He even hates the sign of will in others. It used to cause quarrels between me and him, for the qualities which I thought necessary to success in art or in life seemed to him "egotism" or "selfishness" or "brutality." I had to escape this family drifting, innocent and helpless, and the need for that drew me to dominating men like Henley and Morris and estranged me from his friends.

William Murphy concludes that from the 1890s on William regarded his father as "a mere dreamer unable to make his mark in the real world." But in the world of dreaming, where both sought a more ineffable triumph, John Butler must often have seemed to go before his son. Yeats's late letters increasingly acknowledge his borrowings from his father's ample fund of speculation. John Butler exercised over his son the power of a ubiquitous imagination. What did the failures of the nineties signify when, as Murphy reminds us,

> Every night his father was there, like the Ancient Mariner, at the other side of the dinner table, discoursing on philosophy, art, and literature, and Willie could not choose but hear. It has been said that John Butler Yeats was one of the few fathers who lived long enough to be influenced by his son, and the epigram is so good that one wants to believe it. Yet, it is clear that, except for his forays into the occult, the ideas on literature, art, and politics that William Butler Yeats made known throughout the world all grew from the seeds planted by John Butler Yeats, the sower who could not reap. Try as he might, the demon of Blenheim Road was one Willie could never exorcise.

Perhaps the Cuchulain myth, in its aspect as a family saga, dramatized the simple anxiety that wherever a young man ventures, his father remains the spore of what he is becoming.

John Butler may have seen no reason why a man should fight his father, but Cuchulain, his vision of futurity subdued by a reverence for priority, saw ample reason why not:

    Boy,
If I had fought my father, he'd have killed me,
As certainly as if I had a son
And fought with him, I should be deadly to him;
For the old fiery fountains are far off
And every day there is less heat o' the blood.

The operation of a prior and external constraint—the oath—relieves such confrontations of the burden of choice. Yeats's original contribution to the Cuchulain myth is the arbitrary and fatal oath. Oaths relieve selves of the *need* for motivation. They are mechanisms by which drama is made to go forward even as they obscure the question of motives, a question perhaps too painful to be explored.

Yeats also defends against the burden of the myth's ending by committing action to narration. The play begins with a blind man's narration and ends with a fool's. We do not witness the actual killing, although Cuchulain unwittingly narrates its comic antecedent:

    [*Showing cloak.*
    My father gave me this.
He came to try me, rising up at dawn
Out of the cold dark of the rich sea.
He challenged me to battle, but before
My sword had touched his sword, told me his name,
Gave me this cloak, and vanished.

Through this not-touching of swords the father Lugh passes on his power even as he acknowledges the son's. This is not the kind of drama Yeats found it in his power to represent. The actual confrontation between father and son is a failed recognition scene. No names are bequeathed, no power is transferred. The origins and ends that confirm identity are, in the present of the play, only obliquely approached. Once the father and son do cross swords a blind man, Yeats's Tiresias, must perform the act of recognition: "It is his own son he has slain." In Yeats's revision these words replace Cuchulain's own: "He was my son, and I have killed my son." Even this personal admission is finally denied him. Yeats could get no closer to describing, let alone acting out, the scene which makes the myth compelling for him. His dramatic sense is curtailed by the repression of the very impulses the play is meant to explore.

John Butler Yeats objected to just this sense of a deflected intention in his criticism of the end of *On Baile's Strand*. His letter to William about the play begins with extraordinary praise:

    I cannot tell you how much I enjoyed your play. As I lay awake most of the night I had plenty of time to think about it. The scene between father and son

over the duel was the most thrilling and enthralling experience I ever went
through. You touched at the same moment the fountain of joy and tears.

But I maintain that the end won't do—it is not true to nature to suppose that
the fool would not have had thoughts of dinner driven out of his head by such
a sight as a great knight gone mad and confronting himself with his own fury.
Nor do I quite like the hero's coming on after the fight "in good spirits" as you
say. There would have been something more than this—as it stands it rather
suggests that the father killed the son as you would a chicken—

Yeats himself found the end, on the other hand, "particularly impressive."
So father and son were diametrically opposed as to the heart of the play.
The older Yeats experiences a strange exultation—a thrill—in seeing a
father and son debate their way toward disaster. But he resists the final
turn into comic inconsequence. Above all, the high sentence of the drama
must be maintained. John Butler apparently felt only the dignity of the
tragedy without any of the humiliation. He accuses his son of having
botched the ending, of having failed to take seriously what must have
been so sublimely moving. Where the son wishes to allay the turbulence
of the conflict, the father prefers to keep it fully in view. Thus a father
implies that his son has shirked his responsibility toward his materials,
materials themselves expressive of a son's inability to meet the expecta-
tions of a father. Such a response must have struck William less as
confirmation that he had succeeded in defending against priority than as
one more evidence of the continuing necessity to struggle against it.

The Playboy

Yeats was to survive Synge by thirty years, and might well have heard
something prophetic in Maurya's elegy for her dead son in *Riders to the
Sea:*

In the big world the old people do be leaving things after them for their sons
and children, but in this place it is the young men do be leaving things behind
for them that do be old.

Synge left much behind; most importantly, a myth to undo the myth of
Riders to the Sea. In its haunting suggestion that the death of a child
flows perhaps from some unconscious wish of the parent, *Riders* belongs
as much to Yeats's canon as to Synge's. The play lays out the problem—a
script inherited across a gap of generations—which it becomes Synge's
project to rewrite.

Deirdre also inherits a script—"I am Deirdre of the Sorrows"—but, as
part of Synge's mature vision, finds the resources to resist acting out a
"predestined part." She begins by wanting to shut out the unpredictability
of an open future by living out "what is foretold." But as she debates

within herself the possibility of flight with Naisi, Deirdre finds herself less and less concerned with fulfilling a prophecy: "Isn't it a small thing is foretold about the ruin of ourselves, Naisi, when all men have age coming and great ruin in the end?" All men "end"; Dierdre suddenly confronts the overwhelming importance of how each man or woman *lives*. As the play proceeds, Synge helps Deirdre shed all traces of tragic decorum. She finally cleaves to uncertain life over noble death, free play over mythic inevitability. The last act proceeds through a series of reversals—stay Naisi/go Naisi/stay Naisi/—which display the essential waywardness of human desire. Life here is all an impetuous turning, for all Deirdre's belated claim to have had "the choice of lives." So when she ends by deciding to stay with Naisi forever, the act affects us more as culminating a process of self-discovery than as fulfilling the promised end. Synge's characters do not resolutely make themselves but find themselves by embracing their luck a second time, seconding with an act of will an originating act of chance.

Christy Mahon twice repeats himself. Repetition frees rather than binds him. It is decidedly not a compulsion, some irresistible upwelling of the insistent uncanny. Repetition in the service of free play: this is the heart of Synge's achievement. He claimed that the "aim of literature is to make the impossible seem inevitable or to make the inevitable seem impossible." Yeats, on the other hand, makes the inevitable seem inevitable. Synge reserves his most bitter irony for those who repeat in the service of repetition, who choose through pride or succumb through compulsion to play a foreknown role. The last thing Synge desires is Unity of Being, for he fears to purchase integration at the cost of the power of reversal.

When Synge writes *The Playboy of the Western World*, he takes up the most preordained script of all. Synge's work constantly questions whether the human imagination can renew itself *within* the tradition of the old. The Oedipal myth offers such an ambition a considerable challenge. If the story of Oedipus promises that the begotten can overcome the begetter, the full burden of the myth enforces the more limiting recognition that we *are* only within what *was*. As a myth about myth, Oedipus renounces the option of free play by revealing even our rebellions as contained by scripts that, if human in origin, have become natural in operation. Synge takes up this myth not to reaffirm it but to strip it, once and for all, of tragic necessity. Not only does a son here triumph over a father—that would be, after all, only part of the script. The means here revise the end. It is the *way* in which Synge carries us toward a conclusion which is anything but original that liberates us from the original burden of the conclusion.

The way, of course, is through comedy. The play is both comic in tone and comedic in outcome. The tone counts for at least as much as the final harmony. For more, perhaps, since Comedy also acts as a myth which conditions and finally governs expectation. Synge wishes to avoid any sense of the foregone and so keeps his resolution thoroughly in doubt. Comedy acts as a mythos if it can be foreseen; such are its pleasures that they are never seriously in doubt. But doubt certainly intrudes in the *Playboy*, most acutely at the moment when Pegeen, her Christy bound and gasping, brands him in the leg. Synge's alternative to the tragic is much more like Bergson's than like Frye's. What he requires from "each of us is a constantly alert attention that discerns the outlines of the present situation, together with a certain elasticity of mind and body to enable us to adapt ourselves in consequence." Synge's is a world governed by a law which Yeats, as Harold Bloom argues, could never entirely respect: the law of reversal. His reversals present a life which refuses to render up even the pattern of Comedy, however much it is governed from moment to moment by the elasticity of the comic.

T. R. Henn calls Christy a "comic Oedipus," and he is right, but one wonders why this is put forward as statement rather than paradox. This is the paradox of the play—that these two words can be brought into alignment. Patricia Meyer Spacks responds directly to this contradiction: "Synge somehow manages to treat so dreadful a theme with apparent lightness." The play denies the guilt which is the very mechanism by which the play should go forward. Christy never resorts to self-recrimination; the agent of punishment here is finally society, not the ego. The successful attempt to reverse the relation of father and son, itself an act of revenge, does not receive its traditional psychological reward. Thus the recurring cycle of rebellion and revenge is broken off at the crucial juncture when the self would turn upon itself in an act of self-punishment. Sons may supplant fathers, but fathers do not survive as crippling agents of guilt within the son. The play questions whether the Oedipal complex need be a universal tragedy in human life.

While Christy discovers that one obvious consequence of father-killing is increased female attention—"two fine women fighting for the likes of me"—his crime does not originate from competition within an Oedipal triangle. Christy "kills" his father in order to *avoid* incest. When Old Mahon insists that he marry the Widow Casey, Christy refuses, and for good reason: "'I won't wed her,' says I, 'when all know she did suckle me for six weeks when I came into the world.'" Here the son displays greater respect for taboo than the father, while the father effectively identifies with the traditionally forbidden wishes of the son. Whatever Christy's "dirty deed" means, then, it does not necessarily mean that sons unconsciously wish to supplant fathers in order to possess mothers. Synge seems to have sensed that such a reversal of roles could only occur on a symbolic level, and he is interested in more permanent solutions.

Were the play a matter of rivalry over the mother, it would run up against the brute fact of Christy's origin in a moment in which he was not present. The sexuality of the mother embodies the whole unarguable fact of priority which any son is helpless to reverse. So Synge shifts attention, as had Yeats before him, toward a condition he can reverse: the father's authority.

Shawn Keogh is the complete pawn of his various fathers, yet he originates from none of them. They are simply "authority figures." Throughout the play Synge emphasizes the father's power to command or compel obedience rather than his sheer precedence. Authority is a power Christy actually can assume. The first time he lets fall the edge of his loy across his father's skull, Christy may seem a mere repetition of an instinctive attempt to rid the self of the man who came first. The second time he tries to "stretch" Old Mahon, Christy reinforces something spontaneous with an act of will. When he sees his father "coming to be killed a third time," what may have been tragic before has certainly become a farce. It proves impossible to "kill" a father in this world. It is the highest form of vanity: "Them that kills their fathers is a vain lot surely." Fathers cannot be gotten rid of, let alone subjected to total reversal. One can only emulate and finally acquire their power. Christy's parting declaration—"I'm master of all fights from now"—reveals a grasp of what he really has won. "Mastery" can be passed from one generation to the next; priority creates the gap across which any such exchange is made. Synge simply refuses to acknowledge temporal belatedness as dooming a son to always remaining a son. The generations can stand next to, as well as follow. Synge thus realizes the very fantasy Yeats had failed to consummate in *On Baile's Strand*. In a key stage direction, Synge has Old Mahon exit before his son *"with a broad smile."* Father and son leave the stage defiantly in league. The son gives the commands, but the father leads the way.

The Family Romance

On the night of 4 February 1907, William Butler Yeats rose on the stage of the Abbey Theatre to defend Synge's *Playboy* after a week of rioting. This was to prove the culmination of a relationship begun in Paris ten years earlier. In Yeats's hopelessly a-chronological autobiography, he claims to be "certain" of only "one date, for I have gone to much trouble to get it right. I met John Synge for the first time in the Autumn of 1896, when I was one and thirty, and he four and twenty." Synge was born into Yeats's life two years before he was to become the collaborator of Coole Park. Yeats admits at the end of this episode that his introduction of Synge at this point in the autobiography may have been premature:

"But in writing of Synge I have run far ahead, for in 1896 he was but one picture among many. I am often astonished when I think that we can meet unmoved some person, or pass some house, that in later years is to bear a chief part in our life." Despite this disclaimer of prescience, the episode itself unfolds with prophetic inevitability:

> He told me that he had learned Irish at Trinity College, so I urged him to go to the Aran Islands and find a life that had never been expressed in literature, instead of a life where all had been expressed. I did not divine his genius, but I felt he needed something to take him out of his morbidity and melancholy. Perhaps I would have given the same advice to any young Irish writer who knew Irish, for I had been that summer upon Inishmaan and Inishmore, and was full of the subject. My friends and I had landed from a fishing-boat to find ourselves among a group of islanders, one of whom said he would bring us to the oldest man upon Inishmaan. This old man, speaking very slowly, but with laughing eyes, had said, "If any gentleman has done a crime, we'll hide him. There was a gentleman that killed his father, and I had him in my own house six months till he got away to America."

Yeats is as careful to establish this as a famous scene of instruction as he is to establish the date. In his preface to *The Well of the Saints* he had put the date at 1898. This mistake is corrected in the 1922 autobiography, but another is allowed to stand. While reading this passage, the impression is gathered that Yeats spontaneously enjoined Synge toward Aran on their first meeting. But it was only on one of his "subsequent visits to Paris," Hone points out, that Yeats "finally" gave Synge his famous travel tip. Yeats retreats from further myth-making by admitting that "I did not divine his genius," and modestly disclaims any foresight through a "perhaps." This adverb opens the way, however, for Yeats's master-stroke. Not only does he manage to secure for himself the role of Synge's Prime Mover, he ends by becoming his poetic father. Was Yeats the source of Synge's greatest plot? This is an illusion he never tires of creating. He first claims priority over the story of the "man destroyed his da" a year after Synge's death. And he was to repeat this maneuver in Stockholm on the night the Irish Dramatic Movement received its highest public acclaim:

> When I had landed from a fishing yawl on the middle of the island of Aran, a few months before my first meeting with Synge, a little group of islanders, who had gathered to watch a stranger's arrival, brought me to "the oldest man upon the island." He spoke but two sentences, speaking them very slowly: "If any gentleman has done a crime we'll hide him. There was a gentleman that killed his father, and I had him in my house six months till he got away to America." It was a play founded on that old man's story Synge brought back with him.

The inescapable suggestion in both of these accounts is that Yeats either conveyed this anecdote to Synge, or relinquished it to him, secondhand. If he cannot claim to have fathered the playwright, he can hint at having inspired his greatest play. However calculated this effect, the origin of Synge's plot is dangerously compromised.

From the first Yeats sought to gather Synge into an intricate Family Romance. Augusta Gregory/William Butler Yeats/John Millington Synge: "Man, woman, child (a daughter or a son),/That's the way all natural or supernatural stories run." Synge was anything but a child when he first came to Coole after his initial visit to Aran, but he should have been a prime candidate for such a triangle. His father had died when he was just a year old. In all of Synge's *Autobiography*, the only acknowledgment that men *have* fathers arises from an early bout with atheism: "Incest and parricide were but a consequence of the idea that possessed me." Synge's mother, who died just four months before he succumbed to the tumor in his neck, spent her lifetime lamenting his atheism. Her favorite epithet —"Poor Johnnie"—nicely captures the mixture of pity and irritation he provoked in her. "He writes the most utter folly," she complained to Synge's brother Samuel. She was not without more powerful weapons, and withdrew financial support when Synge strayed beyond atheism into Irish Nationalism. His chronic asthma could scarcely have been helped by her constant attempt to draw him homeward and into the bosom of Jesus. The rejection of Synge's Aran manuscript provided one more proof of his waywardness: "Poor Johnnie! We could all have told him that, but then men like Yeats and the rest get round him and make him think Irish literature and the Celtic language and all these things that they are trying to revive are very important, and, I am sorry to say, Johnnie seems to believe all they tell him." She died without ever having seen one of his plays.

Lady Gregory provided more nourishment. Synge wrote to her soon after its publication that "Your *Cuchulain* is part of my daily bread." She was hardly reluctant to cite such a statement as evidence for her imaginative priority over Synge's language: "I wrote in it before Synge did. He said he was amazed to find in my *Cuchulain of Muirthemne* his desired dialect." Whether Synge would have easily acknowledged such dependency is dubious. For all the help he willingly received—and his stay at Coole in 1898 must have converted him from an outsider to an insider—nothing struck Yeats more than Synge's imperviousness to influence. "Neither I nor Lady Gregory had ever a compliment from him." This approaches the tone of an indebtedness scorned. Yeats appears to have wanted from Synge not so much praise as acknowledgment. But Synge did not seem capable of noticing any authority, imaginative or otherwise. "I do not think he disliked other writers—they did not exist." Yeats to George Moore: "Synge has always the better of you, for you have brief but ghastly moments during which you admit the existence of other writers; Synge never has." To whom does Yeats speak here but himself? The more Yeats struggled to include Synge within his Family Romance, the less Synge appeared to be playing his part.

When Synge did deign to adopt a role toward either of these sponsors, it was in secret, and as the rebellious son. He could betray jealousy of the alliance between his two sponsors: "every now and then Poel launched out into praise of my work, and it was amusing to see Lady G dashing in at once with praise of Yeats' work." Throughout his letters to Molly Allgood he complains of being excluded from his fair share in the professional triangle. He complains of being "inclined to clear away to Paris and let them make it a Yeats-Gregory show in name as well as in deed. However it is best not to do anything rash. They have both been very kind to me at times and I owe them a great deal." Synge's private expression of both rage and gratitude allowed him, it appears, only the public expression of a remarkable indifference.

In Yeats's autobiography, he and Lady Gregory first "conceive" Synge during the summer of 1897. Yeats is as careful to glorify her origins as he is to obscure Synge's. After a reverent genealogy of the Gregorys he brings Augusta on stage: "Lady Gregory, as I first knew her, was a plainly dressed woman of forty-five, without obvious good looks, except the charm that comes from strength, intelligence and kindness." This ideal sponsor-mother, husbandless, of brave lineage, possessed the perfect aristocratic site for the conception of a dramatic movement. Here was a woman who would never withdraw her support:

> On the sea-coast at Duras, a few miles from Coole, an old French Count, Florimond de Basterot, lived for certain months in every year. Lady Gregory and I talked over my project of an Irish Theatre, looking out upon the lawn of his house, watching a large flock of ducks that was always gathered for his arrival from Paris . . . I told her that I had given up my project because it was impossible to get the few pounds necessary for a start in little halls, and she promised to collect or give the money necessary. That was her first great service to the Irish intellectual movement. She reminded me the other day that when she first asked me what she could do to help our movement I suggested nothing; and, certainly, I no more foresaw her genius than I foresaw that of John Synge.

Yet what Yeats denies to foresight he reclaims for intuition. Less than a page later he asks the crucial rhetorical question: "where, but for the conversation at Florimond de Basterot's, had been the genius of Synge?" Thus Yeats recovers what his modesty had just forfeited. This chapter completes the second crucial episode in his imaginative fatherhood of Synge. To the scene of instruction Yeats here adds the primal scene. The relationship was unfolding with the inevitability of myth. Only the third and final act of the drama remained—the trial of the generations. Yeats knew that endings give myths their names. The question that must have haunted him as the three assumed directorship of the Abbey Theatre and moved toward the *Playboy* crisis was this: would the creator of the tragic Cuchulain play only "a predestined part?"

When Yeats rose to defend the *Playboy*, he was not alone. Hone reminds us that while "the author stayed at home . . . Yeats' chief support upon the platform was his father." And Yeats seems to agree, years later, in "Beautiful Lofty Things":

> My father upon the Abbey stage, before him a raging crowd:
> "This Land of Saints," and then as the applause died out,
> "Of plaster Saints"; his beautiful mischievous head thrown back.

Both men had thrust themselves into a highly volatile situation. Synge's attendance at the play had been met with cries of "Kill the Author." Feeling ran so high on all sides that even one of the Abbey's female custodians had been moved to remark, "Isn't Mr. Synge the bloody old snot to write such a play?" The *Freeman's Journal* summed up public opinion of the play: "It is calumny gone raving mad."

John Butler Yeats had taunted the crowd, but William downplays his father's aggressiveness somewhat in *Autobiographies:* "No man of all literary Dublin dared show his face but my own father, who spoke to, or rather in the presence of, that howling mob with sweetness and simplicity. I fought them, he did a finer thing—forgot them." John Butler himself insists that he was even less heroic:

> Of course I did not make a speech in favour of patricide. How could I? Here is what I said. I began with some information about Synge which interested my listeners and then: "Of course I know Ireland is an island of Saints, but thank God it is also an island of sinners—only unfortunately in this Country people cannot live or die except behind a curtain of deceit." At this point the chairman and my son both called out, "Time's up, Time's up." I saw the lifted sign and like the devil in *Paradise Lost* I fled. The papers next morning said I was howled down. It was worse, I was pulled down.

In favour of patricide: as if this were the issue! And yet of course it was the issue, one which John Butler grasped as instinctively as he had the defensive bathos at the end of *On Baile's Strand*. He sensed that this was not a play in defense of which a father might legitimately speak. And so he relinquishes, with some help from his impatient son, the role of heroic defender to that son. "I fought them . . . he forgot them."

None who witnessed the scene that night were to forget the figure Yeats cut upon that stage. Lady Gregory saw the boy inside the man: "Yeats when he rose for the last speech was booed but got a hearing at last and got out all he wanted to say. He spoke very well, but his voice

rather cracked once or twice from screaming and from his sore throat."
Mary Colum saw only the man:

> Yeats took the platform in full evening dress and faced the crowd. Step by step
> he interpreted the play, delivering in the process some of his most complex
> theories of art, one moment cowing the audience, the next shouted down by
> them. . . . Even on the patriotics Yeats was equal to them. "The author of
> *Cathleen ni Houlihan* addresses you," he said. The audience, remembering that
> passionately patriotic play, forgot its antagonism for a few moments and Yeats
> got his cheers. . . . I never witnessed a human being fight as Yeats fought that
> night, nor knew another with so many weapons in his armory.

This was a moment of self-transformation. Apart from all choosing,
Yeats had been cast by events in a heroic role. Moreover, the "weapons"
with which he fought were used in defense of a fantasy of "patricide."
The reversal of roles had finally been completed. John Butler Yeats/
William Butler Yeats/John Millington Synge: Lugh/ Cuchulain/ The
Young Man. What else did this audience witness but Lugh and Cuchulain
in league, rising not to destroy but to protect the third generation? Not
only were two generations of Yeatses now completely allied, but they
found themselves defending the very myth of reversal in which Yeats had
never before been able to believe. On this night the mantle of fatherhood
—like Lugh's cloak—passed from father to son. Yeats had finally become
Cuchulain, but a Cuchulain with a son to fight *for*.

After Synge

In his last year Yeats had achieved such distance from the Cuchulain
story that he could kill his hero with a minimum of feeling. While
watching *The Death of Cuchulain* we feel less for the hero in the play
than for the producer of it. Cuchulain merely goes through the motions
of dying; the greatest imaginative investment appears to be in the figure
who stage-manages the death. He materializes as if in obedience to habit:
"*Old Man.* I have been asked to produce a play called *The Death of
Cuchulain*." Asked, not inspired. This is a man beyond conflict—"so old
that I have forgotten the name of my father and mother"—in a play
beyond guilt. Yeats's version of *Oedipus at Colonus*, its tragedy is the
dismemberment of deed from desire. Aoife and Cuchulain willingly play
predestined parts. Despite "an exchange of remarkable tenderness," both
submit to her right of revenge for a crime against the son which both
have long since forgiven. Yeats had translated Sophocles' play ten years
before, and had found there the same impulse to sever the motivation
from the deed:

> nobody can accuse me of anything. They settled before my birth all that I was
> to do. The oracle had announced that my father was to die by the hand of his

son. How then can I be blamed? I met my father not knowing who he was, and killed him not knowing what I did, but misery is not guilt.

Although faithful enough to the original, such a defense sounds conveniently apt for a Yeatsian hero. By 1928 Yeats had become a defender of Oedipus, not a victim of Cuchulain. The heroes have changed places, but the determinism goes on. Thus Oedipus here denies in himself the wishes that led to his tragic conflict and so ceases to be Oedipus. He becomes the prototype of Cuchulain's final calm: resolution through aphasia. His peace of mind is won at the cost of his identity.

Purgatory (1939) combines both myths and restores their psychological force. Here the Cuchulain Complex seconds the Oedipus Complex to reveal the former as what it has always been—an inversion of the latter. Oedipus becomes Cuchulain before our eyes. The Old Man has killed his father and now, on stage, kills his son. The crime of generation—"of death and birth"—has been kept green by his obsessive memory of the primal scene and so he attempts, like Quentin Compson, to save the life of his son by taking it. *Purgatory* reveals the fantasies on which much of the appeal of the Cuchulain myth was based. In its willingness to explicate them, however, it reads more as an essay at understanding than a drama of discovery. The play even pauses to discourse on the therapeutic project. Souls in purgatory (analysis)

>   Re-live
> Their transgressions, and that not once
> But many times; they know at last
> The consequence of those transgressions
> Whether upon others or upon themselves;
> Upon others, others may bring help,
> For when the consequence is at an end
> The dream must end; if upon themselves,
> There is no help but in themselves
> And in the mercy of God.

This is beautiful and true, but it may not be drama. While it penetrates the heart-mysteries *The Death of Cuchulain* ignores, *Purgatory* puts on its knowledge with some loss of power. If a profound self-analysis is displayed in the play, the moment of its felt dramatization through word and deed seems already to have occurred.

Drama was not, after the death of Synge, the medium through which Yeats acted out his deepest conflicts or achieved his greatest triumphs. This was largely owing to the nature of Yeats's gifts, but also to his success on behalf of Synge. In summing up the events of 1907, James Flannery reminds us that "Yeats thus secured a hearing for Synge and ultimately a recognition in Ireland (and elsewhere) of Synge's genius. But his victory was a costly one, for it all but guaranteed the loss of the very audience that might have supported his own plays." This victory would have been more costly had Yeats's future truly lain with the stage. While Yeats could scorn "theatre business, management of men," his contributions behind stage were no less valuable, both to the theater and to his own development, than those made upon it. Yeats did complain of "sleepless nights, thinking of the time that I must take from poetry," but he was also justified in claiming for his backstage efforts a certain athletic prowess: "It is a long fight, but that is the sport of it."

All along Yeats had displayed traits peculiar in a playwright. Few have failed to notice that the plays often serve to illustrate a system without which they have no independent existence. More importantly, Yeats's passing interest in action, in the instability of character and the uncertainty of fate that make for "dramatic" action, was always to lend his plays the air of something foregone. He conceived of experience much more as lyric epiphany than dramatic narrative. David Clark has convincingly shown that "Yeats's drama . . . takes one moment of the tragic rhythm as the clue to life and action." Yeats's later plays especially become the dilation upon an obsessive or transcendent instant, full of portent, empty of contingency. This may be drama, but there is no reason why it could not just as well be carried on within a poem. Yeats's most suspenseful drama was not written but lived, on the Abbey stage.

In the years after Synge's triumph Yeats found the strength to take direct responsibility for his epiphanies. This is to say he invested more and more of himself in self-conscious lyric. This required a placing of himself in historical, or at least recognizably human, time. (One thinks especially of his transfiguration in "Vacillation," where "My body of a sudden blazed" has all the more force for occurring in a specific year and in "a crowded London shop.") The book written after Synge's premature death in 1909 Yeats called *Responsibilities*. It appeared in 1914, the year in which William assumed full financial responsibility for his father. Since John Butler's departure for America in 1908, the son had begun to discover, in Ellmann's words, "that his father and he were collaborators rather than opponents." As he urged his father to write an autobiography and began to edit his letters, Yeats came to appreciate his substantial borrowings from his father's constant flow of philosophy. It is difficult to imagine the Yeats of ten years ealier (the year is 1914) so openly greeting his most insistent correspondent with "your letter came just in time to give me a most essential passage." As the poet made peace with the idea of inheritance, the responsibility of nourishing as he had been nourished became more compelling for him. He begins *Responsibilities* by apologizing to *"old fathers"*—not for a failure in poetic achievement, but for having sacrificed to unrequited love the task of establishing a link with the generations. These are the lines in which, as Eliot has claimed, Yeats first "fully evinced" the speech of "a particular man":

> *Pardon that for a barren passion's sake,*
> *Although I have come close on forty-nine,*
> *I have no child, I have nothing but a book,*
> *Nothing but that to prove your blood and mine.*

The fulfillment of this claim has been underestimated in its significance for Yeats's development. The birth of his son produced a remarkable poem which, as we shall see, was at once evidence of the Cuchulain Complex and an occasion for further resolution of it.

In the meantime Yeats never ceased elaborating the ties that bound him to his imaginative foster son. He worked him up into the "Receptive Man" of *A Vision*, a strange designation for a temperament there described as "ready to sacrifice every convention, perhaps all that men have agreed to reverence, for a startling theme." Yeats had long since understood Synge's importance as a breaker of taboos, but there remains a resistance to the natural consequence that this leaves him originless, *un*receptive: "he is without a master, and only by his technical mastery can he escape from the sense of being thwarted and opposed by other men." Yeats accomplished two things here; he again vents a forerunner's spleen, and he displaces attention from Synge's stance toward his style. Of course I have been arguing that Synge's *stance* toward the myths through which Yeats also sought to express himself held most significance for the poet. As a radical stance Yeats could never easily adopt, it perhaps required submersion under the less radical claim that "the outcry against *The Playboy* was an outcry against its style, against its way of seeing." Yeats here pays tribute to one kind of originality in order to ignore his much more serious debt to another.

Yeats remained attached to Synge's role as a son rather than a partner. Even while he speaks of him as one of many "friends" in "The Municipal Gallery Revisited," he assimilates Synge to a lament over his prolonged childlessness. The poem concerns itself with patrimony, with what Yeats has to pass on:

> My mediaeval knees lack health until they bend,
> But in that woman, in that household where
> Honour had lived so long, all lacking found.
> Childless I thought, "My children may find here
> Deep-rooted things," but never foresaw its end,
> And now that end has come I have not wept;
> No fox can foul the lair the badger swept—

VI

(An image out of Spenser and the common tongue).
John Synge, I and Augusta Gregory, thought
All that we did, all that we said or sang
Must come from contact with the soil, from that
Contact everything Antaeus-like grew strong.
We three alone in modern times had brought
Everything down to that sole test again,
Dream of the noble and the beggar-man.

The woman who here requites "all lacking" is Lady Gregory, and the
man who completes the triangle Yeats had begun to form with her is John
Synge. Yeats's last flirtation with the Family Romance achieves its dignity
through the surprise of its final line: "Say my glory was I had such
friends." The poem reveals that one of the poet's sustaining fantasies has
led to the enlarging conclusion that we begin and end as surely in
friendship and in kinship as in craftsmanship. In such a mood who knows
but that "John Synge" might not have annihilated the "or" of "The
Choice." The choice had always been, notwithstanding Yeats's hard little
poem to the contrary, not between, but of. Denis Donoghue goes so far
as to argue that "what surrounds Yeats's name is not the aura of an
achieved poetry, a body of work separable from its origins, but an
impression of genius fulfilled chiefly in the multiplicity of its life."
Whichever way the balance was tipped, the fact remains that work *and*
life were always for Yeats mutually constitutive rather than exclusive
categories. And Synge himself was bound to become, along with Maud
Gonne, a symbol of mediation, at once a creation and an experience. The
confusion of realms was a liberating one; Synge was perhaps Yeats's
greatest "work."

But there was also Michael Yeats. "A Prayer for My Son" (1921) again
raises the question of stance versus style. While not as technically dis-
tinguished as "The Municipal Gallery Revisited," Yeats's poem to his son
takes up a posture in every way as original. The first two stanzas expose
the son to the paternal threat:

Bid a strong ghost stand at the head
That my Michael may sleep sound,
Nor cry, nor turn in the bed
Till his morning meal come round;
And may departing twilight keep
All dread afar till morning's back,
That his mother may not lack
Her fill of sleep.

Bid the ghost have sword in fist:

Some there are, for I avow
Such devilish things exist,
Who have planned his murder, for they know
Of some most haughty deed or thought
That waits upon his future days,
And would through hatred of the bays
Bring them to nought.

Who is it that plans such a murder? The fantasy may seem melo-
dramatic but acquires pathos once we realize that Yeats here projects and
then meets as a threat from without the fear that he may play Cuchulain
to his son. The excessive solicitude on behalf of the sleeping woman
suggests that Yeats has already begun to feel the power of the boy's "deed
or thought" to intervene between husband and wife. He now knows in
the flesh what it is to have a son able to deprive his mother of sleep.
These emotions may not be as welcome as those of which John Butler
spoke when he assured Willie that "there is a feeling that of itself unbidden
and of necessity always springs into actuality when a parent meets his
offspring." But they are, to continue his father's line of thought, no less
"animal and primitive." Yeats has been thrust by circumstances into the
role of a father who wishes to protect his son however he may, and
especially against himself.

Once the poem has isolated this threat, it reaches an impasse. Yeats
seeks as so often a myth that can accommodate his response, but turns, as
if against his own emerging system, toward Christ rather than Oedipus.
He ends by admonishing himself that the Supreme Maker felt the necessity
to submit himself to the protection of earthly parents—and survived:

Though you can fashion everything
From nothing every day, and teach
The morning stars to sing,
You have lacked articulate speech
To tell Your simplest want, and known,
Wailing upon a woman's knee,
All of that worst ignominy
Of flesh and bone;

And when through all the town there ran
The servants of Your enemy,
A woman and a man,
Unless the Holy Writings lie,
Hurried through the smooth and rough
And through the fertile and waste,
Protecting, till the danger past,
With human love.

To see Yeats take comfort in the precedent of the Holy Family is to witness a profound reversal of the myths which help to govern his life. Only after having a father's ambivalence and power literally thrust upon him, an experience which allowed him to become the subject of the hostility of which he had previously felt himself the object, does Yeats find a way of moving beyond the Oedipal impasse to a more felicitous myth. And in order for him to make use of the Christian story as a father, he must rehabilitate a forgotten one. Yeats reminds us that in the Holy Writings the abstract Greek trinity coexists with a wholly human triangle: The Father, Son, and Holy Ghost would not be worshipped to this day were it not for Joseph, Mary, and Jesus. In holding up as an example to himself the most emasculated father in our tradition, Yeats displays an extraordinary strength. Despite all the mockery that surrounds the name of Joseph (and about which Yeats was brutally frank in "A Stick of Incense"), he will still raise him up as a usable hero. Yeats's perspective on the Christian story had temporarily shifted: at this moment it seemed less about the victimage of Christ on the cross than of Joseph on the road to Egypt. Joseph faithfully protects the child he has not even conceived. He thus stands as example of the man who has fully confronted and forgiven a son's Oedipal wishes—he has fallen their literal victim and still loves.

This is just the kind of precedent Yeats requires in order to weather the ambivalence called up by his son's recent arrival. It is within this revised sense of the significance of Christian archetype (of the triangle behind the Trinity) that Yeats can consciously accomplish a reversal of roles while remaining a protector of rather than a competitor with his infant son.

This solution was bound to be unstable, founded as it was upon pitting Yeats's conscious aims—keeping "dread afar"—against his unconscious projections—"devilish things." Yeats was nevertheless required henceforth to mediate between both sets of claims. His passive response to an older generation was now met by an active ambivalence about a younger. He was finally caught in a true middle, possessed of an offspring who helped to explicate an ancestor. The ancestor never saw the offspring; John Butler Yeats died in America less than a year after Michael was born. In the year of his grandson's birth, John Butler was still dwelling on his son's mistake in not having remained under his wing:

> Had you stayed with me and not left me for Lady Gregory, and her friends and associations, you would have loved and adored concrete life for which as I know you have real affection. What would have resulted? Realistic and poetical plays—poetry in closest and most intimate union with the positive realities and complexities of life. . . . I bet it is what your wife wants—ask her.

This letter clearly vindicates the son's departure, for it envisions a partnership in which William would have remained Willie. While John Butler rejoiced in the birth of his grandchildren, he could not have been aware that it brought to a close a process in which William's replacement of family with Family Romance had played its necessary part. What he could sense was the significance for them all of his son's new role. In one of his last expressed wishes, he imagines a meeting between the generations, even as he reminds us that for all his debilitating solicitude, he had always wanted Willie to be more than a son:

> I would like to see Willie playing with his own child. From the first, whenever American people came up to me in the American way and shouted: "How you must be interested in your grandchild," I replied "No, not a bit, but very much so in seeing my son as a father."

✑ *Three*

Hemingway's Uncanny Beginnings

Hemingway has a hard time imagining beginnings but an easy time inventing ends. Middles challenge him most of all. His novels constantly anticipate, when they do not prematurely achieve, the sense of an ending. Our surprise at hearing Anselmo say "I am an old man who will live until I die" turns upon the prolonging *until* and measures our disbelief that Hemingway will actually let such a life happen. Living from birth to death through a long life proves difficult of depiction for a writer trying to stave off death by continually adumbrating it. Hemingway's beginnings have the uncanny effect of raising the very specter of the end against which they are so concerned to defend. In the attempt to forestall annihilation by preempting it, Hemingway loses hold on the present. His moments of immediate experience unshadowed by future loss are rare indeed. His present tense, abundant as it is, registers itself as the tension of a consciousness caught between the trauma of the "before" and the fear of the "after." Hemingway's pleasure in the "now" is a largely apocryphal experience. Short stories, consumed in the limit of a single sitting, can protect us from the gathering sense of doom which becomes, in all but one of Hemingway's five major novels, his central effect. For writing novels of any length excites as much tension as it releases. The sense of option felt while beginning to write (or read) proves to be an oppressive irony when all that can be foreseen is the outstretched interval of time that must be filled. Why bother filling, Hemingway everywhere suggests, what will only be certainly lost?

I

The major obstacle to understanding *In Our Time* is ellipsis. Do the spaces between the stories and vignettes connect or separate? Life emerges here as a series of gaps punctuated by crises. Reading *In Our Time* trains us to infer, to search for patterns of continuity underlying seemingly disjointed episodes. The continuity of the book reveals itself as psychological rather than structural. What we uncover is a life history obsessively unified. The reader's attention weaves together Nick's story as the true plot of the book. Hemingway masked this plot in the 1930 edition by placing "On the Quai at Smyrna" before "Indian Camp," where the book originally began. But "Indian Camp" is the true beginning of Nick's story and of Hemingway's novelistic career:

> At the lake shore there was another rowboat drawn up. The two Indians stood waiting.
> Nick and his father got in the stern of the boat and the Indians shoved it off and one of them got in to row. Uncle George sat in the stern of the camp rowboat. The young Indian shoved the camp boat off and got in to row Uncle George.
> The two boats started off in the dark. Nick heard the oarlocks of the other boat quite a way ahead of them in the mist. The Indians rowed with quick choppy strokes. Nick lay back with his father's arm around him. It was cold on the water. The Indian who was rowing them was working very hard, but the other boat moved further ahead in the mist all the time.
> "Where are we going, Dad?" Nick asked.

The darkness which shuts off sight does more than disorient. It presents departure as risky. Origins are murky here, just as ends will prove too certainly known. The one thing we will see clearly in "Indian Camp" is death; the one thing Nick cannot look at is birth. Our not being able to see where we start sharply contrasts with his being able to see how all of us must stop. Yet for all its obscurity about specific contours, this opening makes us confront the fact of priority. We enter a world already filled with objects. "Another" has gone before us. Repetition of definite articles (as in "the Indians") suggests that this is a place with which we are already familiar. Hemingway never questions the givenness of reality. He refuses to deal in epistemological angst. The world is not unknowable; it is just unpredictable. Parataxis conveys the sense that event follows event by only the slimmest logic. "And" reflects Hemingway's honest ignorance of how one thing leads to another. It is not an ignorance he cherishes. Hemingway's project becomes to predict as well as to know.

The casualness of this narrator contrasts with the ignorance of the reader and encourages us to pretend that we are, in fact, at home here. Yet no one is at home here. A relaxed and knowing tone acts as defense against a wholly unfamiliar scene. Hemingway approaches the terror of the sublime through the uncanny, the *unheimlich*. In "The 'Uncanny,'" Freud points out that the German synonym for the "uncanny" derives from the word for home (*heim*) and that its original meaning was "familiar." Hemingway's career follows a similar evolution: what begins as familiar becomes unfamiliar, and yet is sought for as if it were still desired as much as feared. So his goal turns out to be at once "mysterious and homelike." The uncanny is the opposite of the "good place" Nick will spend his life trying to recover, and yet the "good place" (the womb) becomes for Nick the most uncanny place of all.

Nick begins as a lost son. This beginning makes us ask a question basic to Hemingway's fiction: "Where are we going, Dad?" His father cannot know that the prophetic answer is "away from, and yet nearer to, mother." Nick is about to be initiated into the paradox of the uncanny; being forced to live where one is and is not at home. After witnessing the birth of an Indian baby and the suicide of its father Nick will never again *feel* at home. He defends against this untimely exposure to birth confused with death by turning a fear into disbelief: "In the early morning on the lake sitting in the stern of the boat with his father rowing, he felt quite sure that he would never die." Throughout Hemingway's career we can measure the depth of a fear by the strength of a denial.

Nick asks two questions just before the story ends: "Do ladies always have such a hard time having babies?" and "Is dying hard, Daddy?" These are the central questions in Hemingway's novels. To ask one is to ask the other, since to confront any kind of birth is to confront one's mortality. What has a specific beginning very likely has a specific end. But Nick confronts not only the facts of origins and ends—he witnesses them as violent. From this night on, Nick's psyche begins to play the violent extremes of human life against its uncertain middle. Love emerges as the fleeting center of a parenthesis. It only lasts in fantasy. After Nick ends "something" with Marjorie, he enjoys the most extreme fantasy of recovery in Hemingway: "He felt happy. Nothing was finished. Nothing was ever lost." The belief that what we have started never finishes is impossible as an aesthetic principle but compelling as a psychological stance. It suggests that behind this author's anxiety over origins is a fear not so much of having but of losing them. To believe that nothing is ever lost is to recover the mother, the first thing one ever had.

While there is nothing new in calling Hemingway's basic fantasies regressive, we need to look more closely at how difficult this makes it for him to conceive of going forward as satisfying. The recurring experience in In Our Time is of anticlimax. Narrative pathos constantly collapses into bathos: "He loved the mountains in the autumn. The last I heard of him the Swiss had him in jail near Sion." Whole towns are given us to be swiftly reclaimed: "the sails of the schooner filled and it moved out into the open lake, carrying with it everything that had made the mill a mill and Hortons Bay a town." "A Very Short Story" is short because its bottom falls out: "Luz never got an answer to the letter to Chicago about it. A short time after he contracted gonorrhea. . . ." Or stories begin with their endings: *"They hanged Sam Cardinella at six o'clock in the morning."* This vignette explodes into the escapism of "Big Two-Hearted River." It reveals the interchapters as the nightmares which haunt the mind of the main character. They are the dream work in which Nick's unconscious rehearses its appointment with death. They force us to face the possibility of premature arrest. Sam's is a totally closed plot, a fable about the loss of self-control, which becomes so threatening to an imagination concerned to behave as if it were choosing, since it had so little sway over its beginnings, whatever end it must endure.

The story that brackets this execution is Hemingway's most ambitious flight from the world of death. Nick's fishing trip cannot be understood apart from the personal history necessitating it. An elliptical return to the darkness of "Indian Camp," this regression to origins proves how little Nick has moved beyond them. He lives but he does not develop. Nick's initial trauma either predicts or preempts future experience. He sees his father humiliated, ends an affair, confronts incest and homosexuality, has an affair ended, and then passes through a series of veiled avatars—a numb veteran, the friend of a failed revolutionary, the partner in three ruined marriages—and finally reemerges as a nervous husband who plucks his mind out rather than face the "hell" of his wife's pregnancy. The recurrent limitation of this composite character is an ability to adapt. None of these experiences lead to emotional development. Nick's life has no middle. It emerges as pure reaction. It is not by accident that Nick suffers wound after wound. Some inner compulsion leads him to put himself in the way of disaster. Nick's fate reflects his author's lack of faith in life after birth.

Yet cannot "Big Two-Hearted River" be read as Nick's return to his beginnings in order to discover whether going over the same ground will free him to go forward in a new way? This involves reading the story as a repetition made for the sake of renewal. Hemingway certainly tries to make going back seem like going forward. But we do not experience here a sense of growth. The deceptive quality of the prose is that it seems to flow while actually freezing. Nick's movements, apparently instinctive and unhurried, actually reflect an obsessive concern with controlling his every step. His highest satisfaction comes from keeping himself as "steady" as the hovering trout. This is a story about repetition, but of a kind that determines Nick's existence. As Nick finishes his carefully planned dinner, he finds himself remembering the special recipe of an old friend—"coffee according to Hopkins." This leads into an increasingly involuntary regress which Nick cuts off with an ironic twist that makes "a good ending to the story." Nothing can be left loose, surprising, open-ended.

What frightens the spectator of the Greek retreat frightens Nick: *"No end and no beginning.*" Nick transforms his anxieties over stopping and starting into a despair over middles. A lack of closure thus becomes more intimidating than foreclosure. A known death menaces less than unpredictable life. This anxiety originates, as we have seen, in a premature exposure to the dark and uncertain place from which life emerges and of which living and loving must therefore be a part. Sex and birth cross the hard fact of personal limitation with the harder facts that our limits are vulnerable, that we are not the original possessors of our first source, and that our first source must be lost. This anxiety terminates in Nick's confrontation with the swamp, in the place where sexuality merges with mortality. There one has to crawl on one's belly. "It would not be possible to walk through a swamp like that." Going in means being buried alive. The swamp is not "clean and compact" like the male trout Nick disembowels while looking at it. It is dark, interwoven, deep. Nick refuses to enter a genital paradise that has become threatening and unfamiliar. "This *unheimlich* place, however, is the entrance to the former *heim* [home] of all human beings, to the place where everyone dwelt once upon a time and in the beginning." Freud invokes here the future that would be for Nick a true middle, an intermediate way between the womb and the tomb. He chooses rather to put behind him—"He looked back" —what still confronts him; and he comforts himself with a future—"plenty of days coming"—which will never arrive.

II

Robert Cohn was once middleweight boxing champion of Princeton. Do not think that I am very much impressed by that as a boxing title, but it meant a lot to Cohn. He cared nothing for boxing, in fact he disliked it, but he learned it painfully and thoroughly to counteract the feeling of inferiority and shyness he had felt on being treated as a Jew at Princeton. There was a certain inner comfort in knowing he could knock down anybody who was snooty to him, although, being very shy and a thoroughly nice boy, he never fought except in the gym. He was Spider Kelly's star pupil. . . . He was so good that Spider promptly overmatched him and got his nose permanently flattened. This increased Cohn's distaste for boxing, but it gave him a certain satisfaction of some strange sort, and it certainly improved his nose. . . .

I mistrust all frank and simple people, especially when their stories hold together, and I always had a suspicion that perhaps Robert Cohn had never been middleweight boxing champion and that perhaps a horse had stepped on his face, or that maybe his mother had been frightened or seen something, or that he had, maybe, bumped into something as a young child, but I finally had somebody verify the story from Spider Kelly.

Every book is an invitation and a challenge. *The Sun Also Rises* begins by inviting us to believe this voice and challenges us to despise Robert Cohn. If this invitation is accepted, we find ourselves assuming attitudes of which we would normally be ashamed. What accounts for this gratuitous bile? Since it is difficult to resist Jake's narration on impact, this question is one we scarcely have time to pose. Presented with two unattractive options—siding with the narrator or siding with Cohn—we very likely choose to go along with the former. After all, he is a man not easily impressed, one sensitive to racial prejudice, friend of Spider Kelly and of Princetonians, a worldly if somewhat cutting cynic. Yet in the moment of formulating these impressions, their irony becomes unmistakable. Jake's is the story which doesn't hold together. His language simply sounds too defensive. It apparently gives him "a certain satisfaction of some strange sort." Cohn emerges as a massive projection of the speaker's anxieties. Through the literal "snootiness" of this voice we can detect that the speaker is impressed, that he feels both inferior and shy, that he takes abnormal interest in competence. And are we finally not led to wonder whether the fantasy of a child's mother seeing "something," so viciously excessive, arises from mutilation fears wholly original to the speaker? The dominant emotion here is rage at Cohn's inability to appreciate a potency that he possesses and the narrator lacks. Jake's uncanny fantasy becomes explicable once we realize that it reflects a universal fear which for Jake has become a realized fact. So by the logic of Jake's fantasy (mutilation points back to the mother), it is not Cohn's birth he libels, but his own.

This is the only one of Hemingway's major novels which does not begin at a specific season or time of day. Its action will remain the least constrained by rhythms other that those the characters themselves impose. This generation is "lost" to any connection with earlier or later generations and hence to the primary vehicle for forwarding life. *The Sun Also Rises* is a novel about wasting time. Jake's castration has made him unable to participate in the natural rhythms of life. He can never consummate experience; resolution is always withheld from him. Sexual impotence becomes a metaphor for the inability to enter the flow of duration. Only in fantasy does Jake approach the rise, immediacy, and fall of sexual experience: "I was thinking about Brett and my mind stopped jumping around and started to go in sort of smooth waves. Then all of a sudden I started to cry. Then after a while it was better. . . ." His life is all middle, but emptied of any suspense. As the Italian colonel who visits Jake in the hospital says, "You . . . have given more than your life." Jake can lose nothing more. In Hemingway's world, you simply cannot live without a penis.

Style here focuses the repetitiveness which is necessarily Jake's fate.

Chapter 5 opens with a new morning, but the prose soon confines any sense of option within a recurring formula for Jake's movement: "I walked," "I read," "I got," "I walked," "I passed," "I stepped," "I walked," "I walked." Anyone who narrates his experience through such unvarying syntax experiences motion as anything but discovery. Jakes's two experiences of *déjà vu* provide the strongest evidence that he feels himself caught in an uncanny pattern of repetition beyond his control. His most promising attempt at love collapses into "the feeling as in a nightmare of it all being something repeated, something I had been through and that now I must go through again." After Jake fights Cohn and begins to cross the Pamplona square, he experiences a *déjà vu* about returning home: "I felt as I felt once coming home from an out-of-town football game. I was carrying a suitcase with my football things in it, and I walked up the street from the station in the town I had lived in all my life and it was all new. They were raking the lawns and burning leaves in the road, and I stopped for a long time and watched. It was all strange." Jake can never beat Cohn, for he has lost the organ which would permit him to consummate, rather than endlessly repeat, the attempt to get "home." Here the *déjà vu* gets dangerously close to exposing the original experience for which the feeling of "something repeated" acts as a screen memory. Jake here remembers a homecoming experienced as a dream. It is a *déjà vu* about *déjà vu*—an uncanny repetition of the feeling of the uncanny. If Hemingway's fiction continually strives to get back home, the greatest irony awaiting it would be to achieve the return only to find it "all strange." Through the defenses of such screen memories, Jake is doomed to repeat, rather than free to overcome, the traumatic effects of some original loss of the "good place."

It may be more appropriate, then, to read Jake's actual castration as a literalization of the original castration-anxiety that threatens to make home feel unhomelike. Jake's conscious drive toward competency expresses his author's unconscious anxieties about potency. Jake's narration is an instruction manual—how to drink, kiss, fish . . . and pimp. Technique culminates in the bull ring. Bullfighting is the great orgy of a repressed culture: competence killing potency. What makes this more than just another "how to" is the prospect of death. Hemingway finds here a game like life, one played for mortal stakes. And yet in *Death in the Afternoon* he admits that it is the opposite of a truly existential sport: "Rather it is a tragedy; the death of the bull, which is played, more or less well, by the bull and the man involved and in which there is danger for the man but certain death for the animal." As Jake teaches Brett, bullfighting is something "with a definite end." Watching a bullfight, Hemingway unconsciously identifies with the doomed animal. He has no more sense of hope for his own end than for the bull's. Jake's irony is to be granted the comparative immortality of a "steer." He drifts onward in a life promising no final climax. By insisting upon the analogy between the tragedies of the ring and the ironies of the café ("It's no life being a steer"), Hemingway again confounds anxieties over death and sex. *The Sun Also Rises* can be read as the story of an impotent animal submitted to repeated gorings.

Jake speaks for his author when he says that "people went to the corrida . . . to be given tragic sensations." The consolation for ironic life can at least be tragic death. That death is a reality that will not dodge us. Yet this most antiepiphanic of novels questions whether life offers any culmination. Even Belmonte no longer feels "sure that there were any great moments. Things were not the same and now life came only in flashes." What is intermittent for the matador is undifferentiated for Jake. With nothing to look forward to, the cure for Jake's wound is a ritual context that precludes foresight.

Once the fiesta begins, choice becomes nearly impossible. On the morning it starts, Jake orders a drink in a quiet square. Before the waiter can return, the fiesta explodes. The prose tries to manage this sensory overload through a series of subordinate clauses that capture and disperse the scene's energy: "By the time the second rocket had burst there were so many people in the arcade, that had been empty a minute before, that the waiter, holding the bottle high up over his head, could hardly get through the crowd to our table." The waiter gets lost in the crowd, and we get lost in a sea of activity. "Everything became quite unreal finally and it seemed as though nothing could have any consequences." Life ceases to move in any kind of line. We are immersed in an unrelenting buzz: "This hum went on, and we were in it and a part of it." It becomes hard to move except as part of a mass. "We could not make our way through but had to be moved with the whole thing, slowly, as a glacier, back to town." The fiesta concentrates in a single experience what has heretofore been Jake's way of life. His wound has made eschatology irrelevant. Jake prefers to work nothing out in advance: "Perhaps as you went along you did learn something. I did not care what it was all about. All I wanted to know was how to live in it. Maybe if you found out how to live in it you learned from that what it was all about." So morality becomes afterthought: "things that made you disgusted afterward."

Our belated disgust with the book's beginning exemplifies this morality at work. Hemingway so skillfully gets us to "go along" with Jake that only afterward do we learn "how to" understand what his beginning is all about. If we do not resist the opening, the increasingly simple demands the novel makes on us—just to go along—become more and more easy to accept. The moral contexts that permit judgment are precisely those that the book tries to tease us out of. It finally asks us to abandon all

prejudices except the love of style. The obsession with "how to" do
something is the only forethought Jake allows himself. We tardily realize
that the novel opens with a display of Jake's skill at how "to get rid of
friends." While the middle does not justify the tone of the beginning, it
explains it. We come to understand that Jake is jealous of Cohn for his
unmistakable potency. His symbolic castration of Cohn (flattening his
nose) attempts metaphorically to convert a bull into a steer. Language is
the only weapon Jake has left.

Yet this first person narrator, upon whom the prolonging of the
narrative depends, finally disbelieves in language: "You'll lose it if you
talk about it." Jake talks because he has already lost everything. Yet he
expresses a theory that where language is not necessary as a defense, it is
not necessary at all. For whom, then, does he speak? We can speculate
that Hemingway invents an impotent male who is still the "hero" of the
novel in order to establish that impotency is a crisis that a man can
actually survive. Yet his project ends in a draw, for it appears that in the
case of this wound, talking or not talking finally makes little difference.
Hemingway begins by marshalling his best rhetorical skills in a sneak
attack on the threat, and ends once he realizes that even direct talk
"about it" will only confirm the loss of what has been already lost.

III

A Farewell to Arms is Hemingway's most fatal book. While it promises
the most life, it delivers nothing but loss. The imagination of disaster
intrudes even into the strenuously pacific opening:

> In the late summer of that year we lived in a house in a village that looked
> across the river and the plain to the mountains. In the bed of the river there
> were pebbles and boulders, dry and white in the sun, and the water was clear
> and swiftly moving and blue in the channels. Troops went by the house and
> down the road and the dust they raised powdered the leaves of the trees. The
> trunks of the trees too were dusty and the leaves fell early that year and we saw
> the troops marching along the road and the dust rising and leaves, stirred by
> the breeze, falling and the soldiers marching and afterwards the road bare and
> white except for the leaves.
>
> The plain was rich with crops; there were many orchards of fruit trees and
> beyond the plain the mountains were brown and bare. There was fighting in
> the mountains and at night we could see the flashes from the artillery. In the
> dark it was like summer lightning, but the nights were cool and there was not
> the feeling of a storm coming.

At first this voice appears simply to report what it sees. It sounds in
touch with seasons and elements. We stand aside here and conserve
ourselves. The water flows, the troops pass, the leaves fall. Everything

else spends itself. Yet high summer—a time of ripeness—somehow becomes late fall. We are manipulated into the season of loss. Parallel syntax presents an army of falling leaves. Men are "marching" and leaves are "falling," and through this parataxis they become all too easily confused. The leaves last; the men disappear. What remains is the emptiness of landscape—"a road bare and white"—which the human presence interrupts but cannot master.

The narrator subtly repeats this involvement of the reader in a fall that is at once natural and human. To say that "the nights were cool and there was not the feeling of a storm coming" is to protest too much. Yes, the storm is denied—but why is it ever envisaged? In *A Farewell to Arms* potential turbulence has more presence than actual peace. What Frederic Henry anticipates, Hemingway actually precipitates. A storm is exactly what Catherine fears: "I'm afraid of the rain because sometimes I see me dead in it." The storm looms over the entire novel, and inevitably breaks.

Yet this is not the only disaster the beginning obliquely foreshadows. More striking is Frederic's projection of pregnancy. As he watches the troops march by he notices "under their capes the two leather cartridge-boxes on the front of the belts, gray leather boxes heavy with the packs of clips of thin, long 6.5 mm. cartridges, bulged forward under the capes so that the men, passing on the road, marched as though they were six months gone with child." Through abundant detail Frederic attempts to establish the probability of what he sees. But the metaphoric leap from carefully measured cartridges to carefully measured pregnancy is so idiosyncratic as to reveal more about the mind of the beholder than what he beholds. Even before Frederic fathers a child, he seems to "feel trapped biologically." Projection allows him to assign to others what he feels as threatening to himself. Yet he no more negates this possibility than he does the chance of a storm. Frederic is trapped within *superstitious* narrative. While seeming to open into possibility, it really *stands still over* the very fear that it starts out to exorcise. As if to prove this, a storm quickly develops. The sudden reversals of *In Our Time* are condensed into single sentences: "One day at the end of the fall when I was out where the oak forest had been I saw a cloud coming over the mountain. It came very fast and the sun went a dull yellow and then everything was gray and the sky was covered and the cloud came on down the mountain and suddenly we were in it and it was snow." The storm is upon us before we have time to feel it coming. Yet we will learn to get ready. The novel educates us in anticipating the worst.

Such presentiments are uncanny. They make us uneasy because they so often come true. They express a fascination with death that recurs throughout Hemingway's work. Such recurrence suggests that every encounter with death aggravates rather than allays the fear of it. It is a repression which continually fails and so must repeat itself—a repetition compulsion. Freud argues that an anxiety which "can be shown to come from something repressed which *recurs* . . . would then be no other than what is uncanny." Repetition is a home away from home. What we repeat must be familiar, yet why would we repeat it if that were so? The "uncanny is in reality nothing new or foreign, but something familiar and old-established in the mind that has been estranged only by the process of repression." Freud speculates that "many people experience the feeling" of the uncanny "in the highest degree in relation to death." But the feeling can proceed as well from another source:

> An uncanny experience occurs either when repressed infantile complexes have been revived by some impression, or when the primitive beliefs [e.g., fear of the dead] we have surmounted seem once more to be confirmed. Finally, we must not let our predilection for smooth solution and lucid exposition blind us to the fact that these two cases of uncanny experience are not always sharply distinguishable. When we consider that primitive beliefs are most intemately connected with infantile complexes, and are, in fact, based upon them, we shall not be greatly astonished to find the distinction often a rather hazy one.

Hemingway's version of the uncanny certainly blurs this distinction. As we have seen, his career formally begins with a story that fuses birth trauma, castration anxiety, suicide, fear of dying, and fortune telling. Frederic Henry is the legitimate heir of Nick Adams. His primitive fascination with ends rehearses a universal anxiety over origins.

Caught in the middle, Frederic is a man with no belief in middles. His one memory of childhood defines this sense of limbo:

> The hay smelled good and lying in a barn in the hay took away all the years in between. We had lain in hay and talked and shot sparrows with an air-rifle when they perched in the triangle cut high up in the wall of the barn. The barn was gone now and one year they had cut the hemlock woods and there were only stumps, dried tree-tops, branches and firewood where the woods had been. You could not go back. If you did not go forward what happened? You never got back to Milan. And if you got back to Milan what happened?

Here Frederic's inability to go either forward or backward proceeds from one anxiety. Later, his thoughts about his dead child show how a fear of dying derives from an ambivalence over the conditions of birth:

> He had never been alive. Except in Catherine. I'd felt him kick there often enough. But I hadn't for a week. Maybe he was choked all the time. Poor little kid. I wished the hell I'd been choked like that. No I didn't. Still there would not be all this dying to go through. Now Catherine would die. That was what you did. You died. You did not know what it was about. You never had time to learn. They threw you in and told you the rules and the first time they caught you off base they killed you.

Frederic renounces Jake's hope that learning to live in the world might help one to know what it was all about. In this world, dying is what one learns how to do.

In one of the endings he ultimately rejected, Hemingway admits through Frederic that life is open-ended in a way his stories refuse to acknowledge:

> I could tell about the boy. He did not seem of any importance then except as trouble and god knows I was bitter about him. Anyway he does not belong in this story. He starts a new one. It is not fair to start a new story at the end of an old one but that is the way it happens. There is no end except death and birth is the only beginning.

Once the belief that death is the only plausible ending has been raised to the level of an aesthetic principle, the end of a novel cannot coincide with the birth of a son. Something has to give, and in the final version starting gives way to stopping. Hemingway had to reject this ending if he was not to dramatize openly the conflict between the rules laid down by his technique and the "way" things really happen. He chooses to kill the boy and so avoids having to expose his art as a defense against the facts of life.

So the book is stillborn. Like the child, "it had never been alive." It never knows an interval of time free from intimations of mortality. We do not experience its middle as a discovery of its end. Nothing is allowed to seem lasting. Our insecurity is founded on untimeliness. Wounds inevitably come, but, what is worse, at wholly improbable moments: "I was blown up while we were eating cheese." The rule governing the future is that what cannot be predicted cannot be imagined.

Yet Hemingway finally does get love into a book. "I do what you want" announces a kind of consummation never before represented by him. But it will not be represented here; with these words Chapter 16 ends. Our disappointment with *A Farewell to Arms* comes less from fastidious omission, however, than from Hemingway's refusal of this "splendid chance to be a messiah." Love is always something had on leave, stolen from fate. Throughout, Frederic treats his love for Catherine as something already over—as recollection. His "mistake was this," Kierkegaard argues in *Repetition*, "that he stood at the end instead of at the beginning." Yet he goes on to admit that

> the man who in his experience of love has not experienced it thus precisely at the beginning, has never loved. Only he must have another mood alongside of this. This potentiated act of recollection is the eternal expression of love at the beginning, it is the token of real love. But on the other hand an ironic elasticity is requisite in order to be able to make use of it. . . . It must be true that one's life is over at the first instant, but there must be vitality enough to kill this death and transform it into life.

Frederic has the requisite irony but not the elasticity and so begins and proceeds by "seeing it all ahead like the moves in a chess game." Would we begrudge Hemingway his oft-criticized romance were it not betrayed from the start to so bitter an irony? If books can be defined by how they end—tragedy with the death of the hero, comedy with the birth of a new society— then romance never ends and irony ends before it begins. The two modes are simply incompatible. *A Farewell to Arms* might have been Hemingway's best novel had he opened himself more to the awkward and sometimes silly lovemaking many readers find so embarrassing. Embarrassment is precisely what Hemingway dreads and what he must overcome. But he cannot imagine a future that is not foreclosed in advance because he cannot trust in the basic facts of human continuity: procreation and married love. While Hemingway remains capable of depicting a series of carefree sexual encounters, he fails to invent a hero who truly domesticates the uncanny place.

IV

They started two hours before daylight, and at first, it was not necessary to break the ice across the canal as other boats had gone on ahead. In each boat, in the darkness, so you could not see, but only hear him, the poler stood in the stern, with his long oar. The shooter sat on a shooting stool fastened to the top of a box that contained his lunch and shells, and the shooter's two, or more, guns were propped against the load of wooden decoys. Somewhere, in each boat, there was a sack with one or two live mallard hens, or a hen and a drake, and in each boat there was a dog who shifted and shivered uneasily at the sound of the wings of the ducks that passed overhead in the darkness.

Four of the boats went on up the main canal toward the big lagoon to the north. A fifth boat had already turned off into a side canal. Now, the sixth boat turned south into a shallow lagoon, and there was no broken water.

Across the River and into the Trees returns to the mode of "Indian Camp." Darkness and uncertainty dominate. As before, we are belated —"other boats had gone on ahead." We travel in someone's wake. The narrator knows no more about this world than the reader. Things are just "somewhere." Directions are given which do not direct. We are not only cut off from shore but from the action. "They started" makes the novel's beginning simultaneous with a fictive moment of beginning but leaves us ignorant of and distant from these third persons. Movement goes on here, but only its aftermath—broken ice—testifies surely to its presence. Human presence is once again an interruption. After that presence turns aside "there was no broken water," and the world becomes quiet, still, seamless again.

In this world to make something (movement) is to break something (water). Men are made by being broken. As Colonel Cantwell's precursor, Frederic Henry, asserted twenty years earlier, "The world breaks every one and afterward many are strong at the broken places." The novel is the story of a "heart broken": the Colonel wonders "why that one, of all the muscles, should fail me." It is broken not by love but by life. It simply lacks the strength to keep on beating. "When it stops, you just do not know the time." If the beginning of the novel establishes the uncertainty of going forward, it is because there is so little to go forward for. This is a book about going back. The Colonel is a man without a future. All that is left to him (except one more day of love) is cleaning up old messes, paying old debts, opening old wounds—"merde, money, blood."

The book opens on the day the Colonel dies. To go forward would be to write a short story. Hemingway buys narrative time through a flashback. There can be little surprise in this action since we know it is already over. We suspect from the outset that the Colonel will soon die: "Every time you shoot now can be the last." The middle of the novel is a nostalgic interpolation of nostalgia. Hemingway sounds throughout the old theme of *carpe diem*, but with a dying fall. Play has become self-conscious work: "let us resume the having of fun." The real work is remembering, as memory replaces hope altogether.

Yet the Colonel is a man who has made his living by looking ahead. Shooting ("he swung the gun . . . well and ahead of the second duck") and strategy go by foresight. He is a professional diviner. He has little time for peripheral vision, for turning aside into the present. In a striking reversal of Sartre's metaphor for Faulkner's experience of time, Hemingway captures the Colonel's habitual stance within the temporal flow:

> They were on a straight stretch of road now and were making time so that one farm blended, almost blurred, into another farm and you could only see what was far ahead and moving toward you. Lateral vision was just a condensation of flat, low country in the winter. I'm not sure I like speed, the Colonel thought. Breughel would have been in a hell of a shape if he had to look at the country like this.

That is the difference between Faulkner and Hemingway. One looks backward and the other forward. Their present usually blurs. But appearances are deceiving. Hemingway is simply more highly defended than Faulkner and so makes a frontal attack on the death he anticipates with fascination and fear. Both writers are fundamentally "regressive" in that, while they are borne into the future in different postures, it is the past that moves and attracts their imaginations. Of course the apparent stance here is all-important. If such regressions are more or less universal, then what makes for difference is the ways in which they get expressed —the defenses that are the essence of "style." The Colonel questions here a stance expressed as the love of speed. He tries to take his eyes off the death moving so swiftly toward him. Can we learn to see like that most reluctant of apocalyptic painters, the one so open to the fullness of the world?

"I know now is enough," the Colonel says, but he kills time remembering when. His war stories *are* dull. Unpracticed in the presentation of ruminative consciousness, Hemingway must rely on the awkward device of having Renata ask the Colonel to remember. No narrative requirement governs these forays into the past, so their beginning and ending simply corresponds to the length of the Colonel's stay in Venice. This is not a novel but an essay about impending death. All the action (with the exception of one "act") is past. Hemingway, against his best impulses, chooses to tell rather than show, and thus the book is as revealing about how Hemingway thinks as about who its hero is: "Death is a lot of shit, he thought. It comes to you in small fragments that hardly show where it has entered." The threat as usual is less death than consciousness of dying. Hemingway here replaces death with a metaphor and reduces it through synecdoche. There are no longer "plenty of days coming" when he can fish this swamp. These tropes are his only remaining arms against death.

Though the book itself is not a spatial form, it does contain one —Renata's portrait. The Colonel responds to "the static element in painting" as a stay against the confusion of dying. Yet this nostalgia for a life arrested by art Hemingway's art cannot requite. The Colonel is a man who has made fatal decisions at every stage in life: "I made them early. In the middle. And late." His life has nevertheless decomposed even while exhibiting the classic and neatly punctuated contours of a composition. Only one more decision awaits him—to opt for the present one last time. He must turn from the portrait toward the actual woman:

> The Colonel said nothing, because he was assisting, or had made an act of presence, at the only mystery that he believed in except the occasional bravery of man.
> "Please don't move," the girl said. "Then move a great amount."
> The Colonel, lying under the blanket in the wind, knowing it is only what man does for woman that he retains, except what he does for his fatherland or his motherland, however you get the reading, proceeded.

Hemingway here steps out of the novel to challenge his reader in one of the most self-conscious moments in his fiction. If it is not well done it is bravely done, for it admits that this writer can no longer create meaning alone in a world of death. And it implies one of his guiding premises—that language separates us as surely from experience as death does. When one is present to an act, one says nothing. Speech testifies to the absence of immediacy, to the death of the moment. The novel that contains this moment returns to the marshes where it began, thereby implying that its middle, a saving digression into love, is not its final truth. This act of presence comes to be felt, in fact, as all too much like loss. When the Colonel thinks "how close life comes to death when there is ecstasy," he evokes the loss of control in the sexual act that causes Hemingway to fear lovemaking as practice for the ultimate loss of control in death. Such fears lead to emotional inertia, yet the last act which the Colonel performs is to spare, as his author has, the life of an animal, allowing it to live one more day. If the swaying of the wounded drake is "a movement without hope," so is the Colonel's swerve toward Venice, yet within the arc of that movement we forget, if only for a moment, that he must end so soon after his story begins.

V

For Whom the Bell Tolls is a long book about a short time. It reverses the mode of *In Our Time* by leaving nothing out. Almost every moment of these four days (even during dreams) gets accounted for. In the other novels, large stretches of time are empty, unworthy of description. Except for periodic love-making, Hemingway is unable to find a compelling vocation for his heroes. In *A Farewell to Arms* Frederic Henry admits that "All I wanted was to see Catherine. The rest of the time I was glad to kill." At first Robert Jordan also feels bound to "make up in intensity what the relation will lack in duration and in continuity." But reading fuses intensity and duration into an experience where every moment brims with value. This is a book that fills rather than kills time. Although it is not Hemingway's last novel, I want to end with it, for Robert Jordan's story not only consummates Hemingway's development but takes great and welcome exception to it:

> He lay flat on the brown, pine-needled floor of the forest, his chin on his folded arms, and high overhead the wind blew in the tops of the pine trees. The mountainside sloped gently where he lay; but below it was steep and he could see the dark of the oiled road winding through the pass. There was a stream alongside the road and far down the pass he saw a mill beside the stream and the falling water of the dam, white in the summer sunlight.
> "Is that the mill?" he asked.
> "Yes."
> "I do not remember it."
> "It was built since you were here. The old mill is farther down; much below the pass."
> He spread the photostated military map out on the forest floor and looked at it carefully. The old man looked over his shoulder.

The novel begins on a summer morning. We see a man seeing at a distance. Nothing is melodramatically foreshadowed or withheld. The

scene is both familiar and strange. The landscape is known; the mill is
new. Yet far from producing an uncanny effect, the scene unfolds as one
more stage in its viewer's education. An old man gives information to a
younger one. It is a scene of instruction innocent of any resonance of a
primal scene. Knowledge passes from an older to a younger generation
with no apparent loss of power.

The relaxed tone of the opening contrasts sharply with the ultimate
objective of the book: the proper timing of an explosion. As usual,
Hemingway gives away the end at the beginning: "To blow the bridge at
a stated hour based on the time set for the attack is how it should be
done." We also learn—or are encouraged to expect—that Robert Jordan
will be killed. Twenty pages into the novel Pablo asks his prophetic
question: "If you are wounded in such a thing as this bridge, you would
be willing to be left behind?"

How then does Hemingway help us to live through the book rather
than anticipate the end of it? By encouraging us to commit an act of
presence, of forgetting. The first stage of Robert's education is to stop
"looking into the future in English" and to start conjugating the phases of
the word *now:* "Now, *ahora, maintenant, heute. Now,* it has a funny
sound to be a whole world and your life." But it is less the overt instruction
to enter into the passing moment than the patient recording of the least
remarkable of them that commands our attention. Certainly the novel
can be read as apocalyptic, but we are allowed throughout to participate
in a sense of reprieve. While we remain torn between the impulse to finish
and the impulse to prolong, it is making the most of time that truly
distinguishes character here.

In a "time waster" like Raphael, Hemingway takes little interest. Pablo
embodies the familiar Hemingway hero—the man without a future. His
response to Kashkin's death—"That is what happens to everybody. . . .
That is the way we will all finish"—marks the apotheosis of morbidity.
But it does not go unchallenged. Anselmo speaks for a new patience
when he makes the crushingly obvious reply—"That is the way all men
end"—and so reduces old shibboleth to self-evident cliché. Fascination
with the way men end dominates Pilar's imagination. She is Hemingway's
most seductive agent of divination. The "best time" of her life (eating and
making love in Valencia) has passed. However informed Pilar's "notions
about the value of time," it is through her that her author questions his
lifelong obsession with the future.

Hemingway knew that he carried his fortune in his hand. When he
could no longer write with it, he turned it against himself. What had
made him was used to break him. Yet the novel literalizes this metaphor
in order to reject it. Pilar literally reads Robert's palm to give the ending
away a second time. But he refuses to believe this prophecy. Pilar has

already given Maria better advice: "She said that nothing is done to oneself that one does not accept." During a prolonged discussion about divination, Robert is asked the question all of Hemingway's novels make us ask: "Do you believe in the possibility of a man seeing ahead what is to happen to him?" Robert answers that such forebodings are only "evil visions," projections of what one fears, and therefore need not be accepted: "Seeing bad signs, one, with fear, imagines an end for himself and one thinks that imagining comes by divination. . . . I believe there is nothing more to it than that." But Pilar forces the debate into a confrontation between rational insight and uncensored fantasy. She gives explicit instructions for divining "death-to-come" through the senses:

". . . it is important that the day be in autumn with rain, or at least some fog, or early winter even and now thou shouldst continue to walk through the city and down the Calle de Salud smelling what thou wilt smell where they are sweeping out the *casas de putas* and emptying the slop jars into the drains and, with this odor of love's labor lost mixed sweetly with soapy water and cigarette butts only faintly reaching thy nostrils, thou shouldst go on to the Jardín Botánico where at night those girls who can no longer work in the houses do their work against the iron gates of the park and the iron picketed fences and upon the sidewalks. It is there in the shadow of the trees against the iron railings that they will perform all that a man wishes; from the simplest requests at a remuneration of ten centimos up to a pesata for that great act that we are born to and there, on a dead flower bed that has not yet been plucked out and replanted, and so serves to soften the earth that is so much softer than the sidewalk, thou wilt find an abandoned gunny sack with the odor of the wet earth, the dead flowers, and the doings of that night. In this sack will be contained the essence of it all, both the dead earth and the dead stalks of the flowers and their rotted blooms and the smell that is both the death and birth of man."

"In this sack will be contained the essence of it all": here all of Hemingway's fantasy material coalesces. It is a lurid triumph of the uncanny. But it is also a triumph *over* the uncanny. Hemingway presents this less for effect than for scrutiny. The fantasy is unique in its explicitness, its self-consciousness, and its patent absurdity. Those elements which make "Indian Camp" so unsettling are so compressed here as to become indistinguishable. "That great act that we are born to" assumes a form unrecognizable as love. It is fugitive, rotten, cast out. Life beings and ends in a "dead . . . bed." The site of love houses the oracle of death.

Yet this is precisely the site that the novel seeks to become familiar with. *For Whom the Bell Tolls* divests love of all its vestigial uncanniness. The first thing Robert must learn about love is to make time for it. From believing only "in my work" Robert moves toward believing in "making believe." He gives in to "a complete embracing of all that would not be."

This reverses Hemingway's typical attitude toward the future. To embrace
what will not be is to embrace a fiction, not a fate. Love is the supreme
fiction. If it has previously been left out of the novels, here it is consciously
brought back in. The two notorious and extended descriptions of *"la
gloria"* mark important stages in Robert's (and his author's) development.
During the first lovemaking Robert repeatedly goes "nowhere." He
experiences love as a recurring "dark passage" toward the unfamiliar. But
in the second love scene Robert is carried into the "now." A Hemingway
hero finally becomes present to the act of love, finally has time to become
familiar with the woman he loves. A new kind of heroine emerges
here—one both pure and impure. Maria is an experienced virgin. Her
rape is a fact; her sense of newness, a shared fiction. Both Robert and
Maria must face her past before they can share a true present. They
cleave to the liberating principle "that nothing is done to oneself that one
does not accept and that if I loved some one it would take it all away."
Forgiven is the guilt Maria carries from her traumatic past. Her story
couples catharsis with the insight that resolves the aftereffects of the
trauma. Hemingway breaks through here, against the entire history of his
defenses, to the freedom implicit in love, the great fiction of reversal.

The journey into Maria's past counts for no more than going back into
Robert's. His growing acceptance of life and death in time corresponds to
a revived awareness of being part of a line of descent. The novel does not
seem to promise this. Early on Robert repudiates his roots: "I would
rather have been born here." He is not at home at home. But he makes the
discovery that the human solidarity for which he fights can only be
achieved once he acknowledges his unique origins. The gypsy has lost his
specific patrimony—*"I had an inheritance from my father"*—and so
inherits the sun and the moon. He can never finish spending it, but to be
at home everywhere is to belong nowhere. Robert begins familiarizing
himself with his rejected home by lying about it. When he tells Maria that
his father shot himself "to avoid being tortured," he tells at best a half-
truth. The suicide must have been committed in response to pain, yet
Robert must also learn to admit its basic cowardice. He tries to defend
against the influence of his father's priority through the fantasy of skipped
generations: "maybe the good juice only came through straight again
after passing through that one?" His recurring response to his father is
embarrassment. He is "embarrassed by all of it" when his father says
good-bye at the train, apprehensive lest at any future meeting "both he
and his grandfather would be acutely embarrassed by the presence of his
father." This embarrassment is authentic and difficult to criticize. Em-
barrassment is a minor version of the uncanny: shame at something
familiar which ought to have remained hidden and secret, and yet comes
to light. What is striking is that Hemingway *chooses* to bring it to light.
Robert is distinguished from Nick Adams not by his traumatic upbringing

—Nick's is traumatic too—but by the chance he is given to work directly back through it. Robert's overt rehearsal of his embarrassing past (his father proves a "coward"; his mother, "a bully") helps him to understand it, and "To understand," he ventures, "is to forgive." He can contemplate the forgiveness (of himself and his origins) that will integrate his past with his present and free him to grow into the future. A past no longer repressed loses the power to return as an anxiety experienced as unavoidable fate.

This marks the victory of insight over repression. The potentially crippling force of Robert's past is not denied its return but openly assimilated to a more inclusive imaginative scheme. The single obsession which has dominated Hemingway's fiction—waiting for the end—is absorbed into a multiplicity of truths. The ending of *For Whom the Bell Tolls* celebrates the power of "making believe" over fantasies which the traumas of our personal history make us believe. The beauty of the "high plateau" is just "as true as Pilar's old women drinking the blood down at the slaughterhouse. There's no *one* thing that's true. It's all true." The power of the imagination over a sense of fate culminates in Robert Jordan's good-bye to Maria. When he says "I go with thee," he gives his entire life up to a saving fiction. Metaphor here *is* truth. Robert will always "go" with her in her heart. Wounded and lying alone at the very end, he knows that truth comes down to getting the tenses right. "I have tried to do with what talent I had. *Have, you mean. All right, have.*"

Robert Jordan is alive until the end. His novel does not end—it recommences. Its last words carry us not into loss but return us to the first sentence: "He could feel his heart beating against the pine needle floor of the forest." This is a repetition which knows nothing of the uncanny. These words are familiar; we have heard them before. But they return us to a point of origin unshadowed by loss. The book draws a circle and thus spatializes our sense of return. It overcomes the sense of being bound by unwilled recurrence and creates instead a sense of eternity, of being still in the place and time where we began. Of course between the first and last sentence everything has changed, but these words *say* the ending as if it had not. Here Hemingway's end truly does create the fiction of recovering his beginning. Robert Jordan refuses to take his life by his own hand: "I don't want to do that business that my father did." He understands his father and forgives him but will not emulate him. That Hemingway ultimately chose to emulate his father's final act suggests that the vision of possibility held out by his greatest novel did not at last help him to live until he died. Yet however Hemingway ended, his most generous novel authorizes us to remember him not as the man who took his own life, but as the creator of Robert Jordan, who can say, facing certain death, "I wish there was more time."

ᴥᷱ Four

FAULKNER AND THE BURDENS OF THE PAST

Folks dont have no luck, changing names. —Dilsey

The Burdens

In the middle of Chapter 11 of *Light in August*, Faulkner interrupts the violent affair between Joe and Joanna to relate the Burden family history. The story focuses upon three generations of Burdens: Calvin the grandfather, Nathaniel the father, and Calvin the brother. Thirty-four years younger than the second Calvin, Joanna experiences her family more as a fourth-generation heir than as a third-generation participant. Faulkner underscores her distance from her family history by telling most of it for her:

> Calvin Burden was the son of a minister named Nathaniel Burrington. The youngest of ten children, he ran away from home at the age of twelve, before he could write his name (or would write it, his father believed) on a ship. He made the voyage around the Horn to California and turned Catholic; he lived for a year in a monastery. Ten years later he reached Missouri from the west. Three weeks after he arrived he was married, to the daughter of a family of Huguenot stock which had emigrated from Carolina by way of Kentucky.

Fanatically opposed to slaveholding and always on the move, the Burden family wanders around the plains until its three generations make the fatal decision to settle in Jefferson. Here their confused migrations assume tragic shape when the first and second Calvin are shot in the town square "by an ex-slaveholder and Confederate soldier named Sartoris, over a question of negro voting." Nathaniel spirits the bodies away for burial in a cedar grove, remains to father Joanna, and contents himself with passing on the legacy of revenge to her: "The only time I can remember him as somebody, a person, was when he took me and showed me Calvin's and grandpa's graves." Nathaniel's one moment of presence seems to turn upon this uncanny scene of instruction: "I didn't want to go into the cedars. . . . I think it was something about father, something that came from the cedar grove to me, through him. A something that I felt that he had put on the cedar grove, and that when I went into it, the grove would put on me so that I would never be able to forget it." With Joanna reiterating the lasting effects of this trauma, her story ends.

Joe's immediate response is to reduce the Burden family history to one unanswered question: "Why your father never killed that fellow—what's his name? Sartoris." Joe here raises the largest possible issue in Faulkner —the problem of unconsummated revenge. How to live with a past that has not been avenged proves the most consistent threat to the stability of the Faulknerian present. Joanna resorts to genetic determinism as a way of explaining Nathaniel's failure to act. "I think that it was because of his French blood." Joe proposes a more conventional answer: "I guess your father must have got religion." Joe is probably closer to the truth. Getting religion could obviate the need for revenge. Based as it is upon the trope of sacrifice, or substitution, religion proposes that what is owed one, or what one owes, can be paid for by a mediator. In taking revenge upon a substitute (a ram, Christ), religion guarantees a displacement of wrath away from a human victim and onto an intercessor that has assimilated guilt. Art is the other great form of human mediation, as Faulkner was fond of reminding us: "those who can, do, those who cannot and suffer enough because they can't, write about it." This is perhaps his most famous formula for the way in which words can take the place of deeds. Art intercedes between the artist and his experience, the artist and his audience, as a vehicle that expresses and even partially resolves those desires and grievances that cannot be confronted through action. To Joe, anything but a man of words, such displaced revenge can only look like surrender. As he prepares to listen to the Burden chronicle, Joe sardonically observes that "when they [women] finally come to surrender completely, it's going to be in words." But what Joe registers as surrender Faulkner himself may experience as something like victory. In telling Joanna's story he achieves one more figurative revenge through language against the past that provoked him into writing. The actual shape of this past can best be sketched in after giving closer attention to the way the past returns in *Light in August*. If we look at *how* Faulkner treats this material, we can better understand why he finds it so compelling.

Joanna finally does go beyond words in her attempt to escape the burden of her forefathers. No other woman in Faulkner seems to achieve so violent a break with her past. Her "wild throes of nymphomania" attempt at once to repudiate past time and to recover lost time. Yet as her quest for a release from Puritan self-consciousness and the debt of revenge she owes it proves increasingly obsessive, her promiscuity looks more like the return of the repressed. As a product of three generations of violent release and stubborn restraint, Joanna can find no middle ground between the two. Her apparent rupture with the past proves to be just one more repetition, and one that even fails to take revenge.

So Joanna begins to crave resolution through begetting a new generation. "She began to talk about a child, as though instinct had warned her that now was the time when she must either justify or expiate." A child would act both as a revenge against a repressive past and as a potential avenger of it. It would compensate for the "frustrate and irrevocable years" and assert the survival of the line. Above all, Joanna wishes her ancestors could see it: "A full measure. Even to a bastard negro child. I would like to see father's and Calvin's faces." The child, she knows, would rebuke them in complex ways; as the objectification of the Burden belief in the merging of the races, it would also be the product of a union they could not abide. Once Joanna discovers that she cannot carry her revenge forward into the future, she regresses into a mere woman of words. As Joe listens to the "calm enormity which her cold, still voice unfolded," he witnesses a retreat to a position where all that will be left to Joanna is prayer. In the severe economy of Faulkner's fiction, those who live by words die by words: Joe kills Joanna while refusing her entreaty to kneel.

The split in Joanna's experience between restitution through deeds and restitution through words is fundamental to Faulkner's perception of his own situation. His profound mistrust of words is only slightly exceeded by his indebtedness to them. Faulkner was not inclined to take solace in the paradox that words become deeds through the alchemy of the creative "act." Words remain words; they can never actually "do" anything. Yet they can register a shift in attitude toward the past to which they refer, and hence, if not a change in those antecedents, a change in what they mean for their inheritor. The very way in which Faulkner presents Joanna's family history indicates the changing significance for him of its highly charged material.

The sheer fact of the Burden chronicle requires explanation. Why is it even there? Do we need this much background about this character? Joanna's ambivalent attitude toward Joe's blackness could be explained without all the invention of three generations and a fatal shoot-out in the town square. The excessive detail and length of the story is no more suspicious than its form. The mode is epic chronicle, full of messengers, flights, heroic deeds. The third person narration (which Joanna's voice only partially recovers as it proceeds) is a throwback to a more traditional form of presentation than the elliptical flashbacks through which much of the novel unfolds. Even the revisions in the manuscript reflect Faulkner's attempts, once he had invented the Burdens, to elaborate their story within a linear framework. As Regina Fadiman has shown, the Burden history was "composed independently" of, and probably before, the developing affair between Joanna and Joe. The manuscripts at the University of Virginia indicate that the story underwent two major revisions. The story originally began with Joanna's father: "Her father, Calvin Burden, was a stocky, dark man with black eyes and hair and a pale beak of a nose." Faulkner then cut up this version and inserted a flashback dealing with the "older Calvin," Joanna's grandfather. In the second and final revision Faulkner rewrote the story as we have it, starting with the grandfather and changing the father's name to Nathaniel. The linked fate of the first and third generation is emphasized and clarified through the final name change: Calvin—Nathaniel—Calvin rather than Calvin—Calvin—Calvin. The final emphasis is upon genealogy and chronology, upon an orderly disposition of Joanna's legacy.

We witness here a fulfilled will to digress, one bent upon dominating material hardly necessary to the successful development of the novel. Faulkner's novels are full of material unassimilated to any obvious formal purpose, and the generosity of the digressive style is often invoked as a convenient way of justifying such excesses. Here Faulkner's purpose seems very likely beyond the control of his creative will. The mode of presentation conveys the sense that life is simple enough to be *told;* the telling is of a pattern of repetition and revenge. As John Irwin has shown, this is a pattern Faulkner continually rehearses. In *Light in August* the pattern insinuates itself where we might least expect it. As outsiders, the Burdens are unlikely candidates for a genealogy developed to express the uniquely repetitive nature of Southern doom. In *Light in August* Faulkner tries to master this doom through his own voice rather than allowing it to emerge through the multiple soliloquies of clearly obsessed speakers. But the sheer fact that such mastery proves gratuitous in view of the larger purposes of the novel leaves open the question whether Faulkner has full control of the material this chronicle is meant to order.

If the Burdens embody a story Faulkner cannot seem to forget, his treatment of Hightower reveals his attitude toward such a story. With the Burdens, Faulkner works from cause to effect. Joanna's "revenge" directly follows and is meant to be understood as the inevitable result of a family history she at once rejects and extends. With Hightower, Faulkner works from effect to cause. He presents Hightower as paralyzed by a memory of his grandfather before filling in the history which would make his behavior explicable. Since Faulkner does not locate any objective correlative for Hightower's obsessive behavior in the present, we are left to assume that Hightower's grandfather is himself the cause of Hightower's obsession with his grandfather. Richard Chase accuses Faulkner of being an implausible psychologist here:

> Hightower has projected his sexual and spiritual impotence back upon a myth
> of his grandfather. Faulkner goes along with Hightower on this point, assuming
> too that a fantasy projected from some center of real causation is the cause
> itself. He nearly allows Hightower to determine the quality of his (Faulkner's)
> consciousness.

This is a curious charge. What does Chase mean by the phrase "goes
along with Hightower?" How does a character one has created turn upon
one "to determine" one's consciousness? Only if the character himself
originates from material unavailable to introspection. If we take Chase's
analysis as a point of departure, the largely unconscious workings of
Faulkner's creative mind can be thrown into relief. By the logic of Chase's
argument, what is not true of the character (determination by ancestry)
may well be true of his author: Faulkner risks psychological implausibility
with Hightower because Hightower allows him to express a fantasy he is
determined by. Faulkner apparently has little choice but to create fictions
in which an imaginative relation to one's past proves as formative as any
"center of real causation" in the present. He displaces onto Hightower his
predicament of being determined by "a myth of his grandfather." High-
tower is a symptom of the very symptom he falsely diagnoses in himself.
Faulkner's statements about him thus reveal as much about Faulkner as
about Hightower. It is Faulkner who "produces" stories "out of his
subconscious . . . without volition." It is Faulkner who, in confronting his
own past, "skipped a generation." And it is Faulkner who discovers that
his "only salvation must be to return to the place to die where my life had
already ceased before it began." How he survives that return is the drama
of his career.

The Burden

"History shall never forget you!": the praise shouted by Beauregard
during Colonel William Falkner's gallant charge at Manassas must have
returned, at times, to haunt rather than cheer his great-grandson. Perhaps
the Colonel's most stubborn trait was his unforgettability. In every
important sense he was, for a Falkner reviewing his past, the beginning.
William's first biographical sketch begins with the fact of the first William:

> Born in Mississippi in 1897. Great-grandson of Col. W. C. Faulkner, C. S. A.,
> author of "The White Rose of Memphis," "Rapid Ramblings in Europe," etc.
> Boyhood and youth were spent in Mississippi. . . .

As Joseph Blotner has observed, "It is hard to do justice to William Clark
Falkner in a short space." My purpose will be to abstract the pattern from

his life, and that of the family he founded, which often seems controlling in Faulkner's work. The full account of the Falkner family history can be found in *Faulkner: A Biography*, pp. 3-58. Blotner's article "The Falkners and the Fictional Families" provides the best summary of this material, as well as some interesting speculation on the ways in which it passed into fiction. Blotner ends his article by asserting that "William Faulkner used and transformed more of his own family for his fictional purposes in more books than any other major author." But when Blotner poses the question "how close is art to life?" he implies by the very form of his question that the answer is less a matter of transformation than of merely establishing proximity, of holding the mirror up to nature. The whole tone of Blotner's argument suggests that Faulkner's family history is something reflected in the work, material lying passively in wait for the author's conscious mind to appropriate. Blotner does not possess a theory of psychological determinism or one of Faulkner's artistic development. Thus he is unable to abstract, even from his own biography, a convincing description of the interplay between Faulkner's life and work.

Faulkner's imagination performed an extreme abbreviation of the stories handed down to him about his ancestors. He seems to have reduced this legacy to one episode, its "repetition," and the response to the first and second event by a figure caught up between the two. Of course Faulkner's fiction is overdetermined, and much of its variety derives from experience unrelated to any controlling patterns we might isolate in it. We should not, on the other hand, refuse to acknowledge the existence of such a pattern, especially when it exerts so much more influence over Faulkner's work than the random details he consciously borrowed from his past.

The pattern centers on three figures in Faulkner's male line: the Old Colonel, William's great-grandfather; John W. T. Falkner, his grandfather; and Murry, his father. It is tempting to linger over the details of the Old Colonel's turbulent life—his flight from Missouri to Mississippi at fourteen, his mysterious wounding in the Mexican War, his two acquittals for murder, his short tenure as commander of "The Magnolia Rifles," his career as a novelist, railroad builder, and aspirant to the state legislature. But for William, the essence of the Old Colonel is summed up in his end. For all that happened to his great-grandfather—much of which Faulkner repeatedly incorporates—it was the way he died that made it necessary *to write* about him. It was an end that had to be written about, as we shall see, because it was unfinished, unresolved, unrevenged.

Even William's brother John, writing in *My Brother Bill*, feels it appropriate to introduce the Old Colonel at the moment of his death. John has been talking about the difficulty he had as a child grasping the age difference between himself and William. His thoughts suddenly shift:

Mother finally explained it to me one day and after that Bill left me alone
about it.

The Old Colonel was killed by a man named Thurmond. Their differences
had extended back over the years. They had grown more bitter with time. The
final edge was reached when the Old Colonel defeated Thurmond for a seat in
the state legislature in 1892. When the Old Colonel came back from Jackson,
Thurmond shot him down on the street when he walked up to the Square from
the depot. He died three days later.

The very abruptness of this transition testifies to the familiarity (despite a
number of inaccuracies) of the facts it introduces. They were familiar to
William as well. After reminding Robert Cantwell that "he wasn't armed
the day Thurmond shot him," Faulkner stresses the lasting effects of the
Old Colonel's murder. "The feeling in Ripley did not die out with Colonel
Falkner's death and Thurmond's leaving. I can remember myself, when I
was a boy in Ripley, there were some people who would pass on the
other side of the street to avoid speaking—that sort of thing." Yet William
(writing in 1945) could be remarkably forgetful about a story of which he
must have heard, like Quentin, all *too much.*" In a letter to Malcolm
Cowley he casually ticks off the Old Colonel's achievements and ends
with this sentence: "He built the first railroad in our county, wrote a few
books, made grand European tour of his time, died in a duel and the
county raised a marble effigy which still stands in Tippah County."
There was no duel, and the marble effigy, an eight-foot statue of Carrara
marble, had been purchased for the eventuality by the Colonel himself.
His death was an episode about which the great-grandson remained at
once intensely concerned and curiously vague. The facts are as follows:

THE MURDER: In 1886 Colonel Falkner assumed control of the Ship
Island, Ripley & Kentucky Railroad by buying out his business partner,
Dick Thurmond. The two men had long since become hardened rivals,
fond of competing with each other by expanding the dimensions of their
palatial estates. When Falkner declared for the Mississippi legislature,
Thurmond tried unsuccessfully to finance his defeat. Two weeks before
the election, Falkner arranged his affairs with his lawyer, who warned
him to arm himself against the aggrieved Thurmond. On election day the
apparently victorious Falkner walked down to the Ripley town square.
He stood directly in front of Thurmond's office, talking with a friend,
Thomas Rucker. "Suddenly," as Blotner tells it,

> Thurmond was there beside him, and Falkner turned to see a .44 pistol pointed
> at his head. "Dick, what are you doing?" he said. "Don't shoot!" But the pistol
> roared and Falkner fell, his pipe clattering on the pavement. He looked up at
> Thurmond. "Why did you do it, Dick?" he asked. Then he lost consciousness.

The bullet had hit Falkner in the mouth, knocked out teeth, and lodged in
the right side of the neck under the ear. The Colonel regained conscious-

ness on Wednesday morning, bequeathed his affairs to his son John W. T., and died at 10:40 that evening.

THE REACTION: John W. T. Falkner was forty-one when his father was shot. Thirty miles away in Oxford at the time, it took him over a day to reach the Colonel's bedside. In the meantime, two of Thurmond's men had secured the services of Judge Stephens—a widely respected barrister—for the defense. Apparently John W. T. had decided against taking the law into his own hands. When the trial began in February, the defense managed to secure a charge of manslaughter. John W. T. Falkner served as one of the assistants to the district attorney. Two days after the trial began it was finished: Thurmond had been acquitted. John W. T.'s friends talked him out of taking revenge against Thurmond, but he did experience the minor satisfaction of assualting Joe Brown, one of the men who had pumped a handcar to Judge Stephens's on the night of the shooting.

THE REPETITION: About a year after his grandfather's murder, Murry Falkner became embroiled in an ugly feud. His sweetheart, Miss Pat Fontaine, enlisted Murry's aid in suppressing gossip being spread about her by a seamstress named Mollie Walker. Murry approached Mollie's brother, Elias, with the blunt command, "Tell your sister to stop making remarks about Miss Fontaine." Elias protested; Murry knocked him down twice. Later in the day Murry stopped in at Herron's drugstore to get a powder for his headache. "A moment later," Blotner relates,

> the door swung open and Herron dropped to the floor. Falkner turned his head to find himself looking at the barrel of 'Lias Walker's twelve-gauge shotgun. The blast hit him in the back and knocked him off the stool. In two quick strides Walker was standing over him, a pistol in his hand.
>
> "Don't shoot me any more," Falkner groaned, "you've already killed me."
>
> "I want to be damned sure," Walker said, and pulled the trigger. The slug hit Falkner in the mouth, knocking out teeth, damaging his jaw, and lodging against bone near the roof of his mouth.

John W. T.'s response to the shooting of his son was more precipitous. He pumped a handcar thirty miles from Oxford and cornered Walker behind a hardware store. Armed with his big Navy revolver, standing at point blank range, John W. T. took aim at the would-be murderer of his son. The gun failed to fire. It proceeded to misfire six times. In the meantime Elias had pulled his own gun and shot John W. T. in the hand. "If it had hit me in the stomach it wouldn't have hurt so much."

Back at Nelson's Boarding House Murry lay in critical condition. Sallie Murry, his mother, undaunted by the failure of the doctors to extract the bullet from Murry's mouth, tried an expedient of her own. She poured liquid gum resin in his mouth, Murry began to vomit, and the bullet popped out into the basin. Six years later Murry fathered William Cuthbert Faulkner.

What conclusion can we draw from this chain of events? In his abstract of the biography, Blotner omits important similarities between the two shootings while obscuring the pivotal role played in both by John W. T. "Looking at the eldest sons in the four Falkner generations, one notes that all of them except the author had been shot at least once, two of them twice. And if his father had not killed anyone, his grandfather had tried his best, and his great-grandfather had succeeded at least twice." Here being "shot at least once" is advanced as a connecting link between three generations of Falkners. But surely what matters here is *how* one was shot, and *whether* one was revenged. Blotner misses the woods for the trees. John W. T. is shot not as a heroic victim but as a failed avenger. The shootings of his father and son are linked not only by the similarity of their wounds* and the exact repetition of the plea "Don't shoot," but, in each case, by the ineffectuality of John W. T.'s response. It was a pattern such as this, in which three generations are brought together in an ordeal of suffering and unfulfilled obligation, which made the generations an obsessive subject for fiction. The pattern is at once repetitive and unfulfilled; while two generations, in the act of flaunting their courage, suffer a remarkably similar act of revenge, the intervening generation proves unable to achieve requital. Thus a fourth generation is bound to feel adumbrated by a pattern of repetition that exercises sway over the family destiny, as well as by the more painful fact that the logic of the pattern (similar fates befall alternating generations) links it with a figure who has contributed to the pattern by failing decisively to alter it. Out of such an inheritance may very likely have been born the recurring feeling in Faulkner "that an ancestor's actions can determine the actions of his descendants for generations to come by compelling them periodically to repeat his deeds." The saddest word in Faulkner is not "was" but "again." He is threatened less by a past that is unrecapturable than by a past which continually recaptures him.

Critics have overemphasized Faulkner's tendency to identify with the figure of the Old Colonel. Had the second William actually identified with the first he might never have been compelled to revise the family fate by writing about it, since such an identification would have presumed a mastery of his fate through deeds rather than words. And if such a resolution was available to him, why did William emphasize his imitation of the Old Colonel under his aspect as a man of words? Jack Falkner maintains that Bill "more or less unconsciously patterned his life after the old Colonel's. He spoke of him often, and it has been said that, as a

*Donald Duclos, who interviewed uncles and aunts along with Faulkner himself, emphasizes their awareness of this pattern: "The bullet (and this is what amazes the family) struck Murry in the face, doing the same physical damage to him as had been done to his grandfather by Thurmond's bullet."

child, he was asked what he wanted to become in life and he replied, 'A writer like my great-grandfather.'" This was, at best, an oblique sort of emulation. To reduce the Old Colonel to a "writer" was to confer upon him a role none of the Old Colonel-figures in the fiction embody. Clearly William did not conceive of his great-grandfather as a writer when it came to writing about him. Thus a conscious abbreviation of the Old Colonel's experience may have provided a way of making his achievement less overwhelming. Certainly the desire to be originless, however manageable one's antecedents, was strong in Faulkner: "I would have preferred nothing at all prior to the instant I began to write, as though Faulkner and Typewriter were concomitant, coadjutant and without past on that moment they first faced each other at the suitable (nameless) table." When the first biographers began moving in, Faulkner protested any alignment of his work and his life. "I will want to blue pencil everything which even intimates that something breathing and moving sat behind the typewriter which produced the books," he wrote Malcolm Cowley in 1949. A month later he added that "it is my ambition to be, as a private individual, abolished and voided from history, leaving it markless, no refuse save the printed books." Writing was his first line of defense against the past; perhaps his most direct assault upon originality was to change his name.

While Faulkner downplayed the name change as a merely practical matter — "no outsider seemed able to pronounce it from reading it" — the act acquires some irony in the context of his first major novel, which ends with an acknowledged authority (Aunt Jenny) protesting the vanity of changing names. Clearly the name change was part of a process of rebegetting himself, but for what purpose? Faulkner himself admits that any practical motive was probably insufficient to account for the change: "Maybe when I began to write, even though I thought I was writing for fun, I secretly was ambitious and did not want to ride on grandfather's coat-tails, and so accepted the 'u,' was glad of such an easy way to strike out for myself." This passage can be interpreted in two ways. On the one hand, it may mean what it says. If so, it is the only acknowledgment I know of that John W. T. was a figure who stood too much in William's way. On the other hand, no one was likely, as the history of criticism has shown, to assume that John W. T. had coat-tails anywhere near as long as the Old Colonel's. *He* was the man who apparently stood in the way. But if so, why would someone so concerned to gain filial independence (to be "without past") mistake/misstate the very figure from whom he had tried to gain it? Surely Faulkner means "great-grandfather." Blotner suggests as much in the biography when he edits the letter to read "I secretly was ambitious and did not want to ride on [great] grand-father's coat-tails." This slip makes it possible to emphasize Faulkner's strategy of

defending against the legacy of his grandfather by displacing attention
toward his great-grandfather, a strategy which here fails him. John W. T.
is the far more problematic figure for his grandson. He is, as I have
shown, decisively linked to William through a pattern of repetition; if the
first and third generations suffer nearly identical wounds, the second and
fourth generations are bound together by having arrived too "late" to
take any effective revenge. Given the inevitability of William's identifica-
tion with John W. T., his burden became less a heroic end he was unable
to match than a belated revenge he could not fail to imitate. The decision
to become a "writer," in its displaced or passive aggression, bears much
more resemblance to John W. T.'s failure to "do" it than it does to the Old
Colonel's life of deeds and his heroic finale. By reducing the Old Colonel
to a "writer," and then by trying openly to dispel his influence through a
name change, William effectively distracts attention away from his more
complex ambivalence about writing born of his identification with John
W. T.

If the pattern I have isolated came to function as part of Faulkner's
unconscious, it is because it converged so easily with a universal activity
of the unconscious—the quest for mastery over one's origins through
revision of them. For John Irwin, Faulkner's obsession reduces to belated-
ness itself. Irwin's argument everywhere implies that Faulkner's specific
personal inheritance converges with a psychological predicament ex-
perienced by all writers who have any ambitions with respect to the past.
Thus an analyst listening to a patient resembles a critic listening to a
strong career:

> The analyst who listens while a patient repeats again and again the story or
> stories of his life is simply trying to understand the relationship between the
> narrator and the story or stories that he tells, trying to decipher a hidden story
> by analyzing the variations among the patent translations of that story, trying
> to discover the laws of condensation, distortion, substitution that govern the
> different oblique repetitions of that same hidden story. And it is, I think, not
> unjustified to say that the motive force of those repetitions is, in a very real
> sense, an oblique revenge against time, for if revenge means trying to get even,
> then in light of Freud's economic model for psychic energy exchanges and the
> principle of constancy, those repetitions are attempts to stabilize or equalize a
> tension, attempts "to get even" in terms of energy levels for an insult or affront
> to the psychic apparatus.

The particular affront to Faulkner's psychic apparatus inflicted by his
past was that time had taken revenge against him, leaving him a fourth
generation heir of a pattern he could well feel powerless to reverse and
even compelled to extend. His response was, in Irwin's words, "an oblique
attempt to get even with that irreversibility of time that has rendered the
original affront immune to direct action." He became a storyteller.

In the course of trying to rewrite his family history, and thus his place in it, Faulkner came to understand and embrace the impossibility of his task. Irwin argues that it was the very nature of narration itself—its foredoomed attempt to get even—that led Faulkner deeper into the conflicts narration was meant to resolve. Thus his works become at once self-perpetuating and self-defeating, eventuating wholly out of themselves. Since Irwin views the entire process of Faulkner's career as so circular and self-reflexive—"to use narration to get even with the very mode of narration's existence"—he treats the novels as occupying "a multidimensional imaginative space . . . in which every element could be simultaneously folded into every other element." The great strength of this method is in its tyrannizing unity. It can endlessly multiply examples of the elements which bind the works together in a set of mutually constitutive relationships. But it implies that Faulkner did not develop, and it obscures the relationship of the work to anything beyond the logic of its internal struggle against belatedness. Irwin brilliantly establishes Faulkner's career as the ultimate example of the anxiety of influence. In the course of proving this, however, he generalizes Faulkner's predicament into one so prevalent as to make it uninteresting. Such anxiety derived as much from deeply personal sources as from the paradox of creation itself. It was thus subject to a kind of resolution, since these sources stood in a dialectical (rather than a self-reflexive) relationship to the activity of creation. The meaning of Faulkner's work is not only to be found *among* the texts (in what Irwin calls "interstitial" space) but *between* the texts and the life. As Faulkner's understanding of his inheritance grew, his works changed. In the following pages I intend to show that Faulkner's struggle for a revenge against time was also an ambition which changed through time.

Starting with John W. T.

The central human act in Faulkner is the act of listening. Joe listens to Joanna, Quentin to Rosa, Ike to the hunters, Chick to Gavin Stevens. A relentless voice pours forth into an inevitable ear: narration typically preempts conversation. People relate by telling stories. The test of a good listener is his ability to retell with a difference. Verbal mastery of a verbal inheritance becomes the sign of maturity. Ike celebrates his majority by wresting the narration of his life away from the third person: "then he was twenty-one. He could say it, himself." Development comes to be measured by the growing authority and autonomy of voice. One has grown up when one has learned to resist being entrapped by the "rhetoric of retellings" into a mere repetition of the past.

Since Faulkner was born into a world of stories, it is perhaps no accident that the book he called his first "personal" novel begins with one man listening to another. The immediate impact of *Sartoris* flows directly from being in the felt presence of ancestors. The "spirit of the dead man" John Sartoris has been fetched by old Falls, the custodian of his life story. It is the *influence* of this spirit which interests Faulkner; throughout, Colonel John Sartoris is a figure mediated by the subjectivity of his son old Bayard. (*Flags in the Dust*, the first version of *Sartoris*, opens with the story and largely dispenses with its effects. Whoever revised this opening, its final form, in which we move from effect to cause, has proven more characteristically Faulknerian). On the opening page we witness only the effects of the father's presence; as with Hightower, Faulkner gives us the burden of the past before the past itself.

Old Bayard is deaf. This ailment seems perfectly tuned to his predicament—having heard too much. (He will later protest against old man Falls's interrogations "every time you tell me this damn story.") As if to emphasize the deafness as a defense against a burden passed on by the mouth, Faulkner ushers in the spirit of Colonel John through the transfer of his pipe from old man Falls to Bayard: "The bowl of the pipe was ornately carved, and it was charred with much usage, and on it were the prints of his father's teeth, where he had left the very print of his ineradicable bones as though in enduring stone." The bequest of the pipe suggests the bathetic conceit of Old Bayard following less in his father's footsteps than in his toothprints. (This transfer acquires more resonance when we remember that William inherited the very pipe his great-grandfather had been smoking when he was shot.) The passing on of family identity will prove, for the Sartorises, a burden passed on from mouth to mouth.

The mere sight of the pipe a few pages later can thus function as a *petite madeleine* to conjure up the story which precipitates the opening scene:

> Through the cloth of his pocket his hand had touched the pipe there, and he took it out and looked at it again, and it seemed to him that he could still hear old man Falls' voice in roaring recapitulation: "Cunnel was settin' thar in a cheer, his sock feet propped on the po'ch railin', smokin' this hyer very pipe. . . ."

This recollection begins with Colonel Sartoris's narrow escape from the Yankees and ends with the circumstances of his death:

> "That 'us when it changed. When he had to start killin' folks. Them two cyarpetbaggers stirrin' up niggers, that he walked right into the room whar they was a-settin' behind a table with they pistols layin' on the table, and that robber and that other feller he kilt, all with that same dang der'nger. When a feller has to start killin' folks, he 'most always has to keep on killin' 'em. And when he does, he's already dead hisself."

It showed on John Sartoris' brow, the dark shadow of fatality and doom, that night when he sat beneath the candles in the dining-room and turned a wineglass in his fingers while he talked to his son. The railroad was finished, and that day he had been elected to the state legislature after a hard and bitter fight, and doom lay on his brow, and weariness.

"And so," he said, "Redlaw'll kill me tomorrow, for I shall be unarmed. I'm tired of killing men. . . . Pass the wine, Bayard."

The similarities between the death of Colonel Falkner and the death of Colonel Sartoris do not again need to be emphasized. The central issue here for our purposes is the first intersection of the Sartoris family fate with that of the as yet unnamed Burdens.

In order to understand the curious symmetries between these fatally linked families, consider the following genealogies:

Falkner	*Sartoris*	*Burden*
Col. William Clark Falkner (1825-89)	Col. John Sartoris (1823-73) Bayard Sartoris (1838-62)	Calvin Burden (1804-65)
John W. T. Falkner (1848-1922)	Bayard Sartoris ("old Bayard") (1849-1919)	Nathaniel Burden (1827- ?)
Murry C. Falkner (1870-1932)	John Sartoris (d. 1901)	Calvin Burden (1845-65)
William Cuthbert Faulkner (1897-1962)	Bayard Sartoris ("young Bayard") (1893-1920) John Sartoris (1893-1918)	Joanna Burden (1879-1932)

The relevant incidents in the Sartoris genealogy can best be understood in light of old man Falls's theory that people can be made "kin" not only by the way they come into but by the way they go out of the world. "'Bayard,'" old man Falls said, 'I sort of envied them two Nawthuners, be damned ef I didn't. A feller kin take a wife and live with her fer a long time, but after all they ain't no kin. But the feller that brings you into the world or sends you outen hit. . . .'" Given this theory of kinship, blood ties can be reinforced—even created—by intervening in the process of death. Intervention is precisely what old Bayard forgoes when John Sartoris is shot by Redlaw. He lives out a long and peaceful life punctuated only by the death of his son, the second John, from "yellow fever and an old Spanish bullet wound." After his grandson John is killed in aerial combat, old Bayard's namesake returns home as a guilty survivor. If old Bayard had failed to assert his kinship with his father by not avenging the way he was sent out of the world, young Bayard insists upon assuming responsibility for the way in which his brother died. Young Bayard's relentlessly suicidal behavior culminates in the automobile crash in which old Bayard is killed, directly under the figure of "John Sartoris' effigy." A few months later young Bayard finally destroys himself in a plane crash on the very day that his son, the fourth John, is born. This is the child Narcissa tries to unname.

Perhaps the most striking aspect of this story is the inconsequence of the third generation. In every account of the Sartoris family, the second John Sartoris is the man left out. William's "melancholy excision" of Murry Falkner's "opposite number" leads Blotner to this conclusion: "There seems to have been almost no rapport between these two Falkners, father and son." Very likely so, but an interpretation more useful for our purposes has been suggested by Faulkner himself. "The twins' father didn't have a story. He came at a period in history which, in this country, people thought of and think of now as a peaceful one. That it was an optimistic one, nothing was happening. There would be little brush-fire wars that nobody paid much attention to, the country was growing, the time of travail and struggle where the hero came into his own had passed. From '70 on to 1912-14, nothing happened to Americans to speak of. This John Sartoris, the father, lived in that time when there was nothing that brought the issue to him to be brave and strong or dramatic—well, call it dramatic, not brave, but dramatic, nothing happened to him. But he had to be there for the simple continuity of the family." If the second John Sartoris was conceived as Murry's "opposite number," the one happening Faulkner had to draw upon was Murry's youthful wounding. John Sartoris dies, in fact, from a wound of the sort that Murry survived. The major similarity between these two fathers still resides, however, in the utter uneventfulness of their lives as compared to the other males in their line. (Even William had fabricated the story of surviving a plane crash so as to acquire his share of vainglory.) Murry's wound at the hand of Elias Walker may have been enough to fulfill a pattern of repetition and to raise the issue of revenge, but the specific episode is apparently not one Faulkner feels the need to recapitulate in *Sartoris*. Only in the Burden genealogy does Faulkner link the third generation more dramatically to the family history through the one repetition which confirms Calvin's (as it did Murry's) place in the line.

Taken together then, the Sartoris and Burden genealogies reveal the ways in which Faulkner incorporates the patterns of repetition and revenge derived from his family history. In both families we find the device of the skipped generation: Calvin and Calvin shot by the same gun, Bayard and Bayard linked in their quest for self-destruction. The Sartorises especially display the pattern of spatial doubling within, and temporal doubling across, generations singled out by Irwin. Seen from the perspective of the present, both families contain a second generation which has avoided a clear call to revenge the first. These similarities become more remarkable when we consider that the fates of these two families intersect *because* of their mortal differences. Why should Faulkner, who so self-consciously patterned the Sartoris family after his own, bequeath such a similar genealogy to the Burdens? According to old man Falls's logic, the Burdens become "kin" to the Sartorises once the two Calvins are murdered by the Colonel. But their "kinship" antedates this episode; both families were grafted, as we have seen, from the same family tree. It is as if Faulkner cannot imagine a genealogy without relying upon *his* genealogy.

Perhaps we can now put the importance of old Bayard's development into clearer perspective. A generalized passivity shadows Bayard throughout *Sartoris*. This can be explained less by his old age than by his having failed to commit a purgative act of revenge. Revenge is continually held up by this novel as a means of resolving obligations and relieving guilt. It becomes a primary mode of releasing tension: Horace seeks "revenge on perfection" (meaning the sister to whom he is incestuously bound); women, Miss Jenny admits, "take our revenge wherever and whenever we can get it"; young Bayard takes revenge against the future, "the long, long span of a man's natural life," through suicide. If the constant reiteration of stories (old man Falls's revenge?) keeps Colonel John alive, they are kept lively for old Bayard by his not having imposed closure upon his father's end. Bayard's one attempt to do so is reminiscent of the ineffectuality of John W. T.'s. His father's tombstone had originally borne the words

> For man's enlightenment he lived
> By man's ingratitude he died
>
> Pause here, son of sorrow; remember death

"This inscription," Faulkner relates, "had caused some furore on the part of the slayer's family, and a formal protest had followed. But in complying with popular opinion, old Bayard had had his revenge: he caused the line 'By man's ingratitude he died' to be chiseled crudely out, and added beneath it: 'Fell at the hand of — — — Redlaw, Sept. 4, 1876.'" But this is a revenge of words, not deeds. It leaves old Bayard unfulfilled, as Aunt Jenny's meditation by his grave clearly shows:

> Old Bayard's headstone was simple too, having been born, as he had, too late for one war and too soon for the next, and she thought what a joke They had played on him—forbidding him opportunities for swashbuckling and then denying him the privilege of being buried by men, who would have invented vainglory for him.

That Faulkner felt Bayard's history to be an unresolved dimension of the novel becomes abundantly clear when we consider his major revision of its plot. *The Unvanquished* not only gives old Bayard a childhood, but grants him the opportunity to fashion his unique and triumphant "revenge."

Sartoris (1929) and *The Unvanquished* (1938) are the two coordinates between which I would like to plot my discussion of Faulkner's development. Cleanth Brooks rejects the possibility of such development out of hand:

> It may be difficult to recognize the Bayard Sartoris of *The Unvanquished* in the rather crotchety old banker who is fussed over by Aunt Jenny and by his coachman Simon, and who sputters or blusters at Simon in return, putters about his office, and exchanges reminiscences with old man Falls. One may be tempted to say that since *Sartoris* (Faulkner's third novel, published in 1929) appeared five years before *The Unvanquished*, the author had not at that time thought about the dilemmas of character and courage to which he would expose the young Bayard when he came to write *The Unvanquished*. This way of accounting for the discrepancies may well be sound, though it is perhaps risky to assume that Faulkner would not have had in mind at a very early date the events in "An Odor of Verbena." Faulkner apparently carried many of his novels in his head for years before he actually wrote them down. But in any event, the more interesting way of handling this problem—and one tidier in terms of aesthetic theory—is to say that a young man who has his heroic hour may very well subside into a lifetime of rather conventional duties, and that in any case the man of seventy, however heroic his conduct at twenty-four, will seem stodgy to those who know him only as an old man. To have read *The Unvanquished* before reading *Sartoris* should enrich the latter book, not necessarily contradict it.

In typical New Critical fashion, Brooks sacrifices the history of Faulkner's work to its supposed structure. Is it not just as "risky" to assume that Faulkner had a younger Bayard in mind when he wrote of him, as an old man, *nine* years before he wrote "An Odor of Verbena"? "Tidy" aesthetic theories do injustice to complex personal developments. While not a view Irwin would actively endorse, Brooks's dismissal of the temporal sequence of the novels for the sake of analogies between them is a necessary consequence of Irwin's method as well. It leads him to interpret Bayard's actions in *The Unvanquished* as one more example of the revenge *upon* the father he finds everywhere in Faulkner:

> In defeating his father's killer, Bayard is symbolically killing his father, and when Bayard confronts Redmond, the man who actually did what Bayard had unconsciously desired to do as an implicit part of his incestuous desire for his stepmother, i. e., kill his father, Bayard confronts a double of himself. It is a theme that Faulkner never tires of reiterating; by courageously facing the fear of death, the fear of castration, the fear of one's own worst instincts, one slays the fear; by taking the risk of being feminized, by accepting the feminine elements in the self, one establishes one's masculinity.

This is high praise, reserved by Irwin for the Bayard of *The Unvanquished*. More troublesome here, however, is the fact that within the terms Irwin has set for himself, it becomes impossible for any character in Faulkner to act on his father's behalf. All revenge becomes Oedipal revenge. Every act of revenge, even against the murderer of one's father, is a revenge *against* the father. I would like to treat Bayard's "revenge" less as constituting its own opposite than as an act almost unique among those committed by Faulkner's major characters. But first it is necessary to discuss the major works which along with *Light in August* intervene between Faulkner's first and second novel about the Sartorises.

Words or Deeds?

Faulkner himself claimed that readers of his work should "begin with a book called *Sartoris* that has the germ of my apocrypha in it." Faulkner found himself the legatee of a "false" text which he had to restore to its authentic dimensions. His work stands in the same relation to his inheritance as the Bible does to the Apocrypha: it will assert itself as the "true" version of a rival story. *Sartoris* was merely the beginning—Faulkner had not yet learned that retelling must become revision. In his essay on the composition of *Sartoris*, Faulkner admits the possibility that his material may have *written him*. In response to Ben Wasson's criticism of *Flags in the Dust* that *"you have about 6 books in here,"* Faulkner experienced the following:

> I realised for the first time that I had done better than I knew and the long work I had to create opened before me and I felt myself surrounded by the limbo in which the shady visions, the host which stretched half formed, waiting each with it's portion of that verisimilitude which is to bind into a whole the world which for some reason I believe should not pass utterly out of the memory of man, and I contemplated those shady but ingenious shapes by reason of whose labor I might reaffirm the impulses of my own ego in the actual world without stability, with a lot of humbleness, and I speculated on time and death and wondered if I had invented the world to which I should give life or if it had invented me.

It *had* invented him, insofar as in *Sartoris* Faulkner had discovered the shape of his material rather than its significance. In *The Sound and the Fury* (1929), Faulkner displays an intuitive grasp of this significance and invents the crucial figure of Quentin Compson. *As I Lay Dying* (1930) explores Faulkner's ambivalence toward narration as an act of revenge. *Sanctuary* (1931) digresses from Faulkner's quest for a revised relation to his genealogy but looks forward to revision in light of the theme—for-giveness—which will dominate the second phase of his career. *Light in August* (1932) attempts a more direct assault on the burden of the past than anything since *Sartoris*. The unpublished introduction to *The Sound and the Fury* (1933) expresses Faulkner's growing understanding of his project as one of substituting words for deeds. *Pylon* (1935) acts as little more than a diversion from the strain of completing *Absalom, Absalom!*, a book first conceived in 1931. *Absalom* (1936) completes Faulkner's romance with Quentin Compson and the revenge of words. In "An Odor of Verbena," finished in July 1937, Faulkner returns to Bayard with a fully achieved understanding of the pressures upon him and the solutions available to him. "An Odor of Verbena" acts as the climax not only of *The Unvanquished* (the first six stories of which were written in February-October 1934; published in 1938), but of the first and major phase of Faulkner's career.

The movement from Sartoris to *The Sound and the Fury* is one in which Faulkner internalizes the quest for revenge. As he approaches the universal psychological basis for revenge—the desire to take the father's place—it becomes less a unique family inheritance and more a generalized human predicament. Quentin directs his revenge inward against himself rather than outward toward an enemy. The self-inflicted punishment of guilt replaces the other-directed punishment of murder. Quentin's guilt eventually leads, however, to an end no less destructive. *The Sound and the Fury* can be read as an explanation of Quentin's suicide.

Irwin sees Quentin as Hamlet, paralyzed by the need to carry out a revenge against a crime (incest) that he desperately wishes he could commit. Any analysis of Quentin's conflict would seem to rest here, grounded in his frustrated desire to violate the ultimate taboo. Yet Irwin manages to imply that the desire for incest may be less a cause than a symptom. "The desire to return to the womb is the desire for incest." But what experience can account for this regressive quest, this inability to grow forward into otherness and time? Irwin brings this question momentarily to rest before the figure of Quentin's father, who has performed a "psychological castration" of his son. Yet a further interpre-tation of Quentin's impotence suggests itself: the problem of simply *being a son*. "For Quentin, the psychological problem that has made him impotent (the castration complex whose origin is generation) becomes merged with the problem of whether man, in relation to the flow of time, can ever be anything but helpless, passive, and impotent, and to solve the former problem he must solve the latter." But this latter problem cannot be "solved." It can only be met with a host of defenses. Quentin's most adaptive defense in the struggle with the father is to "prove that he is a better man by being a better narrator." Retelling the story of Charles and Henry becomes his attempt to convert a sense of psychic belatedness into one of imaginative priority. As his cynical father took revenge upon him, so he will take revenge upon a substitute—his audience. Yet the very act of telling precipitates Quentin's final doom, for through it he discovers himself as the fated repetition of those earlier events his narration had hoped to master. His struggle to take a "revenge against time" by fathering the true story of the Sutpens leads him inevitably back into those obsessions which he can only escape, as he does, through death. Thus Quentin's suicide cannot finally be understood until we read another book, *Absalom, Absalom!*

The Sound and the Fury contains an implied alternative to the problem of repetition in its invocation of the Christ story. This is the myth of the second chance. Christ's story is also a story of repetition, but one that redeems repetition itself. The son becomes the father by accepting his place as the son. He transforms the fact of priority (Old Testaments) into his own authority (New Testaments) by giving the story he receives and forwards a better ending. By forgiving himself his place in time he absolves himself of the guilt produced by a revenge against time. The experiences of conversion and absolution can undo what has been done. Forgiveness, as Blake knew, was the only idea in the gospel which could not be found elsewhere. It is also, in the form of cathartic insight, the basis of any cure in psychotherapy. The myth of forgiveness, that one's acts and destiny can be understood and reversed through an act of imagination, assumes that human fate is not determined by outer historical process but by inner psychological conditions. All this the novel implies, however much it does not understand. The challenge to Faulkner is to make this a basis from which he consciously operates. He admitted that *The Sound and the Fury* was almost entirely a spontaneous production, written out of "that emotion definite and physical and yet nebulous to describe: that ecstasy, that eager and joyous faith and anticipation of surprise which the yet unmarred sheet beneath my hand held inviolate and unfailing, waiting for release." The novel includes everything which Faulkner will use to overcome the burden of the past, but not yet in a form which suggests conscious mastery of the burden. It will take eight years for the myth of forgiveness to overcome the appeal of the myth of repetition.

The difference between *As I Lay Dying* and *The Sound and the Fury* is the difference between deliberation and ecstasy. *As I Lay Dying* is an entirely *written* book, and reveals almost nothing new about its author except that he was involved in the problems of writing. The first draft took only forty-seven days and the finished novel required fewer revisions than any of his others. It was, as Faulkner admits, a wholly conscious creation:

> When I began As I Lay Dying I had discovered what it was and knew that it would be also missing in this case because this would be a deliberate book. I set out deliberately to write a tour-de-force. Before I ever put pen to paper and set down the first word, I knew what the last word would be and almost where the last period would fall. Before I began I said, I am going to write a book by which, at a pinch, I can stand or fall if I never touch ink again. So when I finished it the cold satisfaction was there, as I had expected, but as I had also expected that other quality which The Sound and the Fury had given me was absent. . . . It was not there in As I Lay Dying. I said, It is because I knew too much about this book before I began to write it.

No one is more deserving of such a description than Darl. He always has the last word. He is the cold-blooded novelist Faulkner here portrays as himself, the man made out of words who fills an inner void by staring into other people's most private lives. *As I Lay Dying* is the first novel in which Faulkner fully deploys his tragic dichotomy between words and deeds. Darl's facility with words (he narrates nineteen of the fifty-nine chapters) stands in direct proportion to his alienation from the sources of power, from home. His mother, who believes only in deeds, must suffer the fate of confronting the reader entirely through her own words. "I would think how words go straight up in a thin line, quick and harmless, and how terribly doing goes along the earth, clinging to it, so that after a while the two lines are too far apart for the same person to straddle from one to the other." For Addie a word is just compensatory, "a shape to fill a lack." Like a penis, the other weapon of male revenge, the pen can only produce something unvirgin. Nowhere in the novel do words make something whole.

As I Lay Dying is the novel in which Faulkner begins to purge himself of his deepest ambivalence toward his craft. It is thus possible for him to write, two years later, the unpublished introduction to *The Sound and the Fury*. This central Faulknerian document indicates that he had begun to reconcile himself to writing as an act of substitution. Looking back upon the period during which he began *The Sound and the Fury*, Faulkner projects onto it his growing recognition of his project:

> One day I seemed to shut a door between me and all publishers' addresses and book lists. I said to myself, Now I can write. Now I can make myself a vase like that which the old Roman kept at his bedside and wore the rim slowly away with kissing it. So I, who had never had a sister and was fated to lose my daughter in infancy, set out to make myself a beautiful and tragic little girl.

As Irwin perceptively observes, "What Faulkner describes here is the author's sense of the loss of the original virgin space . . . and his mature acceptance of repetition." It would take Faulkner four more years to dramatize this acceptance in a work of fiction.

In the meantime, Faulkner had finished *Sanctuary* and *Light in August*. The second of these novels, as we have seen, again confronts the problems of repetition and revenge through an overt attempt at mastery (the Burdens) and a covert analysis (Hightower) of Faulkner's relation to this burden. As for *Sanctuary*, Faulkner admitted its waywardness by trying, in *Requiem for a Nun* (1951), to redeem its place, and the significance of its heroine, in the canon. When he has Temple quote *For Whom the Bell Tolls* on forgiveness, we realize that the struggle to bring this solution to light has been, for some time, completed:

> Because suddenly it could be as if it had never been, never happened. You know: somebody—Hemingway, wasn't it?—wrote a book about how it had never actually happened to a gir—woman, if she just refused to accept it, no matter who remembered, bragged.

Temple has long since learned, although *Sanctuary* gives no hint of such a possibility, that the most difficult crimes to forgive are those we commit against ourselves. She repudiates guilt. In *Requiem for a Nun*, Faulkner forgives himself for the "crime" of having written *Sanctuary*.

In his life, Faulkner apparently confronted family as archetype and as experience. His work provides abundant evidence that what had happened to him before he was born influenced him as much as what kept happening while he was alive. We are encouraged to make the radical claim that he was shaped as much by what he had heard as by what he had lived. Such is certainly true of the Sartorises. Their concept of family controls their ongoing interaction in a family. The character who appears to take major exception to this pattern is Quentin Compson, who has been understood almost entirely as the product of his Compson upbringing. The Compson genealogy was merely an appendix Faulkner added years later; it does little to explain the behavior of the Compson children in the present. Yet we have seen that even Quentin seeks out, through narration, a genealogy into which he can assimilate himself. If *The Sound and the Fury* is Quentin's biography, *Absalom, Absalom!* is his novel. In *Absalom* Faulkner again examines the power of story to preempt experience as a shaper of the self.

With the writing of *Absalom*, Faulkner seems to have fully understood his project. The novel self-consciously engages the central question of his career: how successful can an imaginative re-creation of the past be as a defense against the past? The difficult answer is "Not very," since Quentin's suicide nine months after completing his narration of the story testifies to the failure of narration to free him from its compulsions. Quentin's story is, as Irwin has shown, the double of Henry's. His aim is to supply his prototype with increasingly more compelling provocations for the murder of Charles Bon: bigamy—incest—miscegenation. But the generosity of Quentin's imagination toward Henry fails to relieve Quentin of the burden Henry represents. The moral of the story is that repetitions keep happening: *"Maybe nothing ever happens once and is finished."* The life he lives recapitulates the story he tells. Faulkner here directly confronts the ambition to undo the past through narrative, but he proves unable to imagine such an attempt as successful. The impossibility of the task is registered by the sustained hysteria of the voices throughout, all of which blend together and none of which can be said to have authority. The way forward, as it turns out, is not through afflatus but understatement. We can be grateful that in *Absalom* Faulkner has provided us with a moving analysis of his own dilemma, and that he goes beyond *As I Lay Dying* in inventing a narrator who is generous rather than voyeuristic. But can we not ask that an author go beyond analysis to resolution? In *Absalom* Faulkner proves a brilliant analyst of failure, but he is most courageous, in "An Odor of Verbena," as an unrhetorical imaginer of success.

Redeeming John W. T.

Faulkner's solution to the problem of old Bayard's passivity is not to invent for him a catharsis through action, but to arrive at a more generous interpretation of what Bayard "failed" to do. In the same way that Quentin supplies his dark double (Henry) with stronger and stronger motives, Faulkner learns to invent for his (John W. T.) a usable past. The issue in both cases of identification is one of failed revenge, and how not to repeat the failure without becoming entrapped in the cycle of revenge itself. By 1937 Faulkner had discovered that deeds are little help at all in response to deeds. When committing an act, one can neither truly imitate nor entirely avoid imitation. The challenge becomes to find some means of participating in one's family destiny without simply reconfirming that destiny as an unavoidable fate.

Little in the first six stories of *The Unvanquished* would have predicted the resolution achieved in the seventh, "An Odor of Verbena." Almost three years separate the completion of the last story from the composition of those which precede it, years which Faulkner spent finishing *Absalom, Absalom!* Like "Big Two-Hearted River," "An Odor of Verbena" can be read alone. But also like Hemingway's story, it gathers together and fulfills a book of stories which would not be a book without it. Faulkner admits this when he writes to Morton Goldman about "the Civil War

Stories we sold the Post. . . . They needed one more story to finish them, which I have just completed, named 'An Odor of Verbena.'" While the seventh story beautifully completes the first six, it does so by utterly reversing the direction in which they seem to move.

Bayard narrates the whole of *The Unvanquished*. Twelve at the beginning, in "Ambuscade," he is twenty-four at the end. Just as *The Unvanquished* was a book allowed to mature, so Bayard is one of the few Faulkner narrators allowed to age. While the entire narration is retrospective, Bayard's voice actually seems to grow younger as he gets older. He begins with the melodramatic impatience of a Quentin Compson, a boy grown old before his time. Thus his miniature Vicksburg can provoke "a prolonged and wellnigh hopeless ordeal in which we ran, panting and interminable, with the leaking bucket between wellhouse and battlefield, the two of us needing first to join forces and spend ourselves against a common enemy, time, before we could engender between us and hold intact the pattern of recapitulant mimic furious victory like a cloth, a shield between ourselves and reality, between us and fact and doom." He ends with a tone of resolution and calm unsurpassed in Faulkner, less knowing, more hopeful. One can hear, in the quiet phrases which close the book, the acceptance of a whole life coming forward to meet Bayard. Faulkner allows him a farewell beautifully understated in its promise of a new start:

> As I passed down the hall the light came up in the diningroom and I could hear Louvinia laying the table for supper. So the stairs were lighted quite well. But the upper hall was dark. I saw her open door (that unmistakable way in which an open door stands open when nobody lives in the room any more) and I realised I had not believed that she was really gone. So I didn't look into the room. I went on to mine and entered. And then for a long moment I thought it was the verbena in my lapel which I still smelled. I thought that until I had crossed the room and looked down at the pillow on which it lay—the single sprig of it (without looking she would pinch off a half dozen of them and they would be all of a size, almost all of a shape, as if a machine had stamped them out) filling the room, the dusk, the evening with that odor which she said you could smell alone above the smell of horses.

Bayard's voice changes because he has come to terms with his place in time.

The overriding emotion provoked by the first six stories is the desire to get back at an enemy. The reader is lured into a series of comic acts of revenge which gradually darken into tragedy. Granny turns the tables on the Yankees only to die at Grumby's nervous hand. While she claims that "I did not sin for revenge," her mule-swapping has the effect of drawing her sixteen-year-old grandson into a fatal quest after it. The book is structured in so linear a fashion—one thing simply leads to another—that the reader never has a chance to question the direction he finds his allegiances carrying him. The one thing we want to do is give back, as we do in "Vendée." The pleasure we take in Bayard's tracking and killing Grumby may strike us as ominous, but is not felt as objectionable. Faulkner successfully manipulates the reader's impatience for closure into an acceptance of every aspect of the grisly hunt, even up to pegging the mutilated "murdering scoundrel" against the old compress door.

So Bayard proves his place in the line by revenging affronts to that line. The supreme conclusion Uncle Buck can draw from his triumph over Grumby is a genealogical one: "Ain't I told you he is John Sartoris' boy? Hey? Ain't I told you?" (The ascendancy of names later forces itself upon Bayard once his father is shot: "I was now The Sartoris.") The Sartorises are unquestioning of the code of *lex talionis*. It is perhaps therefore not surprising that the one warning against revenge in the first six stories is expressed by someone else. On the note Grumby leaves to frighten the boys off his trail, a postscript in another hand offers the boys *"one more chance,"* the chance to quit before they are killed. *"Take it, and some day become a man. Refuse it, and cease even to be a child."* It is just this advice which Bayard unwittingly follows in "An Odor of Verbena." He becomes a man on the day he declines the further pursuit of revenge.

The external events of this climactic story are easily summarized, although the internal ones hold the key to the action. "Skirmish at Sartoris" ends with Colonel John Sartoris murdering the Burdens and marrying cousin Drusilla on the same day. "An Odor of Verbena" opens eight years later as Bayard, a law student in Oxford, receives news of his father's murder at the hands of Ben Redmond. Bayard immediately rides the forty miles back to Jefferson, musing upon all that his father has now "relinquished along with the pipe which Ringo said he was smoking, which slipped from his hand as he fell." A flashback then intrudes in which Bayard recalls an argument with Drusilla over Sutpen's "dream." This memory merges with one of the preceding August, in which Drusilla had challenged Bayard to hate Redmond and to kiss her. Bayard kisses her twice and immediately tries to confess to his father. The story then returns to the present with Bayard's arrival home and refusal of help from his father's friends. That night Drusilla confronts him with her offer of two duelling pistols. Bayard refuses them, Drusilla collapses in hysteria, while Aunt Jenny, once she has packed Drusilla upstairs, assures Bayard that "I know you are not afraid." The next morning Bayard walks to the town square, unarmed, and enters Redmond's office. Redmond, seated behind his desk, fires two shots to the side of Bayard, staggers out of the room, and flees Jefferson forever. Bayard returns home to find Drusilla gone.

The one thing this story lacks is suspense. As he departs from Oxford, Bayard makes his first refusal of a pistol and betrays his intention not to kill by speaking of himself as "one still young enough to have his youth supplied him gratis as a reason (not an excuse) for cowardice." The question then becomes not will Bayard shoot Redmond, but what will support him in his resolve not to? *The Unvanquished* is a novel which turns upon itself, Faulkner's revenge against revenge. The common reader's surprise—even frustration—at this reversal finds expression in George Wyatt, who grudgingly accepts Bayard's unique solution:

> "You ain't done anything to be ashamed of. I wouldn't have done it that way, myself. I'd a shot him once, anyway. But that's your way or you wouldn't have done it."
> "Yes," I said. "I would do it again."

The Unvanquished is a novel of education, and of no one more than the vengeful reader himself.

Bayard's solution is to refuse to repeat. By not killing again as his father had killed, by not killing for his father's sake, Bayard asserts his originality within his society and his indebtedness to a code older than the Southern tradition of honor which surrounds him. His reliance upon the wisdom of "the Book" expresses itself in the form of proverbs. *"Who lives by the sword shall die by it"* is perhaps the central proverb in Faulkner, positing as it does the repetitive fate of all those who seek revenge. An unspoken proverb dominates the story, as Drusilla reminds us when she tells Bayard that "you will remember me who put into your hands what they say is an attribute only of God's." "Vengeance is mine, saith the Lord." We may balk at experience reduced to proverb, even if the proverb is right. Proverbs beg, rather than answer, the question of Bayard's motivation. His willingness to repeat proverbs which express his decision not to repeat suggests that he has passed through analysis of his dilemma and on to resolve. But what has made this resolution possible?

As Bayard rides back to Jefferson, Drusilla rises to the surface of his memory. She returns almost as if in response to his father's death, as if thinking about her will in some way help Bayard to decide upon the course of action he should take. Yet by this point in the story we are already aware that Bayard has decided. Remembering Drusilla gives Bayard access to the process which freed him to make such a decision. His recollection centers about the kiss:

> . . ."Kiss me, Bayard."
> "No. You are Father's wife."
> "And eight years older than you are. And your fourth cousin too. And I have black hair. Kiss me, Bayard."
> "No."

"Kiss me, Bayard." So I leaned my face down to her. But she didn't move, standing so, bent lightly back from me from the waist, looking at me; now it was she who said, "No." So I put my arms around her. Then she came to me, melted as women will and can, the arms with the wrist- and elbow-power to control horses about my shoulders, using the wrists to hold my face to hers until there was no longer need for the wrists; I thought then of the woman of thirty, the symbol of the ancient and eternal Snake and of the men who have written of her, and I realised then the immitigable chasm between all life and all print—that those who can, do, those who cannot and suffer enough because they can't, write about it. Then I was free. . . .

Bayard will kiss her again, but not before insisting that "I must tell Father." His father's reply is a scene out of *The Sound and the Fury*, and also very likely reconstructs what once passed between Colonel William and John W. T.:

You are doing well in the law, Judge Wilkins tells me. . . . I acted as the land and the time demanded and you were too young for that, I wished to shield you. But now the land and the time too are changing; what will follow will be a matter of consolidation, of pettifogging and doubtless chicanery in which I would be a babe in arms but in which you, trained in the law, can hold your own—our own. Yes, I have accomplished my aim, and now I shall do a little moral housecleaning. I am tired of killing men, no matter what the necessity nor the end. Tomorrow, when I go to town and meet Ben Redmond, I shall be unarmed.

The next day John Sartoris is shot, and that night Bayard sets out to return to the home he had ridden away from so soon before.

The basic genius of "An Odor of Verbena" lies in its overt linkage of the Oedipal conflict with revenge tragedy. Eliot might have puzzled over Hamlet's inaction as an aggrieved son, but Faulkner is careful that we will not lack an objective correlative for Bayard's motives. Bayard is Hamlet with insight. In the kiss scene he and the reader are made to acknowledge that wishes for a mother lead to ambivalence toward the father. Bayard at oncé commits and refuses incest; the kiss is a measure of how far he will not go. (His subsequent refusal of the duelling pistols confirms his resolve to take nothing more from Drusilla than two kisses, least of all his father's pistols.) His immediate response is "Now I must tell Father." Here he openly admits and renounces his claim to his (step)mother. If he has done so, he should feel no further need to pursue that claim through a revenge upon the father, or even (as Irwin has it) through a revenge upon his father's killer that really acts as a symbolic revenge upon the father. (Of course Bayard "unmans" Redmond, but through an act of the imagination which only he fully understands.) It is as if Hamlet were relieved of his conflict over revenging his father's murder by being made to confront (by Gertrude) and accept *and* forgo his wish to do what the murderer had done. Bayard "forgives" Redmond because he has been given the chance to forgive himself.

Bayard does not speak for himself alone in the kiss scene. He speaks for Faulkner as well. If we examine the progression of his thoughts, we see that they move swiftly from sexual and physical to verbal conquest. Taking the "woman" in the flesh is precisely what Bayard will not "do," just as revenging his father's murder is something he will not "do." His not "doing" seems to be expressed as a limitation, as something he "cannot" do. "Those who can, do, those who cannot and suffer enough because they can't, write about it." Yet Bayard's not doing, however despairing his tone here, ultimately affects the reader as anything but a display of impotence. Taken out of context, the quote means what it says; writing, like all *not* acting, is a mere substitute for doing, a weak man's way out. But within the context of the story, an entirely new attitude is encouraged toward the admittedly still "immitigable chasm" between life and print. The story posits substitution—of passive for active resistance, of the words of the Book for the deeds of the code—as the only truly adaptive solution open to Bayard. Unlike Quentin, Bayard understands and can articulate the difference between literal and symbolic action, and this allows him to substitute the one for the other. To all outer appearances, Bayard does no more to avenge his father than did John W. T. He does *not* kill for him. But for the first time Faulkner fully embraces the belief that symbolic or internalized actions can be made to take the place of literal ones, and so redeems, not only his hero, but the grandfather for whom he stands.

This triumph over the literal finds oblique confirmation in Bayard's meditation upon his dead father's hands:

> the empty hands still now beneath the invisible stain of what had been (once, surely) needless blood, the hands now appearing clumsy in their very inertness, too clumsy to have performed the fatal actions which forever afterward he must have waked and slept with and maybe was glad to lay down at last—those curious appendages clumsily conceived to begin with yet with which man has taught himself to do so much, so much more than they were intended to do or could be forgiven for doing.

Faulkner here redefines the verb "do." He implies that hands were at best intended to "do" something on paper, that they should bear, if anything, not the "invisible stain" of blood, but the visible one of ink. Writing and killing are both works of the hands, but Faulkner learned better than Hemingway the difference between picking up a pen and picking up a gun. When you pick up a gun with resolution in mind, he could have warned his great rival, you turn your hand against no one as surely as yourself.

In revising the stories he had inherited about his grandfather, Faulkner completed his quest for authority as an artist. *Not* doing is finally made good, in the history of the ancestor, in the life of his grandson. *The Unvanquished* displays a fully conscious grasp of the conflicts which had possessed Faulkner since the writing of *Flags in the Dust*. If the conflict was not resolved, it had at least been understood. The decade of the great formal experiments was over. Faulkner had made the one discovery which he had to make—that understanding *is* forgiveness. Irwin does not pay enough heed to Faulkner's development toward understanding of his obsessive material. After *The Unvanquished* the familiar patterns may recur, but within a context which reduces them more and more to objects of inquiry.

Faulkner's distance from material which would previously have led him into extreme technical innovation can be felt, for instance, in *Go Down, Moses*, which makes rather clear its scorn for Ike's premature unburdening of the weight of the past. When Ike, a budding genealogist, turns upon his family to relinquish it, he reenacts the familiar revenge against time. Ike has tried to compose a History which will serve him as a platform from which he can view history, but this is too ambitious a substitute of imagination for experience. The book's qualifying ironies —especially Ike's "salvation" of his son by refusing to beget him—everywhere suggest that his is a project which his author sees as evasive and self-destructive. *Go Down, Moses* is a reprise of Faulkner's entire career in which he finally lays to rest his quarrel with genealogy. Thus the novel can invent a new kind of hero, Lucas Beauchamp, who has *"fathered himself."* He can never be convicted of a sense of belatedness. He is "durable, ancestryless." He moves through a world filling up with Snopeses, equally durable, equally ancestryless. The problem to which Faulkner turns himself in the second phase of his career is not the past and its burdens but the lack of one.

Being fathered proves less oppressive than being unable to father for Harry, Flem, Ike, Lucas, and Gavin. By the time Faulkner writes *A Fable*, he can imagine a world of fathers unable to make any legitimate claim upon sons. No longer does the Corporal need the acknowledgment which Quentin, Henry, Charles, and Bayard once craved. Thus he can refuse what would have been, twenty years earlier, the ultimate gift, the final triumph. In a single phrase of promise, Faulkner's "magnum o" at once sums up the deepest yearning of a career and reminds us of how long since it has been requited, so much so that a son no longer listens to or answers a father as he speaks the wished for words, "I will acknowledge you as my son."

ᴥᔥ Five

GENERATING VOICE IN
A DEATH IN THE FAMILY

James Agee's *A Death in the Family* is haunted by the problem of inexpressibility. The writing of the novel constitutes a troubled passing of silence into voice. The unsaid and unheard define the sublime, even forbidden, origins of experience that the novelist must literally render prosaic. To speak or to hear is to fall. Yet a sense of personal urgency —that the time has come to "choose a name" for death—propels Agee into this autobiographical fiction to which we, as well, feel compelled to listen. In a shared anxiety over generating voice (writing) or attending to voice (reading), author and audience are bonded together into a relationship which parallels and illuminates those family bonds which are the origin and end of the story.

"Oh, it's just beyond words!" Mary, in one outburst, relegates the utterance of the story to where it *should* be. During its every crisis, its characters long for a place beyond telling. Continually thrust into speech, Mary feels it always a compromise of silence. "I want to tell you about Daddy." In saying this, Mary assumes the burden of the novelist, the voicing of the unspeakable. "But upon his name her voice shook and her whole dry-looking mouth trembled like the ash of burned paper in a draft." She has been elected to speak, the coal has been put to her mouth. Trembling on the edge of voice, Mary must appeal to an audience she has not chosen. In the threat of being consumed by what she utters Mary experiences the dilemma of creation and selectivity which is Agee's. His autobiography befell him. But the telling of it is his choice. Every choice of words, every voicing in the novel, resonates with the author's anxiety over violating the silence of works already written by adding to them his own voice.

In Rufus's relationship to Jay we can discover the most crucial image of Agee's to his own past. The gap between father and son is not so much bridged as measured by voice. Only in silence do they come close:

> Rufus seldom had at all sharply the feeling that he and his father were estranged, yet they must have been, and he must have felt it, for always during these quiet moments on the rock a part of his sense of complete contentment lay in the feeling that they were reconciled, that there was really no division, no estrangement, or none so strong, anyhow, that it could mean much, by comparison with the unity that was so firm and assured, here.

It is the quietude of this moment which makes reconciliation possible. "There were no words, or even ideas, or formed emotions, of the kind that have been suggested here, no more in the man than in the boy child." At such times "silence was even more pleasurable" than speech, because speech bespeaks a distance between. Voice breaks this communion: with "*Well . . .*" the moment is over and the walk home resumes. Here voice registers a gap dividing generations even as it establishes an intimacy between them. Jay's interjection is both authoritative and gentle. If voice possesses both qualities, it is the most appropriate vehicle through which to realize life in a family. If the eye is democratic, voice is hierarchical. It asks us to acknowledge our place. Agee shares Milton's sense of the distancing power of authoritative voice. Leslie Brisman says of *Paradise Lost* that "voice is everywhere the emblem of the distance the recognition of which is creative, the failure of which is fall. Voice separates speaker from listener, author from image, in a way that distinguishes fertile brooding from the sterility of narcissistic self-confrontation." In order to escape from the sterility of isolated selfhood, each of Agee's characters is challenged to generate a voice in which he can brood upon the events befalling him. Yet because voice enforces acknowledgment of distance, and because Agee also wishes to create the impression of relaxed intimacy with his materials and among his characters, his narrative proceeds whenever possible through silence.

The act of writing the novel itself constitutes Agee's most ambitious generation of voice. When he admits to Father Flye that the book is autobiographical and that it leads up to the moment of his "father's burial," we can surmise that more than his biological parent is being buried in it. The story is not only about surviving one's creator; the act of telling it embodies Agee's will to assume a creator's role. If the book narrates Rufus's growing independence of his father, this act of narration accomplishes Agee's full assumption of imaginative independence from his literary fathers. It is his first major *fiction*. The separation anxiety implicit in such a project fittingly eventuates in a story about such separation.

Agee was not always able to make his personal loss an overt theme. *The Morning Watch*, Agee's autobiographical novella, takes as its apparent subject his complicity in the death of Christ. Only at the vigil's end does Agee recur to what proves, in retrospect, to be the story's hidden stimulus. For the boy, the words "Ever any more" refer more powerfully to the impossibility of his dead father's return than to the imminence of Christ's. Agee appears so far from the recovery of his subtext that he can only reveal it on the story's last page.

Agee's filial ambivalence emerges most dramatically in his closet drama "Menalcas," where a king, after an incestuous marriage with his daughter, kills the son of that union. Alfred T. Barson concludes that it is the issue of creation itself which is here at stake: "Agee is describing the relationship between God and His creation and, on another level, the relationship between the artist and his art. In each instance there is an inability of the Creator to properly love His creation, to see it for what it is and to respect its essential otherness." In writing *A Death in the Family*, Agee simultaneously becomes a participant in both of these relationships while generating voice which respects the "otherness" of his characters and his creation. That the novel was nevertheless generated by guilt over asserting this distance as well as by pride in having attained it is supported by Victor Kramer's speculation that Agee intended to introduce it with "Dream Sequence." In this short story the dreamed murder of John the Baptist—the forerunner of the true creator—is confused with Agee's guilt over his dead father:

> I've betrayed my father, he realized. Or myself. Or both of us.
> How?
> He thought of his father in his grave, over seven hundred miles away, and how many years. If he could only talk with him. But he knew that even if they could talk, they could never come at it between them, what the betrayal was. . . .
> He thought of all he could remember about his father and about his own direct relations with him. He could see nothing which even faintly illuminated his darkness, nor did he expect ever to see anything, yet if he could be sure of anything except betrayal and horror, he could be sure that was where the dream indicated that he should go. He should go back into those years.

The decision not to use this as an opening for the novel suggests an editorial reluctance to include such a direct violation of the novel's seemingly benign casting of generational conflict. Yet the mere writing of the novel forced such a conflict upon Agee. J. Douglas Perry reminds us that "*A Death in the Family* is an epic about Agee's father and his father's people, his mother and her people. Agee is simultaneously Homer and

Telemachus, bard and participant." To become the bard is to stop being the son. Agee's inability absolutely to assume either role is not only a measure of his humanity but the source of tension between creation and reception, voice and silence, which each of his characters recurrently experiences.

The dreamer concludes "Dream Sequence" by admitting that "all his life he had fiercely loathed authority and had as fiercely loved courage and mastery." The very harshness of this self-judgment seems to effect a softening in the speaker's attitudes, and he feels himself relaxed in his father's imagined presence: "And here he was, and all was well at last, and even though he was more rapidly fading, and most likely would never return, that was all right too." It is as if the decision to write his autobiographical novel, and the insight into its originating motives, together allay much of the conflict which generates the project. From the beginning of *A Death in the Family*, the father-son relationship seems anything but troubled. Agee presents the relationship between Rufus and Jay as remarkably quiet. Allen Shepherd remarks the atypicality of this project: "If it seems that *A Death in the Family* is an almost un-American novel in that it is about death, but not about violence, and about love, but not about sex, we may go two steps further and say that the novel is at least atypical in that it is about the achievement of identity, but not about alienation, and in that it is about a family, but not about a facilely allegorized Every-Family." The novel begins in a mood of passionate harmony, but in writing it Agee came to discover that a strong sense of alienation helps not only to create an artist's identity, but a son's. It is precisely at that moment when Rufus feels most alien from his father that he commits the act that initiates the search for his own independent identity. The task of the novelist and his boy-protagonist coalesce as Rufus gives voice to a knowledge of death: he "looked towards his father's face and, seeing the blue-dented chin thrust upward, and the way the flesh was sunken behind the bones of the jaw, first recognized in its specific weight the word, *dead.*" To accept the weight of this word is to begin shouldering the consequences of one's mortality, one's original birth out of, and separation from, a mortal source. The assumption of voice here coincides with a distancing from the father achieved through a metonymy—Jay's sunken face—which empties him of further power to influence or enliven the son. It is remarkable that Rufus must learn the facts of death before the facts of life. In the face of Catherine's impending birth his parents go to considerable trouble to prevent him from making *"see-oh-en-en-ee-see-tee-eye-oh-en-ess, between—between one thing and another."* Yet Rufus will be empowered by his experience of death to begin making his own connections, to grow up and become a father himself. The limited challenges one can impose upon the sexuality of a boy of six may account, however, for the generalized anxiety over generation that pervades the novel. Agee displaces such anxiety throughout into the one activity which for a writer constitutes the essence of identity: generating voice.

"We are talking now . . .": the novel opens with an acknowledgment of voice. Agee might not have chosen to begin in this way; the editors have nevertheless discovered a point of departure to which the action constantly recurs. A novel of a family talking, *A Death in the Family* turns upon moments when a voice chooses to break silence. This opening is appropriate insofar as it presents the beginning of the novel as depending upon the simultaneous decision to begin talking. There is no dramatic voice in "Knoxville: Summer 1915." The prelude is narrated, by the voice of a child that is also the voice of an elegist. Agee establishes no firm distance between these two voices, just as he blurs the distinction between narrator and reader through *"We."* All these identities diffuse here into a shared lyric experience. James Sonoski argues that "Agee's narrative techniques are designed to convey the distances between the voices in the novel and the way in which they are bridged." Yet this initial narrative voice, by retaining total possession of its story, prevents any other from distinguishing itself. Of the speakers in the family the narrator can only say that they have *"voices gentle and meaningless like the voices of sleeping birds."* Conversation among them is described, not enacted. If the prelude ends with the boy-elegist wondering who can *"ever tell me who I am,"* it may be because he has assumed so early and so absolutely the burden of narration. "If a premature assertion of the 'I' masks an anxiety about power of voice, then the listening relationship, in which one's own voice is silenced before voice more authoritative or more distinctly separated from the self, images the successful resolution of that anxiety." In the novel proper, Agee separates the voice of the boy from this more self-conscious adult intelligence to restore the gap between them which, if threatening to an independent "I," is also a primary force in determining its identity. It is inevitable that this restoration of authoritative voice does not fully resolve Rufus's temptation toward premature self-assertion, since the loss he experiences forces independence upon him. Giving voice to his identity remains for him an anxious task, compounded of both pride and shame. This is movingly illustrated during his encounter with the boys who tease him with the question *"What's your name?"* In suffering this challenge from a disbelieving audience to assert himself as the son of his father, Rufus is made to anticipate the situation in which he will have no other choice. What had been an anxiously obeyed prohibition from the living father—*"Don't you brag"* —becomes, after his death, a command that may be ignored.

If a listening relationship permits a lessening of separation anxiety, if "silence" is "less mistaken than trying to speak," this condition is most fully realized in Chapter 12, when Jay silently returns. Communication is here effected without speaking. Telepathy—what Joel calls "thought transference"—permits the family to feel Jay's *"presence"* without having to hear his voice. Except for Joel, who remains deaf to these unheard melodies, everyone present participates in this moment. That Catherine, normally unable to share easily in family conversation, *hears* Jay return only intensifies the sense of silence through which everyone else registers it. The attempt to articulate this experience serves to dispel it: "It just —means so much more than anything we can *say* about it." For Mary, speech succeeds not in reaching Jay but in "driving him away." Voice is here not so much a mediator as a threat to the purity of the immediate.

The mediating agent to which voice is all too often committed is the telephone. It breaks silence, like a "persistent insect," without allowing us to face each other. Telephoning parodies the distancing voice naturally establishes—"the voice seemed still to come from a great distance"—by creating the illusion that we are present to a voice from which we are actually absent. For Father Jackson, therefore, the telephone is the appropriate instrument of communication. When Hannah phones him all we or the children can hear is her voice, a premonition of his inability to speak to anyone. Yet in anyone's hands the telephone cannot but further the avoidance of love. Even the calls which send Jay after his father and Andrew after Jay reduce personal utterance to news. Aware that such communication imparts all the burden of knowledge with none of the release of confrontation, Andrew refuses to phone:

> he knew it was more than I could stand to *hear* over a phone, even from him, and so he didn't, and I'm infinitely grateful he didn't. He must have known that as time kept—wearing on in this terrible way, we'd draw our own conclusions and have time to—time. And that's best. He wanted to be with me when I heard. And that's right. So do I. Straight from his lips.

Straight from his lips: only the deepest love risks voicing itself without mediation. And only the strongest compassion would take upon itself this burden of saying. When Andrew finally arrives, Mary literally takes the words out of his mouth. "He's dead, Andrew, isn't he?" Here the breaking of silence becomes not a "sacrilege" but a restoration of presence, of the direct assumption of personal responsibility.

Once these words have been said, the telling of the whole story cannot be stopped. Agee even includes a character with limited powers of audition to ensure that "we can all hear." At the heart of this novel listens a deaf person. Catherine's presence sanctions the continued utterance of the unspeakable. The one pun in the novel—"grandmaphone"—ironically confuses Catherine with an instrument which preserves disembodied voice (gramophone) while meaning to link her with one (telephone) which conveys it. Yet Catherine's function as an embodied but defective listener is to reveal the inadequacy of anything but directly heard human voice. "Uncle Andrew says she's crazy even to try" to listen to or through anything else. She exists in relation to the bereaved family as the reader does to the authorial voice. Her malady forces what might otherwise be whispered, or left unsaid, into words. Narration becomes by virtue of her need to hear less a violation than a consideration. So must the story be told to the reader. We are "we." It is for us that Agee makes this personal tragedy audible. The reader's will to listen finds image in Catherine's trumpet: "It required immediate speech. That trumpet's like a pelican's mouth, he thought. Toss in a fish." Andrew's bitterness here partakes of the author's conflict between reluctance to speak any more than he must to keep the attention of his audience and his eagerness to speak so much as to capture it completely. Agee admits in a letter to Father Flye that a reader can completely consume, while being consumed by, a text: "I would suspect a chemical rule of reading as in 'influence,' 'imitation,' and 'plagiarism'; that in reading or in being influenced 'successfully' one does as much work as the authors did originally." The knowledge that in writing this novel of the death of his father Agee was himself fathering his own heirs accounts for much of the care he takes in generating, or in allowing his characters to generate, authoritative voice.

Ambivalence over whether to speak or remain silent resolves into a marriage of opposites in Joel and Catherine. He experiences language as a prison house. "He wished he could think what to say that would make up for it, but he could not think of what to say." She feels no anxiety over assuming voice: "He feels much more than he says, she comforted herself; but she wished that he might ever say what he felt." Catherine finds language a transparent medium. "I've always supposed, it was the business of *words*—to *communicate*—*clearly*." Yet her theory is undercut by her practice, for the single most striking act of communication in the novel takes place wordlessly, between herself and Joel. It happens in Chapter 9, which intervenes between the sound of Andrew's arrival and his actual entrance, and where a temporary suspension of the plot gives us a picture of the married life that, for Jay and Mary, also might have been. At the same time, Catherine and Joel share similar, and then the same thoughts:

> She felt a moment of solemn and angry gratitude to have spent so many years, in such harmony, with a man so good, but that was beyond utterance. . . .
>
> he . . . felt a moment of incredulous and amused pride in her immense and unbreakable courage, and of proud gratitude, regardless of and including all regret, to have had so many years with such a woman; but that was beyond utterance.

It may be less important that these closing identical phrases again define the limits of voice than that they embody the wordless communion which the years of this long marriage have made possible. In such marriages silence is not an evasion but an expression of identity. On the night Jay leaves for the last time, he shares with Mary a similar moment of having "nothing to say." Once two voices achieve identity—grow up —through having been "influenced 'successfully'" by more authoritative ones, the testimony of their mature equality is silence.

If silence is the contrary of voice as well as its eventual fate, the negation of both is noise. A kind of Satanic force, its indulgence is a sin against the limits the novel sets for itself. However much Jay nods his "regret of the racket" his car makes, "the eyes which followed him could not forgive him his noise." Noise originates, in the first interpolated scene, from an unworthy and profane voice: *An auto engine bore beyond the edge of audibility the furious expletives of its incompetence.* The satiric personification of such racket suggests that Agee's anxiety over generating voice can diffuse into a more generalized one over creating *any sound.* That representing sound is for him a problem deeply implicated in the process of composition becomes clear in Jay's departure. The only experimental writing Agee ventures in the novel attempts to capture the noise of the car starting:

```
RHRHRHRHRHRH R
                 H
                  R
                 H
                  R
                   H
                     rh
                     rh
                     rh
                     rh
                     rh
                     rh
                     rh
                     rh
              rh
            rh
            rh
            rh
   C utta wawwwwk:
            Craaawwrk?
            Chiquawkwawh.
                     Wrrawkuhkuhk uh.
                        Craarrawwk.
```

rwrwrk?
yrk.
rk:

This experience stimulates a response beyond the normal range of Agee's style. Such noise represents so wanton a violation of the silence which the author and his characters only carefully break as to drive Agee toward the limits of his art. It is too sheer a display of dissonance in a novel committed to assimilating all phenomena and relationships, however divergent, into an amassing harmony.

Father Jackson is the one character in the novel who most seems to deserve a similar kind of inhuman notation. Rufus and Catherine experience his voice as noise. If the novel's true test of maturity is whether one can speak to a child, the priest fails it. But then he does not speak, he is spoken:

> Father Jackson spoke almost wholly without emphasis and with only the subtlest coloring, as if the personal emotion, the coloring, were cast against the words from a distance, like echoes. He spoke as if all that he said were in every idea and in every syllable final, finished, perfected beyond disquisition long before he was born; and truth and eternity dwelt like clearest water in the rhythms of his language and in the contours of his voice; his voice accepted and bore this language like the bed of a brook.

Having wholly relinquished his voice to a higher power, Father Jackson cannot be expected to possess one of his own. His lack of a personal voice stands as emblem of his inability to beget anything truly original. He remains a perpetual son. This is, of course, Ralph's predicament, although he must admit the further mistake of having prematurely "fathered children." No more than the priest does he display a generating voice, a condition dramatized by Agee's reassumption of almost total narrative control during the chapter Ralph fills. It is clear from Ralph's few attempts to speak that his voice affects others like the sound of that "persistent insect" the telephone, of which Ralph is the novel's most impetuous and persistent user. Since "every tone his voice took, was controlled by his idea of what would make the best impression on others," Ralph experiences even his own voice, into the possession of which he has never entered, as an alien noise.

The redemption of noise is song. Song weaves voice and silence into a harmony in which the virtues of both are temporarily suspended. The novel begins by inducting us into a world in which every noise can modulate into music: *"First an insane noise of violence in the nozzle, then the still irregular sound of adjustment, then the smoothing into steadiness and a pitch as accurately tuned to the size and style of stream as any violin."* With this orchestration (Agee once claimed that "I want to *write symphonies"*) the locusts stay in tune and

> *carry on this noise of hoses on their much higher and sharper key. The noise of the locust is dry, and it seems not to be rasped or vibrated but urged from him as if through a small orifice by a breath that can never give out. . . . The noise of each locust is pitched in some classic locust range out of which none of them varies more than two full tones: and yet you seem to hear each locust discrete from all the rest, and there is a long, slow, pulse in their noise, like the scarcely defined arch of a long and high set bridge.*

Without creating anxiety, this music calls up a memory of generation, of the sounds which register the pulse and origin of our lives, *"the noises of the sea and of the blood her precocious grandchild."* Once the noises that keep time are admitted, the narrator (himself a precocious grandchild) hastens to quiet sound altogether as we hear *"the faint stinging bell; rises again, still fainter; fainting, lifting, lifts, faints forgone: forgotten. Now is the night one blue dew."* Silence prevails; we enter a *"Now"* world in which the family members can lie down together without anxiety. But the delicate balance of sound and silence which is song, and the harmony it celebrates, is shattered by the first phone call in the novel. It necessitates dialogue, the inevitable exchange of "furious and annihilating words." The experience of harmonizing song becomes a condition to which both characters and readers permanently long to return.

Andrew recovers song in Chapter 13. Agee inducts us into this episode in such a way that song emerges not as a fortuitous, but as a permanent (though perhaps unremembered), possession. As Andrew walks home with his parents he finds himself listening to the night: "Andrew could hear only their footsteps; his father and mother, he realized, could hear nothing even of that. How still we see thee lie." Here "O Little Town of Bethlehem" returns as the wonder of unexpected supply, as a voice which unwittingly, yet authentically, sings through us. As the lyrics of the song weave themselves more insistently into Andrew's meditation, Agee ensures that his moment of fully acknowledging their source will be simultaneous with the reader's. *"How still we see thee lie*, he heard his mind say. He said the words over, drily within himself, and heard the melody; a child's voice, his own, sang it in his mind." Here the lyrics are italicized, fully admitted to be of another voice. In Andrew's possession of a voice he is possessed by, the reader finds another image of his being "influenced 'successfully'" by the voice which authors the novel. In reading we are delivered up to being sung—to the authority of a voice which expresses us more authentically than we could alone—while seeming ourselves to sing. Agee realizes the definition of sublimity; the reader feels as if he had produced what he has heard. In its power to effect this sublime cancellation of "otherness" lies the consolation of fiction, of human song.

Jay makes this discovery while singing to Rufus. Song comforts not only by articulating an intimacy between father and son but by recovering a sense of the gap across which the generations have sung it and which it has helped to define and bridge. *"To the child it looked as if his father were gazing off into a great distance and, looking up into these eyes which looked so far away, he too looked far away."* As he keeps singing, the father hears the sound of his own mother's voice: "Don't you fret, Jay, don't you fret." The distance he gazes off into becomes filled with all those who have influenced him:

> she must have lain under the hand of her mother or her father and they in their childhood under other hands, away on back through the mountains, away on back through the years, it took you right on back as far as you could ever imagine, right on back to Adam, only no one did it for him; or maybe did God?
>
> How far we all come. How far we all come away from ourselves. So far, so much between, you can never go home again. You can go home, it's good to go home, but you never really get all the way home again in your life. And what's it all for? All I tried to be, all I ever wanted and went away for, what's it all for?
>
> Just one way, you do get back home. You have a boy or a girl of your own and now and then you remember, and you know how they feel, and it's almost the same as if you were your own self again, as young as you could remember.

Singing voice has here helped to recall, notate, and preserve the sense of a line, of being not only a generator but generated. It restores Jay to a sense of his own father, of his father's fathers, of his dependency upon them as well as his inevitable replacement of them. This is a vision of generations as a communal, not a competitive, labor. Each of us is but a refrain sounded again through our children. All of the anxiety in the novel over a creation independently creating is here fully acknowledged and momentarily dispelled as Jay simultaneously speaks as a father and listens as a son.

In *A Death in the Family* Agee risks generating voice. In doing so he supersedes the earlier limited claim he had made for his own language in *Let Us Now Praise Famous Men* that "words cannot embody; they can only describe." While attempting to father a novel of the death of his father Agee discovers the inadequacy of this theory in the face of his imagination and his experience. If this experience is to be represented, it must be through more than a mere way of seeing. A descriptive or cinematic mode—either documentary or screenplay—would have been an evasion of the challenge to bring his family to life. In order to recover the voices of his past Agee must discover his own. While still conflicted over assuming voice, Agee reveals it as the possession the use of which bespeaks the full acceptance of embodiment. As the most effective means of placing

ourselves in the presence of another, even while it confirms the gap
—generational or imaginative—across which one is speaking, voice must
be generated by any author who wishes to "go back into those years"
which send up the life of a family. This is the project of writing itself, the
assumption of the burden of the past so that it can be reborn—given
voice—in the present.

Six

ROBERT PENN WARREN
The Critic as Artist

A Place to Come To

Warren's novels read like essays about themselves. His fictions continually resolve into apologues. It is scarcely possible while reading them to have the experience but miss the meaning. Where commentary does not preempt drama, it quickly intrudes to explicate it. While in "Pure and Impure Poetry" he acknowledges that ideas may "participate more fully, intensely, and immediately" in poetry by being implicit, his own work typically incorporates ideas "in an explicit and argued form." Such a habit of mind stations Warren on the border between two modes of imagination, between the artist who works from experience and the critic who works toward meaning.

Warren's double career in the creative and critical establishments seems to be the central fact here. There is nothing remarkable about a divided allegiance in a man who set out to devote himself to both worlds. But had Warren never written his major articles on Frost, Faulkner, Conrad, and Coleridge, or his textbooks on *understanding* poetry and fiction, we would still need some term for a writer so concerned to usurp, within the body of his own fictions, the critic's task. Warren has revived interest in Wilde's claim that "it is very much more difficult to talk about a thing than to do it." His works constantly "talk about" themselves. His characters achieve integration in a moment with its own self-reflexive grammar: "*I am me.*" How can one both feel and say this? In such climactic formulations, wholeness asserts itself against a syntax which splits the self into the nominative and the accusative case. The self remains the object of its own *critical* awareness. Oneness proclaims itself in a language doomed to doubleness.

Warren's characters are placed out of themselves, the bemused or obsessive spectators of their own wayward acts. So his newest narrator tells us: "Something is going on and will not stop. You are outside the going on, and you are, at the same time, inside the going on. In fact, the going on is what you are. Until you can understand that these things are different but the same, you know nothing about the nature of life. I proclaim this." We abstract; we embody. Warren has dedicated his career to proving the indivisibility of the critical and the creative imaginations. Even where the self stands next to itself, he tries to convert self-consciousness into ecstasy. He thus joins that central American tradition of speakers —Emerson, Thoreau, Henry Adams, Norman Mailer—who are not only the builders but the interpreters of their own designs.

The stance of a critic is the stance of a son. Both are fundamentally indebted as both take up their positions in response to prior achievement which surrounds and defines them. The price of understanding is belatedness, a sense of remove in time. If the creative spirit repudiates as much of the past as it possibly can, the critical sensibility conserves as much as it possibly may. Warren's central character is a son (or daughter) whose only hope lies in not rebelling against father, tradition, home. In 1960 Leonard Casper nominated "exploration of unbroken years of homesickness" as Warren's central theme. Warren has not been coy about proving him right. *A Place to Come To* depends upon a place one has come *from*. Warren's most recent novel explores once again the psychology of exile and return.

Adam's first word to Eve in *Paradise Lost* is "Return," and it is upon her reluctant but ultimately obedient response to this command that Warren models his plots. The voice of one's origin keeps calling one homeward. Satan wanders; Eve returns. While Warren's strongest characters wander also in aimless selfhood (in *A Place*, through what Jed's mentor calls the *"imperium intellectūs"*), none of his readers is left to doubt the pointlessness of such quest. Warren the critic always shepherds us toward the destination the artist knowingly withholds. The best way out is always back.

In the character of Jed Tewksbury, Warren has found his perfect hero. As if in passing a last judgment upon himself, Warren writes a novel about a critic writing a novel. Just after Jed introduces himself by retelling the primal memory of his father's death—drunk, he fainted while pissing in the road at midnight before the very wagon which then rolled over his neck and broke it—he steps out of his autobiography to tell us how it reads to him:

> I wrote that part very fast. It came rushing out, my ball-point pen rushing ahead—a new experience for me who am accustomed only to scholarly and

critical composition and who, not being of a quick mind or ready to trust my early notions, am inclined to be painfully slow and careful in my formulations.

"Rushing ahead" on into experience is, unfortunately, just what this Dante scholar repeatedly fails to do. Too much the spectator and too little the actor, he prefers telling to doing. Potential ecstasy becomes mere alienation as we read on into this book full of "the passion for the big ideas." Considerable scorn is heaped, as usual, upon abstractions un-tethered to fact. But Warren goes far beyond his earlier judgment in *World Enough and Time* that the world must redeem the idea. It is no longer a question of working from the concrete toward the abstract; there seems little hope here that the two can be brought into any relationship whatsoever. The author of this novel seems to have rejected Wilde's boast and embraced Faulkner's apparent dismissal: "those who can, do, those who cannot and suffer enough because they can't, write about it." All writing comes under indictment here as an evasive sublimation, a criticism of, rather than a participation in, life. When Warren shares this mood, he tries to make it convincing by reducing writing to a merely critical impulse. This book displays a contempt for learning that is downright redneck. Scholarship feeds on the death of life: as Jed's first wife dies, his essay on "Dante and the Metaphysics of Death" grows. Never are we made to feel Jed's work as interesting, let alone valuable. Jed suffers an alienation of word from world that he is never fully allowed to resolve.

This alienation arises from Jed's attempt to use words as a defense against origins. He begins as sick *of* home. Jed's parents confront him in embarrassing postures. His father dies not only drunk but clutching his penis of legendary size. His mother, having worked for a decade to free her son of Dugton, Alabama, is rewarded by having him return from college to find her in bed with a man of somewhat lesser proportions. Such things must be put behind one. When the distancing power of words fails him, Jed tries to escape the continuities of the self through the discontinuous joys of sex.

The best writing in the book is reserved for the return of Rozelle, Jed's rejected high school prom date who becomes his middle-aged mistress. A past rejection becomes a future one must inevitably face; through this fateful and wish-fulfilling logic Warren guarantees that one must re-turn not only to the abandoned parent but to the spurned girl friend. No explanation is offered for this highly coincidental reunion other than the implicit appeal to the return of the repressed. Sex proves, however, less a way to redeem time than to stay it. The critic who would return gives way to the artist who will escape. Sex becomes an antimetaphysic. Making love leads to "the death in life-beyond-Time without which life-in-Time might not be endurable, or even possible." Jed's impossible project here stands revealed. Sex, which promises a transcendence of duration, stands defined by the original repression it undoes and the eventual intepretation it generates. The worlds of before and after catch such a moment up to interrogate and place it. Jed comes to realize that a love founded solely on the instant of conjunction is "nothing":

> What had I had of her? Only what I had had, and that seemed, in that instant, nothing at all. It was as though there could be no possession, not even blind and timeless pleasure, unless confirmed by the sight of a sleeping face.

A Place to Come To is Warren's most ambitious attempt to study "the relation of the concept of Love to that of Time." Love finally proves subordinate to time; the only abiding love is a repetition, not a revolution. Thus Jed must return to the mother before he can begin to live. The conclusion which has been lying in wait consequently presents itself, and this wandering son of Alabama, standing for the first time since a boy in his dead mother's front room, not only returns but understands: "after all the years I was returning to my final self, long lost."

A reviewer of this novel might well feel cheated in having nothing climactic to give away. Surprise endings are impossible in a book which knows from the beginning that there is finally only one place to come to. Home hovers over Warren's novels like the threat of death—it will get you in the end. What one may come to resent about Warren's fiction is not its end but its means. The necessity for return few will question, but where it emerges as inevitability rather than option, we are deprived of the very chance to wander and even lose our way, which makes arrival seem an achievement rather than a gift.

Perpetual Return

Warren's career as a novelist departs from the Miltonic assumption that "true autority" begins and ends in "filial freedom," in the freedom to be and remain a son. In the lines that first introduce Adam and Eve, Milton feels it necessary to make (for the onlooking Satan's benefit?) just this point:

> in thir looks Divine
> The image of thir glorious Maker shone,
> Truth, Wisdom, Sanctitude severe and pure,
> Severe, but in true filial freedom plac't;
> Whence true autority in men

The works of both authors are filled with Satans, but in every case narrative logic, symbolic structure, and overt commentary intrude to undercut even the most charming. "I was the thing that always came back": Jack Burden's self-judgment can be taken as Warren's definition of the human. Any unconscious desire to rebel (Blake's caveat still stands) is played out within a larger myth of accommodation that eventually exposes prodigality to ridicule. Paradise is regained in the apparently modest but heroically strenuous closing of a circle: "he unobserved/Home to his mother's house returned."

The critical question for Warren studies could become the one which has vexed Miltonists: is Warren of the prodigal son's party without knowing it? Does a career so dedicated to revealing the poverty of filial ingratitude not protest too much? The answer probably awaits a full biography, as well as further study of the ways in which the dogmatic aims of the novels are compromised by formal lapses and excesses. It is finally his own originality that Warren's ethical position sets out to curtail, and in a writer of such energy and gifts, this occasions some suspicion, even where it does not actively hobble his prose.

Warren and his various proxies characteristically see the entire circle of falling, wandering, and returning in a flash, as, regardless of their station along the way, a story already complete. So "R.P.W." domesticates Robert Warren's history in *Brother to Dragons:*

> in a cafe once, when an old friend said,
> "Tell me about your father," my heart suddenly
> Choked on my words, and in the remarkable quiet
> Of my own inwardness and coil, light fell
> Like one great ray that gilds the deepest glade,
> And thus I saw his life a story told,
> Its glory and reproach domesticated,
> And for one moment felt that I had come
> To that most happy and difficult conclusion:
> To be reconciled to the father's own reconciliation.

After such understanding, what forgiveness? To *begin* at the end is to assume a limiting responsibility, since an author so knowing can never digress into the least indulgence of revolt without seeming merely to mark time. If Agee suffers a nearly perpetual case of arrested development, Warren's as a novelist is strangely preempted. Warren's novels echo his father's self-judgment, as expressed in "Reading Late at Night, Thermometer Falling": "I reckon I was lucky enough to learn early that a man/can be happy in his obligations." The prototype is "Anchises' son," and in his fiction Warren has never failed to shoulder the *care pater.* Perhaps an immense pride underlies Warren's position, since to begin with such a powerful identification with the father implies that one has but fleetingly accepted one's status as a son. Warren's repeated humiliations of the erring child are so consistent, so predictably cathartic (or tragic when they fail), as to take on the quality of a regimen he has assigned himself for fear of more vagrant impulses.

The climax of *All the King's Men* reveals a fascination with the way fathers exercise authority rather than with how a son gains it. These are

the moments of true suspense in Warren. There is little question that the
son will enjoy his opportunity for accommodation. There is some as to
how the father will arrange it. In ignorance of their true relation, Jack has
returned to Burden's Landing to complete his blackmail of Judge Irwin.
Standing over his surprisingly calm adversary, Jack thinks the Judge has
started to reach for a gun.

> He must have guessed the thought, for he shook his head, smiled, and said,
> "No, don't worry. You needn't be afraid."
> "Look here—" I began angrily.
> "I wouldn't hurt you," he said. Then reflectively, added, "But I could stop
> you."
> "By stopping MacMurfee," I said.
> "A lot easier than that."
> "I could just—" he began, "I could just say to you—I could just tell you
> something—" He stopped, then suddenly rose to his feet, spilling the papers off
> his knees. "But I won't," he said cheerfully and smiled directly at me.
> "Won't tell me what?"
> "Forget it," he said, still smiling, and waved his hand in a gay dismissal of the
> subject.
> I stood there irresolutely for a moment. Things were not making sense. He
> was not supposed to be standing there, brisk and confident and cheerful, with
> the incriminating papers at his feet. But he was.

Jack walks out of the house, and that night the Judge shoots himself.

The Judge certainly steals the show. Here a father acquires nobility by
not conferring upon a son a knowledge of origins. We admire the judge
for not telling Jack what Jack needs to know. It is a scene almost unique
in American fiction, where fathers usually prove so strong (Sutpen) that
they overpower their sons or so weak (Compson) that they unman them.
Judge Irwin suspends his fatherly prerogatives and creates a situation in
which the unwitting son can triumph, can even, in the words of Jack's
mother, "kill" his father. This may seem a mere reversal of roles, a
violently *un*resolved Oedipal conflict. But, in part because of Jack's
ignorance that he is caught in a hidden triangle, the father's sacrifice of
himself does not lead to further conflict. It does not lead, that is, to the
destruction of the son through guilt but to the son's acceptance of his role
as a son.

What looks like kindness may disguise, however, a crushing mag-
nanimity. Jack only gets a stronger father in addition to his weak one (the
Scholarly Attorney), even if the intensity of this collision begins to crack
the ice in which he has long frozen. Almost as if to acknowledge that he
has rescued Jack from alienation only by further indenturing him to
authority, Warren rewrites and inverts this scene at the end of *A Place to
Come To*. There a stepfather, Perk Simms, asks that the "son" he has

never seen accept him as the parent he has never had. If we understand Jed's coming home to his mother's house as significant for the husband who survives her, the inevitability of his return may matter less than the quality of the father's welcome.

> "I'm Perk Simms, I'm Perk what had the luck to find your ma in this dark world and I declare I will love her till the day I die."
>
> By this time, forgetting his abortive handshake, he was grappling for my neck like a spookily inept Strangler Lewis returned from the shades, the formidable old hands on their pipestem wrists getting a grip, and with both arms around my neck, he pressed one of his great, bony, leathery, imperfectly shaven cheeks, as raw as a clutch of cockleburs, against my own, all the while saying it was God's blessing to see me, there was so much to tell piling up inside him, and he claimed me like a blood-kin son, with my kind permission, for he had loved her so. And meanwhile I felt the dampness on his cheek.

Rembrandt could have painted this.

In its gentle recovery of the long lost, this penultimate scene becomes one of the most moving in Warren's fiction, and takes much of its own power from a sense that Jed and Perk accept each other because of their willingness to share their absent third. The adopting proceeds without a hitch, and old Buck Tewksbury seems long forgotten. But Jed's Ma had made one last request, as Perk reveals that night over his empty glass of whiskey:

> "All she done for me —" he burst out, croakingly.
> I waited, for I caught the peculiar inflection.
> "And then what she did," he said, "and on her dying bed."
> I waited, for I now could tell that whatever it was, it had to come.
> "Holding her hand," he said, "setting close to the bed, that's where I was, and she said it. Ast me did I know she loved me. I nodded my head, being a-sudden choked up. Then you know what she said?"
> I shook my head.
> "She said for me to forgive her," he managed to get out, "she loved me and declared she never knowed a better man and more fitter for her, and she said she prayed God I'd come to know it was not to kick dirt up in my — in my —" He did a few contortions in his chair, then took it head on: "To kick dirt in my — in my sweet ole face — no, don't make no mistake. Perfesser, them was the words she spoke, not me."
> After a little: "Do you know what it was on her mind?"
> "No."
> "She wanted to be buried out in Heaven's Hope graveyard," he said. "Next to — to you know who." Then "What kin a man do! You do the best the Lord lets you, and it is like all yore love, it is in vain."

So Perk exacts his last request — that Jed scatter whatever remains of him after his cremation in some place "not too unhandy to Ma." On the day when Jed returns to carry out his promise, he will constitute a perpetually oscillating triangle's living fourth. By ending his novel with an image that blurs distinctions between the first and the second, the natural and the adopted, Warren lays questions of priority and authority quietly but firmly to rest.

Warren's sustained identification with paternal authority, however qualified in his most recent novel, contributes to his anticipatory stance toward the development of his plots. One of his favorite narrative devices is to foretell an outcome that must then be awaited through pages of exposition. In *Flood*, Brad Tolliver actually writes a movie script that heralds the climax of the novel containing it. Casper calls this abbreviated foreshadowing an *"exemplum."* The most famous is the Cass Mastern episode in *All the King's Men*. Faulkner thought this the only part of the novel worth saving: "The Cass Mastern story is a beautiful and moving piece. That was his novel. The rest of it I would throw away." Faulkner's objections to the body of the novel had a good deal to do with the contrast between the heroic past and the banal present. But one wonders whether this master of the twice-told tale was not also urging Warren to tell his story only once. Had Faulkner been challenged on this point, he might have answered that while in his novels multiple narrative strands are kept unraveled until and even beyond the last page, in Warren's the story within the story, or the telegraphing of the novel's destination, occurs at some one point along the way. His foreshadowings are not, like Hemingway's, implicit in hauntingly unsure beginnings, but explicit, calculated, *understood*.

The problem comes down to the manipulation of narrative time, and here again Warren displays almost paralyzing insight into the technique of his immediate forefathers:

> . . . The frozen moment. Freeze time. Somewhere, almost in a kind of pun, Faulkner himself uses the image of a frieze for such a moment of frozen action. It's an important quality in his work. Some of these moments harden up an event, give it its meaning by holding it fixed. Time fluid vs. time fixed— In Faulkner's work that's the drama behind the drama. Take a look at Hemingway; there's no time in Hemingway, there are only moments in themselves, moments of action. There are no parents and no children. If there's a parent he is a grandparent off in America somewhere who signs the check, like the grandfather in *A Farewell to Arms*. You never see a small child in Hemingway. You get death in childbirth but you never see a child. Everything is outside of the time process. But in Faulkner there are always the very old and the very young. Time spreads and is the important thing, the terrible thing.

This brilliant comment designates both authors as impatient with the medium that defines origins and limits originality. By turning this impatience into an overt theme, Warren almost stands aside from an experience of it. The rejection of origins is the given of Warren's fiction, but the fact that nearly every strong character rejects them, and the reason why, remains to be explained. In Faulkner, the past explains the present; in Warren, the present is explained by the *reaction against* the past. But whence the reaction? The violent departures of his sons seem more perverse than motivated. Here too Warren is Miltonic; Satan's rebellion against the very concept of origin ("That we were formed then say'st thou?") springs out of nowhere. It is the first, the "original" sin. Warren seems to agree that further explanation of such revolts is not possible: "Explanations can only explain explanations, and the self is gratuitous in the end." As a philosophical rather than a psychological novelist, Warren is interested less in motivation (an instigating act) than in definition (a concluding act). This interest (along with all the other attitudes and devices that mitigate a dynamic unfolding) renders his novels curiously static, since definitions are not so much earned through time as they are formulations which, however frequently reconceived, remove us from it.

"There will be an end but you cannot see it": if this line from "The Ballad of Billie Potts" fails to capture the experience of Warren's novels, it does ample justice to his career as a poet. In his best poems, he does not stand at a critical distance from the very themes he wishes to affirm. Warren does not develop in his novels, as I have been suggesting, because in them he converts any authentic rage against authority into its opposite, a thoroughly rationalized myth of filial dependence. Warren's poems are the medium through which his true development takes place. "Poems are," he wrote in the preface to *Selected Poems* (1966), "in one perspective at least, always a life record." In his statements about writing poetry versus writing fiction, Warren usually casts the difference as a matter of degree:

> Both fiction and poetry became—poetry very early—for me a way of life. I had to live into them, had to have them. But there is a difference. Poetry is a more direct way of trying to know the self, to make sense of experience.

In the same year he told another interviewer that

> I started as a poet and I will probably end as a poet. If I had to choose between my novels and my *Selected Poems*, I would keep the *Selected Poems* as representing me more fully, my vision and myself. I think poems are more *you*.

Because Warren practices poetry as a running life record, he had to write poems as assignments made to him by experience, not as tasks he set himself. As the ongoing history of a life, his poems asked him to submit to whatever happened next. In his poetry Warren lives through as life what he may already, as evidenced by his fiction, have comprehended as thought. The drama of his career is in watching his life draw his art into time.

The Father's Sublime

The end of Warren's *Selected Poems: 1923-1975* defies prediction. One usually reads such a volume with a gathering sense of a poet's hard-earned maturity. But this selection begins with the poems of 1975 and ends with those of 1923-43. As one reads into the book, the past looms up as if it were the future.

> This
> Is the process whereby pain of the past in its pastness
> May be converted into the future tense
>
> Of joy.

This inverted presentation of his poetic development is Warren's most profound act of criticism. It is also his biggest lie against time.

The most obvious motive for such reversal is to present the best work first. Warren has had the luck to live a long life. It took sixty years for his poetic voice to ripen into his great volume, *Or Else*. Naturally he might wish to begin with his triumph. More compelling, however, must have been the impulse to revolt against a career dedicated to the awful responsibility of Time. (Warren had inverted and jumbled chronology in his two previous *Selected Poems*, but never to such dramatic effect. The last line of all three books has remained the same, and reverberates backward to sum up our passage through these wayward measures: "Borne in the lost procession of these feet.") This is a book in which poem after poem defines man as a creature caught up in irreversible history. Yet all these propositions inhabit a structure which belies chronology. The arrangement of the *Selected Poems* constitutes a rebellion against the priority of an earlier self, and, by extension, earlier selves. Through an illusion of presentation, early Warren becomes indebted to late Warren. In throwing off the yoke of time, the critic/son finally becomes the artist/father.

Watching Warren assume fatherhood creates the drama of this book. If we restore chronology for a moment, the following pattern emerges:

    I Poems 1923-43 (The Fugitive and After)
   II Ten year gap (The Novelist)
 III *Brother to Dragons* (The Poet as "R.P.W.")
 IV *Promises:* 1954-56 (The Birth of the Son)
  V Poems 1957-60 (*Mortmain:* The Death of the Father)
 VI Poems 1960-68 (The Falling Off)
VII *Audubon* (The Recovery)
VIII *Or Else:* 1968-74 (The Father's Sublime)

Brother to Dragons, with a density of metaphor never again equaled in Warren's poetry, marks his turn into direct self-presentation. Not until

Promises, however, does Warren achieve a fully personal voice over the length of an entire book. The birth of his son and daughter suddenly converts the abstractions of Time and History into a continuity of blood in which he has directly chosen to participate. The son is named Gabriel. Warren's paternal grandmother Martha, wife to Gabriel Warren, had died giving birth to Robert Warren, the poet's father. By naming his son Gabriel, Warren celebrates the survival and triumph of the line in the wake of family disaster. He also revives the suppressed "Genealogy," the poem that had once pondered this inheritance:

> Gabriel, Gabriel, if now together
> With Martha you keep any sort of weather
> In fragrant hair and dissolute bone adrowse,
> Your grandson keeps a broken house.
> There's a stitch in his side no plasters heal,
> A crack in the firmament, maggots in the meal;
> There's a mole in the garden, fennel by the gate,
> In the heart a curse of hell-black hate
> For that other young guy who croaked too late.

This poem is almost unique in Warren's canon in voicing an active grievance against a personal past. I take it that the "other young guy" is Warren's father, and it is in documents like this that we should look for the authentic filial ingratitude that Warren chastens so thoroughly in the novels. Victor H. Strandberg argues that this poem expresses "such a *personal* trauma concerning entry into the ruined world" as to explain its deletion from the *Selected Poems* (1944). If so, by 1956 the personal has become the promise. The joy of two successful births seems directly proportional to the curse of that earlier one. In the moment of watching his infant son asleep, we can hear all the voices of Warren's past absorbed into the poet's own:

> Moonlight falls on your face now,
> And now in memory's stasis
> I see moonlight mend an old man's Time-crossed brow.
> My son, sleep deep,
> For moonlight will not stay.
> Now moves to seek that empty pillow, a hemisphere away.
> Here, then, you'll be waking to the day.
> Those who died, died long ago,
> Faces you will never know,
> Voices you will never hear—
> Though your father heard them in the night,
> And yet, sometimes, I can hear
> Their utterance like the rustling tongue of a pale tide in
>   moonlight:
> *Sleep, son. Good night.*

Metrical restraint here still chastens Warren's reach toward a more untrammeled rhythm. This father conserves as much as he invents: this is a lullaby. The poise of these poems is shattered in *Mortmain*, where Warren returns to the bedside of his dying father. The death of his origin releases even more in the poet than the birth of his future. So intensely felt is this sequence that we scarcely notice its beginnings in *ottava rima*. As the dying father reaches out to the awaiting son, perhaps in blessing, the motion stops:

> But no. Like an eyelid the hand sank, strove
> Downward, and in that darkening roar,
> All things—all joy and the hope that strove,
> The failed exam, the admired endeavor,
> Prizes and prinkings, and the truth that strove,
> And back of the Capitol, boyhood's first whore—
> Were snatched from me, and I could not move,
> Naked in that black blast of his love.

This failed embrace had to wait nearly twenty years for requital. The falling off after *Mortmain* is due to the blunting of any possible sublimity through bathos. "There was a time," Warren tells us, "in the middle of the forties and for the next 10 years almost when I couldn't finish a poem." The poems of 1960-68 are finished, but they rebel against any sustaining conclusions. Simply put, "Delight is not to be trusted." Then, in *Audubon*, ugliness becomes the parenthesis of "delight," the poem's last word. The sublime has been established as inclusive rather than exceptional. Now it only remains to make it a Father's Sublime. Warren accomplishes his embrace of the father not through a return but through a repetition with a difference, by doing for his own son what had not been done for him:

> When my son is an old man, and I have not,
> For some fifty years, seen his face, and, if seeing it,
> Would not even be able to guess what name it wore, what
> Blessing should I ask for him?
>
> That some time, in thaw-season, at dusk, standing
> At woodside and staring
> Red-westward, with the sound of moving water
> In his ears, he
> Should thus, in that future moment, bless,
> Forward into that future's future,
> An old man who, as he is mine, had once
> Been his small son.
>
> For what blessing may a man hope for but
> An immortality in
> The loving vigilance of death?

In this act of forgiveness, Warren heals the past by blessing the future. He realizes the great possibility of reversal, and in so doing recovers a sense of rhythm more sure than anything he has previously known. To use Warren's words from "Knowledge and the Image of Man": "The form is the flowing of that deep engagement of spirit, the discovery of its rhythm." Sometime in the late sixties Warren acceded to the fact that his concern with rhythm could best test itself in a genre written in lines rather than paragraphs. In poetry, rhythm is return, and all the pleasure in *Or Else* depends upon Warren's resisting the pull toward premature closure. Suspense builds as he tolls the self forward into an amassing harmony rather than backward into perpetual refrain.

The poem which immediately follows the reconciliation of the generations in "Sunset Walk" testifies to renewed possibilities for a happy timing of response within the generations. In "Birth of Love" Warren develops into what is perhaps most difficult, because least determined: a faithful lover. This is so arresting a poem that I want to read it at length:

> Season late, day late, sun just down, and the sky
> Cold gunmetal but with a wash of live rose, and she,
> From water the color of sky except where
> Her motion has fractured it to shivering splinters of silver,
> Rises. Stands on the raw grass. Against
> The new-curdling night of spruces, nakedness
> Glimmers and, at bosom and flank, drips
> With fluent silver.

This is a poetry of the verb rather than the noun. Warren rediscovers the power of words that enact over those that abstract. Our fate in the poem depends upon its verbs. Stationed at the beginnings and ends of lines, granted a full and measured breath of their own, these carefully positioned action words reach forward to create an anticipation which carries us through the poem. They draw us, like enduring love, into time. Love is also born here in an onlooker:

> The man,

> Some ten strokes out, but now hanging
> Motionless in the gunmetal water, feet
> Cold with the coldness of depth, all
> History dissolving from him, is
> Nothing but an eye. Is an eye only. Sees

> The body that is marked by his use, and Time's,
> Rise, and in the abrupt and unsustaining element of air,
> Sway, lean, grapple the pond-bank.

Suspended in an undifferentiated medium, cut off from shore, the man here contracts into a mere seer. For a moment he seems in the world but not of it, but Warren allows him only a momentary stay. Simple eyesight quickly becomes historical consciousness as seeing leads to remembering. To see "the body that is marked by his use, and Time's" is to dissolve back into awareness of history. However much the eye may enjoy visions unmarked by time, the objects of its sight insist upon their subjection to time's usages. Warren rejects Blake's visionary claim that "the Eye sees more than the Heart knows." However much the heart longs for immutability, it can only feel the loss of memory as the loss of love.

This is a poem of suddenly perceived grace. Love comes back unannounced, as surprise:

> Sees
>
> How, with the posture of female awkwardness that is,
> And is the stab of, suddenly perceived grace, breasts bulge down in
> The pure curve of their weight and buttocks
> Moon up and, in that swelling unity,
> Are silver, and glimmer.

With each "and" conclusion is here delayed while loving attention is extended. These conjunctions testify to her sheer bodily abundance. Within the ingathering the beat comes momentarily to rest upon "grace," and we are given time not only to see "how" she moves him but to feel how she moves us. What may have only penetrated to the eye now stabs to the heart.

The poem now precipitates us toward a fall:

> Then
>
> The body is erect, she is herself, whatever
> Self she may be, and with an end of the towel grasped in each hand
> Slowly draws it back and forth across back and buttocks, but
> With face lifted toward the high sky, where
> The over-wash of rose color now fails. Fails, though no star
> Yet throbs there.

As she withdraws into her private history, the light fails. "Fails," Warren repeats, to emphasize that no fiction of arrest comes between this failure and the acknowledgment of it. Her ongoing withdrawal turns upon the "The's" which begin the next four sentences. Throughout the poem, the formality of definite articles replaces the intimacy of personal pronouns to create a sure sense of otherness. Here the articles build toward a vision of her as an "it," drawing "to itself . . . what light/In the sky yet lingers." What then shall we further be able to see? An abstraction:

> This moment is non-sequential and absolute, and admits
> Of no definition, for it
> Subsumes all other, and sequential, moments, by which
> Definition might be possible.

"This" closes the growing gap between the man and his vision, the reader and the poem. "This" testifies to the presence of a thing and our familiarity with it. We have had our moment; now we savor it through commentary. An immediacy becomes an example. Yet the poet speaks of this moment as still happening. It "is." We again question whether one can speak of a moment and still experience it. The poet's way of saying contradicts the force of his statement. He advances a definition about the inadmissibility of definition. He denies sequence in a poem dependent on it. The moment, we are told, subsumes and dissolves history. And yet the poem, as we have seen, involves us in a necessary sequence of seeings. Our movement through it is as much like walking as stationary looking. In its own words, it is "stair-steep." It is torn between asserting its moment as "non-sequential and absolute," and the necessity of entrusting any such experience to the mediation of language and emotion working in time.

The genius of Warren's poem is to locate this lapse from unconscious grace not after but *within* the swelling present moment. The abstraction interrupts rather than completes the poem's movement. So it is with relief that the reader returns to the unfolding of the actual scene. The woman must still wrap, glimmer, and go. For five syllables the poet prolongs departure and restores her to our sight through repetition: "Glimmers and is gone." This is the freedom of poetry, the power of its repetitions to reassure us that all is not quite yet lost. What the man now hopes for is not so much to stay her going as to stay her forever:

> and the man

> Suspended in his darkling medium, stares
> Upward where, though not visible, he knows
> She moves, and in his heart he cries out that, if only
> He had such strength, he would put his hand forth
> And maintain it over her to guard, in all
> Her out-goings and in-comings, from whatever
> Inclemency of sky or slur of the world's weather
> Might ever be. In his heart
> He cries out.

Here repetition works not to recover but to remind, to remind that what he cries out for he cannot really achieve. Yet what we are moved by is not the impossibility of the hope but its stubborn persistence. (Readers of Warren will note that "Birth of Love" rewrites "A Vision, Circa 1880," perhaps Warren's most beautiful poem to his father, and one in which he first tries to "cry out" to a "hieratic" figure who glimmers in a clearing and then "is gone.") That he cries out again—that is what matters. So he ends as the poet has proceeded, by raising his hand against the very medium—time— through which he expresses his love.

"Birth of Love" confirms the love between men and women which makes generation possible. Any enduring love is profoundly historical, growing through change, confirmed through repetition. Yet poetry represents love less in its confirmation through repetition than in its freshness through transformation. Warren's poem is a repetition *experienced* as a beginning. It fuses, as fully as one might ever wish, the imagination which conserves and the imagination which creates. This birth is really a re-birth. The man has again fallen in love with this woman, as he will, with grace, again. He falls in love again, however, *as if* for the first time, *as if* he were free to choose, apart from all the historical obligations determining such a choice. The whole poem is structured to be experienced as "the non-sequential" moment of which it speaks. It is given greater force than a poem of actual beginning by virtue of the very history it excludes, and yet which surrounds this moment to define and give value to it. We know that the body has been marked by time's use; we know that the day is late. Yet we are left with another image of beginning:

> Above

> Height of the spruce-night and heave of the far mountain, he sees
> The first star pulse into being. It gleams there.

Of course the star is Venus; of course the poem is a repetition in modern time of the myth of her birth. But Warren's mode of indirect allusion frees us from a mere rehearsal of the archetypical—the poem was originally called "The Birth of Love"—and preserves the illusion of an original event. What is lost for mythic inevitability is gained for imaginative free play.

The poet ends by refusing to answer an unasked yet implicit question posed by the evening star:

> I do not know what promise it makes to him.

Is this a question on our lips? Not if we have attentively read the poem. For by the end we should realize that the fact of the star's pulsing forth every night, not what it might symbolically promise, *is* the promise. It too marks a pattern of repetition, yet it too, in its nightly pulsing forth, is always ready to be seen and felt as if for the first time. In this quiet refusal to interpret his own imagery, Warren acknowledges the critic's desire to know while protecting the poet's will to present, a resolution worthy of his most mature and beautiful poem.

~§ *Seven*

DAVIES AND THE MIDDLE OF THE JOURNEY

The Keepers of the Stone

Near the beginning of his autobiographical *Memories, Dreams, Reflections* (1961), Jung tells us that in his tenth year

> My disunion with myself and uncertainty in the world at large led me to an action which at the time was quite incomprehensible to me. I had in those days a yellow, varnished pencil case of the kind commonly used by primary-school pupils, with a little lock and the customary ruler. At the end of this ruler I now carved a little manikin, about two inches long, with frock coat, top hat, and shiny black boots. I colored him black with ink, sawed him off the ruler, and put him in the pencil case, where I made him a little bed. I even made a coat for him out of a bit of wool. In the case I also placed a smooth, oblong blackish stone from the Rhine, which I had painted with water colors to look as though it were divided into an upper and lower half, and had long carried around in my trouser pocket. This was *his* stone. All this was a great secret. Secretly I took the case to the forbidden attic at the top of the house (forbidden because the floorboards were worm-eaten and rotten) and hid it with great satisfaction on one of the beams under the roof—for no one must ever see it! I knew that not a soul would ever find it there. No one could discover my secret and destroy it.

Whenever he feels oppressed by his life Jung visits the manikin and the stone. There he feels secure.

A retrospective jung concludes that "this possession of a secret had a very powerful formative influence on my character; I consider it the essential factor of my boyhood. Similarly, I never told anyone about the dream of the phallus; and the Jesuit, too, belonged to that mysterious realm which I knew I must not talk about." Jung here links his "earliest dream" and his "first conscious trauma" to his most "formative influence."

129

Taken together, these three events give the chapter "First Years" an almost novelistic coherence.

At "between three and four years old" Jung had dreamt himself in a meadow. "Suddenly I discovered a dark, rectangular, stone-lined hole in the ground." He descends a stone stairway, penetrates a heavily curtained doorway, and enters an arched "rectangular chamber about thirty feet long" in the center of which stands a magnificent throne.

> Something was standing on it which I thought at first was a tree trunk twelve to fifteen feet high and about one and a half to two feet thick. It was a huge thing, reaching almost to the ceiling. But it was of a curious composition: it was made of skin and naked flesh, and on top there was something like a rounded head with no face and no hair. On the very top of the head was a single eye, gazing motionlessly upward.

The awe-struck boy fears that the thing "might at any moment crawl off the throne like a worm and creep toward me." Suddenly he hears his mother's voice: "'Yes, just look at him. That is the man-eater!' That intensified my terror still more, and I awoke sweating and scared to death."

"At about the same time," Jung relates, he suffered his traumatic encounter with the Jesuit. While playing in sand near his home he had looked up to see "a figure in a strangely broad hat and a long black garment coming down from the wood. . . . At the sight of him I was overcome with fear, which rapidly grew into deadly terror as the frightful recognition shot through my mind: 'That is a Jesuit.' Shortly before, I had overheard a conversation between my father and a visiting colleague concerning the nefarious activities of the Jesuits. From the half-irritated, half-fearful tone of my father's remarks I gathered that 'Jesuits' meant something specially dangerous, even for my father." The terrified boy runs into the house and hides in the attic. Fear clings to him for days, and only later does he realize "that the black figure was a harmless Catholic priest."

Robertson Davies's *Fifth Business* (1970) begins in the tenth year of Dunstan Ramsay's life. Dunny has been sledding with his "lifelong friend and enemy," Percy Boyd Staunton, on the outskirts of the little Ontario village of Deptford. Dunny's old sled outperforms Percy's new one. An argument begins, Percy starts throwing snowballs, and, before we know it, "the unforeseen" takes over. The Reverend Amasa Dempster and his wife, on their nightly constitutional for her pregnancy, loom in Dunny's path.

> I had a boy's sense of when a snowball was coming, and I knew Percy. I was sure that he would try to land one last, insulting snowball between my shoulders

before I ducked into our house. I stepped briskly—not running, but not dawdling—in front of the Dempsters just as Percy threw, and the snowball hit Mrs Dempster on the back of the head. She gave a cry and, clinging to her husband, slipped to the ground; he might have caught her if he had not turned at once to see who had thrown the snowball.

Dunny stands in awe of emotions he has never before witnessed:

suddenly there she was, on the ground, with her husband kneeling beside her, holding her in his arms and speaking to her in terms of endearment that were strange and embarrassing to me; I had never heard married people—or any people—speak unashamedly loving words before. I knew that I was watching a "scene," and my parents had always warned me against scenes as very serious breaches of propriety.

That next morning, as a result of Boy's throw and Dunny's duck, Paul Dempster is prematurely born.

What Dunny withholds from the reader in this largely self-incriminating account ("I was contrite and guilty, for I knew that the snowball had been meant for me") is the secret that inside the snowball there had been a stone. When he next confronts Boy he accuses him of knowing why "the baby came too soon." Boy's reply is characteristically self-protective: "No I don't." No mention is made of the stone. Some ten years later Ramsay returns to Deptford as a war-hero and ventures into his dead parents' home to collect a few things: "Everything was where I knew it should be, but all the objects looked small and dull—my mother's clock, my father's desk, with the stone on it he had brought from Dumfries and always used as a paperweight; it was now an unloved house, and want of love had withered it. I picked up a few things I wanted—particularly something that I had long kept hidden—and got out as fast as I could." The "something" is Boy's stone, the secreted talisman of their common guilt. The stone attempts to surface once more before its eventual revelation. On the night in Mexico when Ramsay blurts out his story to Liesl, he hears himself "rattling on about Deptford, and the Dempsters, and Paul's premature birth, though I did not tell all I knew of that." Once again the opportunity to bring the stone to light has been acknowledged and rejected.

The stone finally resurfaces in Dunny's clinical report of Boy Staunton's death. He has been found (the year is now 1968) behind the wheel of his Cadillac convertible in the Toronto harbor. "But the most curious fact of all was that in Boy's mouth the police found a stone—an ordinary piece of pinkish granite about the size of a small egg." "Curious" only to a reader who for 250 pages has not been tempted to supply a referent for some of Dunny's more tantalizing abstract nouns. Ramsay goes on to reveal that the night before Boy's death he, Staunton, and Paul Dempster (now the magician Magnus Eisengrim) had enjoyed their first reunion in Ramsay's office at Colborne College. Ramsay tells them both "the story of the snowball," but Boy refuses to accept any responsibility for the incident. Driven beyond the limits of his patience, Ramsay finally points Boy toward his "old paperweight":

> "It is the stone you put in the snowball you threw at Mrs Dempster," I said. "I've kept it because I couldn't part with it. I swear I never meant to tell you what it was. But, Boy, for God's sake, get to know something about yourself. The stone-in-the-snowball has been characteristic of too much you've done for you to forget it forever!"

It has taken sixty years and four times that many pages for Dunny to reveal his secret to Boy and to the reader. After further argument, Boy drives Magnus home. Only the next morning does Ramsay notice that "my paperweight was gone." We last hear of the stone at Eisengrim's *Soirée of Illusions*, where, in response to a cry from the balcony "Who killed Boy Staunton?" *The Brazen Head of Friar Bacon* replies:

> He was killed by the usual cabal: by himself, first of all; by the woman he knew; by the woman he did not know; by the man who granted his inmost wish; and by the inevitable fifth, who was the keeper of his conscience and the keeper of the stone.

Ramsay is not a dreamer, but he also records for the autobiographical record his most striking "conscious trauma." It occurs surprisingly late, two-and-a-half years after Paul's birth. While pursuing his hobby of prestidigitation, Dunny has broken a stone-shaped egg stolen from his mother's kitchen. She misses it and confronts him; he refuses to confess. She goes for the pony whip and begins to beat him:

> "Don't you dare touch me," I shouted, and that put her into such a fury as I had never known. It must have been a strange scene, for she pursued me around the kitchen, slashing me with the whip until she broke me down and I cried. She cried too, hysterically, and beat me harder, storming about my impudence, my want of respect for her, of my increasing oddity and intellectual arrogance—not that she used these words, but I do not intend to put down what she actually said—until at last her fury was spent, and she ran upstairs in tears and banged the door of her bedroom.

That evening Dunny repents, kneels before her, and receives her bene-dictory kiss:

> "I know I'll never have another anxious moment with my own dear laddie."
> I pondered these words before I went to sleep. How could I reconcile this motherliness with the screeching fury who had pursued me around the kitchen with a whip, flogging me until she was gorged with—what? Vengeance? What was it? Once, when I was in my thirties and reading Freud for the first time,

I thought I knew. I am not so sure I know now. But what I knew was that nobody—not even my mother—was to be trusted in a strange world that showed very little of itself on the surface.

It is this confrontation, as much as anything else, which turns Dunny away from the uncanny Mrs Ramsay and toward the "unchancy" Mrs Dempster.

If Ramsay and Jung are both Keepers of the Stone, it is even more remarkable that they bring such similar interpretative strategies to bear upon their secret. One thing quickly becomes clear: both encourage us to collate the secret stone with the other remarkable experiences of childhood. But in both cases it is the keeping of the stone, and not the traumas or dreams with which it is associated, that proves "formative." It is the "essential factor." This is not a little surprising given the ten years of experience which in each case precedes the secreting of the stone. Neither autobiographer regards the obsession with the stone as a reaction; it points forward, not backward. Life for both men can be said to begin with the stone.

The profile such a perspective renders is rather unfortunate, since both men emerge as retentive as the result of having made an initial decision to hold something back. Each becomes what he has hidden. Ramsay's reduction of his home to two privies, his compulsive cleanliness, his "scrupulosity in money matters"—this and more contributes to our sense of him as a man dammed up. There is throughout his narrative the tone of something withheld. He prides himself on having been a "repository of secrets." Liesl comes closer to the truth when she judges him a constipated prude, "grim-mouthed and buttoned-up and hard-eyed and cruel." Jung's retention of the secret threatens to have similar effects. The great anxiety of "School Years" is that he will allow himself to think a particularly forbidden thought. What is it? That "God sits on His golden throne, high above the world—and from under the throne an enormous turd falls upon the sparkling new roof, shatters it, and breaks the walls of the cathedral asunder." If this were not such a marvelous parody of a Gnostic creation myth, it might be disturbing. It becomes so as Jung goes on to connect this blasphemy with the hidden stone: "With the experience of God and the cathedral I at last had something tangible that was part of the great secret—as if I had always talked of stones falling from heaven and now had one in my pocket. But actually, it was a shaming experience." He sometimes feels "an overwhelming urge to speak" of all this, but never does: "It would never have occurred to me to speak of my experience openly, nor of my dream of the phallus in the underground temple, nor of my carved manikin." The rather frightening reward for his "great achievement" of having "resisted the temptation to talk about it with anyone" is to feel part of himself hardening into his secret. "I was but the sum of my emotions, and the Other in me was the timeless, imperishable stone."

Of course neither Ramsay nor Jung sees himself as petrified. Confronted with the challenge of interpretation, both choose to amplify rather than to reduce. Here is Jung's interpretation of the dream. "Only much later did I realize that what I had seen was a phallus, and it was decades before I understood that it was a ritual phallus." And here is his interpretation of the manikin and the stone: "Ultimately, the manikin was a *kabir*, wrapped in his little cloak, hidden in the *kista*, and provided with a supply of life-force, the oblong black stone. But these are connections which became clear to me only much later in life." Jung will proceed to make much of such connections. In the last chapter of the autobiography he concludes that "it is important to have a secret, a premonition of things unknown. It fills life with something impersonal, a *numinosum*." Here the significance of the secret stone is retroactively generalized into the numinous universe of which Jung can claim to be the redeemer and interpreter. But one wonders whether the impulse to impose a teleology upon his development has not triumphed here. *Memories* is littered with remnants of the stone. The great hobby of later life becomes building in stone: "when I came up against a blank wall, I painted a picture or hewed stone." On one occasion he finds a "fragment of stone" which recalls "the underground phallus of my childhood dream. This connection gave me a feeling of satisfaction." He pushes such connections no further; on the contrary, his impulse is to amplify rather than to reduce his associations with the stone. So it becomes a "Christ," the medium for "a confession of faith," a vehicle for the fourfold mystery of being which remains "incomprehensible to others." For Jung the movement toward psychic wholeness culminates in "a feeling as if I were being reborn in stone."

The stages in Jung's understanding of the dream and the stone correspond to the stages (he reads Freud; he moves beyond him) in Ramsay's interpretation of his mother's behavior. Jung begins by reading significance as personal and even sexual. But he matures into a reading that is universal and mythological. Directly after generalizing the "huge thing" into a "ritual phallus," Jung digresses into a strange quibble:

> I could never make out whether my mother meant, "*That* is the man-eater," or, "That is the *man-eater*." In the first case she would have meant that not Lord Jesus or the Jesuit was the devourer of little children, but the phallus; in the second case that the "man-eater" in general was symbolized by the phallus, so that the dark Lord Jesus, the Jesuit, and the phallus were identical.

It quickly becomes apparent that Jung answers "Yes" to the second of these questions, questions which raise the issue of symbolic interpretation.

In Jung's reading of the dream the phallus proves a contingent rather than a necessary symbol. Its form is not *necessarily* correlated with its function. For Freud as well dream symbols enjoy no such correlation, but Jung has hit upon the one symbol which for Freud may prove the exception to the rule. The penis is for Freud the hidden tenor of a host of vehicles; its fate is the secret which defies direct representation. Jung here performs a marvelous sleight-of-hand: by dreaming *directly* of a small boy threatened by a huge penis he invites us to read the dream as literal, yet by the logic of Freud's theory of dream interpretation the phallus surely stands for *something else*. (Later in *Memories* Jung will deny that a "dream is a 'facade' behind which its meaning lies hidden," but this rejection of Freud's method of dream interpretation does not serve his purposes here.) In this way Jung neutralizes or renders incidental a central referent in Freud's system of interpretation. The phallus is simply one of many possible symbols for authority, or for whatever theme the dream is finally understood to explore. The wish and the resultant threat embodied in the stone-Jesuit-phallus complex elaborates itself into a host of symbols instead of focusing itself upon one bodily organ.

In interpreting a dream which fairly cries out the words "castration anxiety," Jung thus deftly directs attention away from the One Reading upon which Freud founds his theory of dream interpretation. But a number of questions are still asking to be asked. Is the "terror" which clings to the boy's limbs as he confronts the phallus not something personal? What is the purpose of fashioning the manikin and secreting the stone but to possess "something that no one knew and no one could get at"? And why does Jung avoid the tantalizing question of the mother's presence here and the threat to bodily integrity she voices? Jung appears unwilling to ponder this as *his* dream, as imaging a drama in *his* family. But as *Memories* makes clear, Jung stood perhaps a little too close to his mother and far from his father to avoid the guilty ambivalence that would attend any usurpation of the latter. "She always seemed to me the stronger of the two. Nevertheless I always felt on her side when my father gave vent to his moody irritability. This necessity for taking sides was not exactly favorable to the formation of my character." Mrs. Jung is the only person to whom Carl "might have communicated" his secrets. Like Mrs Ramsay, she "consisted of two personalities, one innocuous and human, the other uncanny. The other emerged only now and then, but each time it was unexpected and frightening." Jung even relates a scene in which he misbehaves and receives a furious "lecture, spiced with tears, longer and more passionate than anything I had ever heard from her before." For his father his prevailing emotions are "compassion" and "pity." There will even come a time when he can think back on his father as a wounded "fisher king." There is a marvelous moment when Carl, after overhearing his father complain that "I have lost what little I had," suddenly turns into a "serious child" and moves toward an epiphany of self-conscious manhood. In walking the long road from school

> I had the overwhelming impression of having just emerged from a dense cloud. I knew all at once: now I am *myself!* It was as if a wall of mist were at my back, and behind that wall there was not yet an "I." But at this moment *I came upon myself.* Previously I had existed, too, but everything had merely happened to me. Now I happened to myself. Now I knew: I am myself now, now I exist. Previously I had been willed to do this and that; now *I* willed. This experience seemed to me tremendously important and new: there was "authority" in me. Curiously enough, at this time and also during the months of my fainting neurosis I had lost all memory of the treasure in the attic. Otherwise I would probably have realized even then the analogy between my feeling of authority and the feeling of value which the treasure inspired in me. But that was not so; all memory of the pencil case had vanished.

This is Jung's sublimating answer to the upwelling of the uncanny dream. As with so many experiences of the sublime, as Thomas Weiskel has shown, "this recovery has the look of an oedipal crisis 'successfully' resolved." Power that once was felt to reside without now abides within. One no longer needs the stone once one has begun to shoulder, and even to repay, a father's losses. So Jung becomes a man who thoroughly incorporates (these are his own words) the "archaic and ruthless" mother, in all her expansive inclusiveness, without suffering any loss of his fatherly "authority." Certainly his work is characterized by a maternal openness rather than a paternal selectivity. It is founded on a secret the opposite of Freud's. "Mother is mother-love, *my* experience and *my* secret": so he argues in *Psychological Aspects of the Mother Archetype.* But as we have seen, Jung comes into the possession of his secret by way of a conflict entirely recognizable in Freudian terms. While carefully marshalling evidence for such a reading, Jung consistently bypasses the more economical interpretation of the stone complex and its resolution for one more elaborate and esoteric.

This may seem to take us a long way from Davies, but he too attempts to neutralize Freud by tackling him head on. (In *The Manticore* [1972] and *World of Wonders* [1975], David Staunton and Magnus Eisengrim also try to preempt Freud by mentioning him. David turns "Freudians" into a dismissive label, and Magnus, like the magician he is, takes away with one hand what he gives with the other: "Freud has had a great deal to say about the importance of the functions of excretion in deciding and moulding character. I don't know anything about that. . . .") By his very dating of the episode of the stone ("5.58 o'clock p.m. on 27 December 1908") in the first sentence of his autobiography, Ramsay suggests that everything else in his story flows from it. This is the central interpretative act encouraged by the novel. The thrown snowball is an ingenious device for binding together the fates of the Deptford Trilogy's major characters in a "lifelong" triangle of guilt, repentance, and revenge. What we may fail to notice is that the narrator departs ("My lifelong involvement with Mrs Dempster began. . . .") by asking us to believe that his story begins with another man's mother. Two major themes in *Fifth Business*—The Retention of the Secret and The Search for the Mother—are thus bound together from the outset in a reciprocal relation which makes it difficult to place one in a cause-and-effect relation with the other. If asked, the narrator would no doubt answer that the series of events leading to Paul's birth and his own lifelong involvement with Mary Dempster is "one of those coincidences that it may be wiser to call synchronicities." Without the knowledge of the stone, the reader is likely to see Mary's withdrawal from reality as an unmotivated reaction to a little knock on the head. "The snowball that sent Mrs Dempster simple" proves a miraculous boon to Dunny, who discovers her saintliness in the act of caring for her craziness. It proves a manifestation of "a world of wonder" where others only see a world of motives.

This might be sufficient were Dunny's response to Mrs Dempster's trauma not so obviously preconditioned by feelings that themselves require interpretation. (As the first pages of *Fifth Business* make clear, Ramsay assigns motives to others—"when Percy was humiliated he was vindictive"—while obscuring them in himself.) The logic behind the stone's flight need not only be viewed as absent or miraculous. It is also profoundly *psycho*logical. Dunny does not witness the "scene" between Amasa and Mary as a *tabula rasa*. Far from it—as he watches the husband "speak unashamedly loving words" he confronts something of which he has been nervously aware but which he has never before seen brought to light. In his typical fashion, Dunny translates the issues here into those of "shame" and "propriety" when, in fact, they are also of desire. That night Dunny lies awake feeling "guilty and strange." He has had a taste of desire, and now nothing can prevent him from completely supplanting Amasa Dempster. He feels himself none other than Paul's father: "I was directly responsible for a grossly sexual act—the birth of a child." Once Amasa expels Dunny from the Dempster house forever, Dunny feels no compunction about admitting his displaced Oedipal feelings: "I never saw her without a pang of guilt and concern about her. But for her husband I had no pity."

Why then does Ramsay secrete the stone? Because he everywhere displays his greedily retentive self? Because he hopes to preserve a talisman of the miracle that blessed him with a secret mother? Because the thrown stone stands for the crime he wishes to commit against the father? (The kept stone could then symbolize his integrity in spite of the wish, as well as the guilt attendant upon it.) Dunny claims to have fulfilled this last wish "directly," but we will not fail to notice that he has confused the Oedipal Triangle with Family Romance. In witnessing his first (primal) "scene" he plays the role of another man's son: in the consequences that flow from it, the impregnator of that man's wife. (Amasa will eventually seem to fill the role of "Joseph . . . history's most celebrated cuckold.") By ducking the snowball, Dunny accomplishes a forbidden wish. He is anything but direct about acknowledging that this wish might have originally been directed against the "propriety" of another bedroom. In this view the terrible scene with his mother would not *cause* his defection to Mary Dempster; it simply brings to light the inevitable desire and guilt on both sides that can only express itself through violence or displacement. The decorum of his home has been so strictly maintained as to allow for no satisfying expression of the ambivalent feelings which bind it together. Dunny can in no way realize himself within it, and so turns to a surrogate family scarcely aware of his pretensions to sonship. Liesl defines Fifth Business as "the odd man out, the person who has no opposite of the other sex." But Dunny's romance with the Dempsters may be the ultimate definition of Fifth Business: playing Oedipus in an adopted triangle. It is a lesson Ramsay cruelly learns late in his story, when, in revealing to Mary Dempster that her son still lives, he sees her turn against the "son" who has adopted her in an awful parody of the full fury of his own mother's love.

In *Fifth Business*, the stone finally comes to represent something like motivation or causality, and Ramsay proves no less guilty than Boy of withholding from attention this dimension of existence. It is that which can reduce mystery to diagnosis. How much of Jung's amplifying system may we not also be tempted to read as an attempt to mystify the meaning of his secret? We may even have here a clue to Jung's final resistance to Freud, since he jealously guards as *his* secret the wishes and anxieties that Freud asks every man to accept as his patrimony. Would not assent to the Oedipus complex rob Jung of his unique *numinosum?* The irony of their predicament is that Jung and Ramsay are the keepers of a secret everybody knows. They could have learned as much from "reading Freud."

The quarrel between Freud and Jung comes down to the way we read symbols. Jung juxtaposes the two hermeneutics in *Psychological Types* (Baynes translation): "Every view which interprets the symbolic expression as an analogous or abbreviated expression of a known thing is *semiotic*. A conception which interprets the symbolic expression as the best possible formulation of a relatively unknown factor which cannot conceivably be more clearly or characteristically represented, is *symbolic*." For Jung, Freud is clearly a practitioner of the semiotic method, a crude seeker after referents. Jung redefines "symbolic" interpretation to include his own method and so as to collapse, for all practical purposes, the distinction between manifest and latent content. As Freud wrote to Jung in 1911: "the manifest forms of mythological themes cannot without further investigation be used for purposes of comparison with our psychoanalytical conclusions. One has first to ascertain their latent original forms by tracing them back through historical comparative work so as to eliminate the distortions that have come about in the course of the development of the myth." For Freud, symbols of any sort are always vehicles in search of a tenor; for Jung, they function as completed acts of expression. If they do refer, it is as "an expression of the yet unknown." Any symbol viewed in this prophetic light becomes so overdetermined by possible meanings as to remain more determinate than any translation of it. Jung's way of taking symbols thus guarantees that they will remain nearly final in themselves. If such a view seems to eventuate in a literal-minded approach to symbols, Jung's actual practice avoids this by juxtaposing them against other symbols. His vehicles are vehicles for other vehicles: by constantly ramifying an irreducible code into another code, Jung hovers always on the brink of revelation.

In reading Davies, we find ourselves caught up between Freud and Jung. While the text makes explicit claims for the irreducibility of symbol, and directs attention away from everything but coincidence, the symbols themselves call for a semiotic reading that reduces them back into symptoms. We are left standing athwart symbols that can explicate the finished past or prophesy the open future. Davies encourages a simultaneous exercise of the criticism of suspicion and the criticism of restoration about which Paul Ricoeur has written so eloquently. A quotation from his *Freud and Philosophy* sums up the experience of reading this masterful novel:

> From the beginning we must consider this double possibility: this tension, this extreme polarity, is the truest expression of our "modernity." The situation in which language today finds itself comprises this double possibility, this double solicitation and urgency: on the one hand, purify discourse of its excrescences, liquidate the idols, go from drunkenness to sobriety, realize our state of poverty once and for all; on the other hand, use the most "nihilistic," destructive, iconoclastic movement so as to *let speak* what once, what each time, was *said*, when meaning appeared anew, when meaning was at its fullest. Hermeneutics seems to me to be animated by this double motivation: willingness to suspect, willingness to listen; vow of rigor, vow of obedience. In our time we have not finished doing away with *idols* and we have barely begun to listen to *symbols*.

Misdirecting Attention

Davies has a "magical" style. He would not reject this as an impressionistic description. As a profession of very strict conventions, magic

compels its adepts to master a variety of defenses against the limitations
of audience attention. In one of the trilogy's many self-reflexive passages,
Ramsay applauds Eisengrim's technique of "misdirecting" attention, a
strategy that also proves the essence of his author's style:

> Not a day passed that he did not go through a searching examination of several
> of his illusions, touching up one moment, or subduing another, and always
> refining that subtle technique of misdirecting the attention of his audience,
> which is the beginning and end of the conjurer's art.

Whenever we turn to examine the controlling illusions of the trilogy,
Davies directs us toward artlessness rather than art. The question becomes
whether we will accept his effects as expressive of the mysterious (the
uniqueness of a personal style), or as protective of the explicable (the
machinery of a consciously adopted strategy). If seeing here is believing,
more also goes on than meets the eye. By fostering with respect to his
own technique a sense of imminent revelation nearly always qualified by
our inevitable suspicion, Davies creates a style that gently urges us to
enjoy the double-mindedness which is the essence of interpretation.

Each of Davies's narrators creates the impression of something with-
held. I have already adduced this quality of Ramsay's voice as another
evidence of his retentiveness. But how does one explain the consistency
of tone as David succeeds Ramsay and Eisengrim David? And how does
one account for the fact that their stubborn discretion extends from
matters of substance to matters of style? Few will fail to notice that
Davies's speakers withhold key facts. But what are we to make of their
holding themselves back from indulgence in anything but a plain style?
As one reads further into the trilogy, a device that seems to serve the
purposes of character development looks increasingly like an imperative
for the author. For Davies, unobtrusiveness *is* style.

Davies's juxtaposition of rebel Jung against father Freud allows each of
us to participate in a rejection of authority, or "beginnings," or antecedent
facts. The desire not to be bound by the reductive or the definitive
surfaces everywhere in the trilogy, especially in those moments when the
hero-narrators turn away from limiting conclusions with a nonchalant or
studied reticence. But the acts these narrators hide from the reader may
amount to little compared to the insight which their styles allow them to
hide from themselves. When Dunny prattles on about adolescent sex in
the gravel pit as a "frowzy rough-and-tumble," he appears to be facing up
to a fact of life from which he actually distances himself through ironic
jargon. The running argument between Eisengrim and Ingestree reduces
the problem of truth to the problem of decorum. Both embrace the
position that the morality of style necessarily determines the validity of
interpretation: "There are double words for everything: the word that
swells and the word that belittles; my brother cannot fight me with a
word." Whether to amplify or reduce proves for each of Davies's speakers
a decisive stylistic and moral choice.

Roly sees style merely as defense. He tears into Robert Houdin's memoirs, so concerned with the act of "giving things away," with an analyst's glee:

> "What was all that generosity meant to conceal? Because he was concealing something, take my word for it. The whole of the *Confidences* is a gigantic whitewash job, a concealment. Analyse the tricks and you will get a subtext for the autobiography, which seems so delightfully bland and cozy."

With this speech the notion of a subtext is born. (Do we notice that *"Confidences"* at once promises a con and a confiding?) Magnus submits to tell his life story in order to supply an "enriching, but not necessarily edifying, background" to what will be "seen" in the Lind movie. His narration becomes the trilogy's most self-conscious display of style, while proving consistent with the strategies first employed by Ramsay in *Fifth Business*. Both narrators conceive of style as more constructive than defensive. Thus Ramsay answers Eisengrim's first act of autobiographical speaking with one of sympathetic listening:

> "I have spent a good deal of time since last night wondering whether I should tell you anything about my life," said Eisengrim, after dinner that evening, "and I think I shall, on the condition that you regard it as a secret among ourselves. After all, the audience doesn't have to know the subtext, does it? Your film isn't Shakespeare, where everything is revealed; it is Ibsen, where much is implied."
> How quickly he learns, I thought. And how well he loves the power of pretending something is secret which he has every intention of revealing. I turned up my mental, wholly psychological historian's hearing-aid, determined to miss nothing, and to get at least the skeleton of it on paper before I went to sleep.

In the Deptford Trilogy implication everywhere wins out over revelation —this much is obvious. More interesting perhaps is Davies's suggestion that while we typically think of style as the expression of a performer, we might also recognize it as the projection of an audience. The way a reader *takes* an author's style at least partly determines what it will be. Always alive to the dynamics of the stage, Davies reminds us that an actor's intention activates—it does not wholly create—an onlooker's attention. Each of us approaches Davies's text with his unique "hearing-aid"; the generosity of the trilogy lies in its apparent appeal to two very different sorts of ears.

While Davies permits a reader to listen with a wholly "psychological" ear, he clearly prefers that the reader give himself up to the pleasures of a different sort of illusion. While always keeping psychological facts alive, Davies repeatedly "misdirects" attention away from them. The meaning of the text reduces—or expands—to what the reader will notice. And he is not asked to notice detail that helps to reduce behavior to motivation. This is as true in the textural matter of allusion as in the structural problem of interpretation. Davies capitalizes on a "fallacy" of his own invention—The Fallacy of The Casual Example. While in this fictional world casual allusions seem to abound, in fact there are none. A few quick examples: The three women Ramsay numbers among his sexual conquests, as Wilfred Cude has noticed, possess dimensions Ramsay may have missed—Agnes Day (*Agnus Dei*) Gloria Mundy (*Gloria Mundi*) and Libby Doe (libido). And the examples for which Ramsay casually reaches when he wishes to display Biblical erudition prove no less revealing of an anxiety over fatal women that he may never have entirely faced: "I could spot Jael spiking Sisera, or Judith with the head of Holofernes, readily enough." Who could hope to notice that one of Liesl's favorite operas, *Contes d'Hoffmann*, is also Freud's central example of the uncanny in literature? And are we supposed to remember Jung's most famous dream of underground descent (which led him "to the concept of the 'collective unconscious'") when it reappears as David's frustrated attempt to explore the Gothic excavations? These are small sleights, but they contribute (once noticed) to a substantial wariness, and to a sense that at least two subtexts compete here for hegemony.

A more complex patterning of allusion reveals the following: these three novels joke so frequently about excremental functions as to seem scato-logical. Davies's insistence on this function may distract us however from one every bit as important—from what could be called the "oral theme." The trilogy which appears to be an exploration of autonomy and shame can just as consistently be read as about the violation and preservation of boundaries. The great treat in this world is incorporation. Mrs. Ramsay's "idea of a good son was a pretty small potato." Once she has died Dunstan can admit his relief that "I knew she had eaten my father, and I was glad I did not have to fight any longer to keep her from eating me." Magnus sets out "to eat" Sir John, and, according to Ingestree, does so. David Staunton internalizes his image of his father to avoid being consumed by it. The trilogy ends in an orgy of incorporation. While Dunny admits to having "swallowed the pill" of his guilt, Boy swallows the stone—but not before setting out, as Magnus testifies, "to devour me." And what is Liesl's connection with all of this? She is Vitzlipützli, "the least of the demons" (as her satisfying footnote reveals near the end of *World of Wonders*) attendant upon Faust. This belated explication of her baroque stage name meshes with a sufficient number of our impressions of Liesl as to perhaps satisfy any lingering curiosity about her. But through an allusion destined to become legendary, Davies connects Liesl to the "oral theme" through associations carried by her name which she chooses not to mention. If we remember that Ramsay meets Liesl in

Mexico, perhaps we can moderate our astonishment at discovering that "Vitzlipützli" is also the name of an Aztec god of sacrifice given to eating unlucky Spaniards. In the first Joycean footnote to Davies's work, a two-page article in *Canadian Literature* (Spring 1978) dredges up all available allusions to the name of "Vitzlipützli" and puts Davies on the map as a master of the literature of allusion. That Davies gives Liesl multiple identities is interesting; her link to a mode of pagan incorporation more literal and thorough than any other envisioned in the trilogy may even be fascinating; but the way Davies achieves all this is what remains important. He proves himself one of the greatest living adepts of the mode of inconspicuous allusion. He leaves the overdetermined as underdetermined as the most casual reader might wish. This is magical; it reminds us that our existence in multiple contexts promises always to undermine the one-dimensionality of any fact.

The Quality of a Death

Davies ends *The Table Talk of Samuel Marchbanks* (1949) by granting himself three wishes. The first is for "a hearty middle age." From the very beginning of his career (disregarding the 1939 *Shakespeare's Boy Actors*, his one tribute to the value of youth), Davies has written as if middles were a departure rather than a reaction. This is as true for authors as for characters. Middles of lives—of careers—are less determined by origins than preparatory for ends. All one's life can be looked upon as a preparation; not, as Yeats says, "for something that never happens," but for what Davies calls, in *Question Time*, "the quality of a death."

Davies's works are full of people who *seem* to commit suicide. *King Phoenix* (1953) ends with each player left to assess his part in the fatal fall—or was it a leap?—of the king. *Tempest-Tost* (1951) fades into the bathos of Hector and his broken noose; the hero of *A Mixture of Frailties* (1958) finally succeeds in taking his own life. In each case five characters survive to claim some responsibility for the deed. The unknown identities in this "usual cabal" generate the momentum of mystery in the Deptford Trilogy. Do we not keep reading in order to discover why a man's life ended rather than to appreciate how it may have begun?

The consequences of such momentum are anything but morbid. It encourages us to face forward rather than back, as if identity were not behind but something evermore about to be. Determinism can scarcely linger out its claims before the pressures of anticipation. Above all, Davies seems to prize a potential beyond analysis in his characters, his symbols, in himself. He now finds himself, however, in the difficult position of a man who seems to have realized his potential. While the drama of his career *may* be over, our chance to savor it has just begun.

The mystery of Davies's career turns upon the years between 1958 and 1970. What happened to transform the urbane satirist of *A Mixture of Frailties* into the uncanny psychological novelist of *Fifth Business?* How do we account for the happy series of synchronicities that enable Claude Bissel to nominate the Deptford Trilogy "the major piece of prose fiction in Canadian Literature"? Geraldine Anthony speaks of the "final fascinating creation of the real Monica Gall," as if Davies had achieved in the heroine of his first trilogy a fully rounded character. Hugo McPherson argues that "for the first time in his fiction" Davies creates in Monica "a protagonist whom we know fully and through whose eyes we see the action unfold." Monica does become a sympathetic character, and sympathy was what Davies needed to give. But she is still held at a distance through the third person, more told than shown. She possesses none of Ramsay's quality of the unsaid. Davies's later prose invokes *and* represses a sense of the unexpressed. As identity comes to be defined psychologically rather than socially, his theme hovers between guilt and shame. Shame had been the dominating emotion in the Salterton Trilogy, and the struggle to avoid it had turned its characters toward the world. In the Deptford Trilogy Davies moves toward a psychology of guilt, without relinquishing his fascination with shame. We confront characters who seem, even within the framework of a unified interpretative scheme, motivated by opposing if not contradictory impulses. Where they are "motivated" at all—the doubleness and depth of these recent characters depends upon their being allowed to author their own stories and thereby to obscure the question of motivation altogether. Reading the Salterton Trilogy remains an exercise in discrimination and judgment; reading the Deptford Trilogy is self-incriminating and leads, with any courage, to self-judgment. Davies's masterpiece involves us in a truly "speculative" adventure. The text *reflects*. It thus fulfills his epigraph (borrowed from Lichtenberg) to *A Voice from the Attic* (1960): "A book is a mirror. When a monkey looks in, no apostle can look out."

But how did Davies evolve from an author who asks us to point the finger at others into one who directs it back against ourselves? Such processes are easier to describe than explain. Davies published only three plays in the twelve years between the two trilogies. He finished the first trilogy at the age of forty-five; he began publishing the second at the age of fifty-seven. To say that these were the years in which he "was gathering his forces for the decade which was to prove the peak of his literary life" suggests a calculated reservation of strength. Davies apparently began working on *Fifth Business* soon after publishing *A Mixture of Frailties:* in a personal communication to the author he estimated that "it took about ten years to get *Fifth Business* into a shape where I wanted to write it." From the middle of the sixties on it may nevertheless have looked at times as if the future would never arrive; the middle of any crisis can feel all too much like an end. Since this period covers just those "middle" years about which Davies has been such an enthusiastic theorist, perhaps he can best speak for himself about what lies in store for every author who survives his youth. While I have pursued the origin and course of the first half of a career, Davies champions the unique pleasures of the second. Both of us agree that somewhere must come a moment of turning:

> What is the nature of this change? It is part of intellectual and particularly spiritual growth. As Jung explains it, in the early part of life—roughly for the first half of it—man's chief aims are personal and social. He must grow up, he must find his work, he must find out what kind of sex life he is going to lead, he must achieve some place in the world and attempt to get security within it, or else decide that security is not important to him. But when he has achieved these ends, or come to some sort of understanding with this part of existence, his attention is turned to matters that are broader in scope, and sometimes disturbing to contemplate. His physical strength is waning rather than growing; he has found out what sex is, and though it may be very important to him it can do little to surprise him; he realizes that some day he is really going to die and that the way he approaches death is of importance to him; he finds that without God (using that name to comprehend all the great and inexplicable things and the redemptive or destructive powers that lie outside human command and understanding) his life lacks a factor that it greatly needs; he finds that, in Jung's phrase, he is not the master of his fate except in a very modest degree and that he is in fact the object of a supraordinate subject. And he seeks wisdom rather than power—though the circumstances of his early life may continue to thrust power into his hands.
>
> Now, the paradox of this change is that it does not make him an old man. What will make him an old man is a frightened clinging to the values of the first half of life.

Davies gave this speech in 1968, while finishing his masterpiece. What else could have given him the confidence to go on to claim "and I may as well tell you that I regard the writing I have done as little more than a preparation for the work I mean to do." Perhaps the most we can say about Davies's crisis of middle life is that he weathered it by making it his subject.

The three heroes of *Fifth Business* congratulate themselves on having "rejected our beginnings and become something our parents could not have foreseen." Only David Staunton, the man of the next generation, has felt, and chosen to confront, the burden of the parent. David's search for identity begins as if it were merely an inquiry into the quality of a death—his father's. While "the death of his father is always a critical moment in a man's life," David is the first man in the trilogy to pause and discover that such researches lead eventually back to the son. A Jungian analyst makes this pronouncement, but we may remember that the very interpretative scheme David rejects came into its first form (*The Interpretation of Dreams*), in Freud's words, "as my reaction to my father's death." Davies bestows upon each of his characters the opportunity to conduct such analysis, but only in David's case, and then only by way of a system which tends to oppose regressive analysis, does any one voluntarily reach toward it.

The danger in this strategy is that the author of such characters may also seem, in the words which sum up Boy Staunton, "the kind of man who truly believes you can wipe out the past simply by forgetting it yourself." Such a view certainly places strict constraints upon any novelistic imagination. If bound by his psychology not to trace identity backwards, Davies can deprive himself of the ground out of which complex character ordinarily emerges. Does not the thinness in Eisengrim's characterization result from his exploitation of a myth of personal discontinuity? In the portrayal of his magician Davies indulges and exposes the limits of filial impiety.

World of Wonders at first appears to be the weakest novel in the trilogy because it is largely spoken by a character who refuses to believe that he is one. *The Manticore* can be faulted as contrived (the coincidence of his cure in the Bear Cave fits all too neatly into David's psychic schedule), but it never courts ennui. But what except boredom looms as we prepare to listen to a man who does not believe that his story connects with what he is? Eisengrim's story would appear to be a sum of synchronicities. Seven pages before he meets Liesl he is asked to fix a monkey-headed cane. Then she promptly appears as a "sort of monkey." And of course Rango anticipates both. Such coincidences seem to hold his life together. The most one can hope to fashion in a chancy universe is a *role*. A self-conscious theatricality proves the height of integrity in a world which renders up no continuous sense of self. "I am truly Magnus Eisengrim. The illusion, the lie, is a Canadian called Paul Dempster."

Like all the other characters in the trilogy, however, Magnus has integrity in spite of himself. Without in any way dismissing the importance of his self-generated role, we can also come to understand it as determined by what Paul has been. Magnus rejects "Paul" at the end of *The Manticore*. In the three years during which Davies composed *World of Wonders*, the perspective on (and of) Eisengrim shifts. Not only does Davies imply that his past flows into his present; he actually transforms Eisengrim into a spokesman for origins.

The magician's confessional urge itself provides the best evidence of a desire to connect then and now. His motivation for spilling his past begins as an act of revenge against the "educated" Lind and Ingestree.

Along the way Eisengrim succumbs to the romance of authorship. ("But what's an autobiography?" Ingestree asks. "Surely it's a romance of which one is oneself the hero.") The urge to tell a good tale necessitates a conception of character he has previously rejected. The questions of his auditors prod Magnus to make connections he would otherwise repress. The marvelous achievement of *World of Wonders* is to reveal auto- biography as a redemptive act. Its intrinsic conventions compel Eisengrim to form—to reform—himself into a human being.

The measure of this change is in Eisengrim's self-conscious embrace of a psychology he had once abhorred. The pressures of (self) authorship operate on him even before he begins to tell his story. He responds to the mere suggestion that he might do so with the astounding admission that "I suppose whatever I do is rooted in what I am, and have been." Like all autobiographers, he uses the mode for self-defense as well as revelation. Lind rightly objects that "He has let us think that his childhood made him a villain." More remarkable is that Magnus has seen fit to include it in his story at all. He goes so far as to agree with Dunny (where has Dunny ever voiced such a sentiment?) "that a man is the sum and total of all his actions, from birth to death." Magnus even comes to reiterate the trilogy's most insistent refrain, that the uncanny must be brought to light. He is speaking of the

> name of Eisengrim, the name of the wolf in the old fables; but the name really means the sinister hardness, the cruelty of iron itself. I took the name, and recognized the fact, and thereby got it up out of my depths so that at least I could be aware of it and take a look at it, now and then. I won't say I domesticated the wolf, but I knew where his lair was, and what he might do.

Magnus here proves himself, like all our other heroes, the hero of insight.

The wolf repairs mechanical dolls. When Liesl speculates that "there must have been in him some special quality that made it worth his while to invest these creatures of metal with so much vitality and charm of action," she invokes Magnus's uncanny affinity with the uncanny. He has a special closeness with all things which seem lifelike but are not, he fixes clocks, he "understood time." Magnus himself remains uncanny to the reader who persists in seeing him as an automaton masquerading as a human being. But "uncertainty whether an object is living or inanimate, which we admit in regard to the doll Olympia [substitute the automaton Eisengrim] is quite irrelevant in connection with this other, more striking instance of uncanniness." Freud is speaking here of an apparent un- certainty experienced in watching *Tales of Hoffmann*, which, when resolved, does not dispel our sense of estranged familiarity. He proceeds to psychoanalyze the elements of the opera which continue to produce an uncanny effect even after we have settled in our minds the distinction between its animate and inanimate elements. The same lingering sense of the uncanny invests Paul Dempster, even after we have discovered that he is alive rather than an automaton. Freud's final synthesis of the themes most productive of the uncanny in literature reads like a description of Eisengrim's career:

> We must content ourselves with selecting those themes of uncanniness which are most prominent, and seeing whether we can fairly trace them also back to infantile sources. These themes are all concerned with the idea of a "double" in every shape and degree, with persons, therefore, who are to be considered identical by reason of looking alike; Hoffmann accentuates this relation by transferring mental processes from the one person to the other—what we should call telepathy—so that the one possesses knowledge, feeling and experience in common with the other, identifies himself with another person, so that his self becomes confounded, or the foreign self is substituted for his own—in other words, by doubling, dividing and interchanging the self.

As the evidence begins to mount up, it may appear as if in creating Eisengrim Davies had simply followed a recipe for "the uncanny." The magician not only shadows Willard but formally accepts the role of Sir John's "Fetch." As he grows in life his second selves begin to wither. He breathes their breath. Why is Eisengrim's will toward self-extension through a double so strong? Could we not answer this question, the text would stand convicted of fabricating portentous but inexplicable puzzles. Again Freud proves appropriate here. Doubling proves so evocative of the uncanny, he argues, because "such ideas . . . have sprung from the soil of unbounded self-love, from the primary narcissism which holds sway in the mind of the child." The greatest infantile fantasy of all, of one's own immortality, is thus served by the "invention of doubling as a preservation against extinction." Eisengrim seeks everywhere a double—a feat magnificently accomplished in his "duplication" of the world on a stage—so as to never again be the vulnerable creature that suffered so sublimely terrifying an origin.

I have said a good deal about the way Paul was conceived, but little about the way he was born. Paul's birth was a trauma for himself and for his mother. Birth itself is uncanny enough:

> When your mother bore you, she went down in her anguish to the very gates of Death, in order that you might have life. Nothing that you could do subsequently would work off your birth-debt to her. No degree of obedience, no unfailing love, could put the account straight. Your guilt toward her was a burden you carried all your life.

Eisengrim here approaches Hemingway's sense of a beginning, albeit from a perspective more beholden to the bearer than to the one born. Davies expands Hemingway by reminding us that birth obligates as well as alienates. But he too cannot get round the claims of the aggrieved son. Paul's entire life can be understood as an attempt to recover "eighty days in Paradise."

> I was born eighty days before my time. Poor little Paul. Popular opinion is very rough on foetuses these days. Horrid little nuisances. Rip 'em out and throw them in the trash pail. But who knows what they feel about it? The depth psychologists Liesl is so fond of think they have a very jolly time in the womb. Warm, protected, bouncing gently in their beautiful grotto light. Perhaps it is the best existence we ever know, unless there is something equally splendid for us after death—and why not? That earliest life is what every humanitarian movement and Welfare State seeks to restore, without a hope of success. And Boy Staunton, by a single mean-spirited action, robbed me of eighty days of that princely splendor. Was I the man to fret about the end of his life when he had been so cavalier about the beginning of mine?

In this last sentence Davies's fascination with the quality of a death gives way to "the elementary wisdom of caring about the quality of a birth." Again he displays the generous double-mindedness that can countervail its own announced concerns. The admission here goes beyond acceptance of the overwhelming consequences of Paul's birth, his premature exposure to the experience of the uncanny. His becomes a universal claim; he was born too soon, but, given the sweetness of the grotto light, we all are.

Padre Blazon asks for "a Christ who will show me how to be an old man." Davies delivers Jung, but he never assumes that in the search for understanding we will refuse to fall back on Freud. Whichever psychology one adopts orients one in time. Freud's is not simply a myth of fathers; it is a myth *for* fathers. Davies tries to free the middle from the tyranny of origins by attracting attention toward a future that could not have been predicted. He even invents a myth of multiple fathers—"The fathers you choose for yourself are the significant ones"—in which character and author both seem to believe. Each psyche emerges from its primary bonds with an excess of energy still waiting to be shaped into identity through affiliation with a *chosen* authority. Even Magnus has (until he devours them) his Willard, his Sir John. As Jung observes: "A man is only half understood when we know how everything in him came into being." Certainly so, yet Davies's genius is to deny the claims of neither half of life in his effort to liberate the middle. Even his most prodigal son learns to speak for how he came to be. In extending this invitation to experience the tension between archeology and teleology, Davies confers upon his reader the only kind of freedom he, as a reader, truly values. "Where there's a will, there are always two ways." In reading the Deptford Trilogy we move through a true middle, one governed by a conflict of interpretations that continually refreshes both memory and hope.

ᴥᔡ *Epilogue*

CAREER AS CANON

Criticism, like the imagination, is always at the end of an era; it perpetually casts about for strategies to renew its reason for being. We have temporarily exhausted the criticism of works and structures; it is time to turn to careers. Attention to the unfolding shape of the author's development in time strikes more and more critics as a way of reappraising even the most familiar texts. David Kalstone's theory of "refiguration" grounds our sense of the poet less in his key images than in the history of his revisions of them. Stephen Greenblatt's Renaissance scholarship locates the interpretation of any finished work of art within the ongoing artwork of a life. Stephen Railton translates Cooper's apparently fragmented literary output into an integrated emotional career. Gary Lee Stonum reads Faulkner's career as the history of his changing attitudes toward arrest. For each of these critics the search for temporal patterns of renewal refreshes, by proposing new criteria for creative success, the project of criticism itself.

Writing about careers affords its special pleasures. There is the chance to dignify, because of its new-found location in the authorial curve, the heretofore "minor" work. The demarcation of "turning points" between books or poems provides all the drama once generated by locating climaxes within them. The specification of beginnings, middles, and ends can satisfy the critic's nostalgia for narrative. And the belief that literary production ought to be aligned with all those extrinsic forces that operate upon it can more readily be put to the test in a project which traces a motion in time.

150

It is this last possibility which I take to be the most promising new departure for criticism. Why should it be a pleasure to align literary production with the extrinsic forces which shape and are shaped by it? It returns the author to the human community. Attention to births, marriages, friendships, letters, and budgets restores our sense of literature as written by men and women who live with particular hopes and fears, in particular times and places. A student of careers begins by valuing the tension between fact and wish that gives the work power and momentum. He then searches for some destination which, when reached, relieves the tension. As I read careers, they move teleologically, but are to be understood archeologically. As viewed through the parable of the prodigal son, careers naturally reach toward the resolution provided by *insight*, and are set in motion by the inevitability of *conflict*. The meaning of the conflict with the father resides precisely in the act of investigating the meaning of the conflict with the father. The moment in which the struggle with the father emerges into the light—is given conscious shape—is the moment when it acquires its full meaning. In psychological careers (as in critical enterprises) the recognition of form corresponds to the discovery of significance. "I am enacting this story": to say this is to understand as well as to describe. Criticism of careers thus presumes a consonance of form and meaning, but the form and the meaning arise out of the "before" and "after" of a personal history, rather than from the balanced stress of forces in a timeless work of art. And it is a kind of criticism which redefines success in art as very much closer than it has often been taken to be to success in life; it reminds us that we are all authoring, in however unconscious a form, our own beginnings and middles. Emphasis shifts from style to something we might best call *courage*—the courage to take responsibility, in a moment of insight, for the conflicts which shape our stories.

In studying the shape of a career, then, I have become convinced that psychological courage counts for as much as aesthetic achievement, and ought to figure, where it can, in our estimate of an author's worth. Many of the moments of accommodation I discuss occur in works which appear as aberrations in a canon. Valuing a work as part of a career creates a canon altogether different from one which results from the study of individual works or overarching structures. Critics have argued, for instance, that in *For Whom the Bell Tolls* the triumph of Hemingway's vision requires the breakdown of his style. In order to face the experience of family which had previously eluded him, Hemingway turns to a mode of self-conscious exposition that utterly betrays the wintry economies of *In Our Time*. Even those who find this style a falling off have difficulty denying that *For Whom the Bell Tolls* makes a significant psychological advance in its author's fiction. The novel's power flows from the reader's

intuition of the author's struggle to overcome the lifelong fears that still
threaten his new vision of hope. The book deserves praise for this advance
alone. But its new style commands respect and gives pleasure, as I have
argued, by showing how much more of human life than Hemingway had
ever previously acknowledged can be comprehended within it. By
attending to such psychological careers we can learn to recognize in an
apparent breach of style the strictest observance of a new and renovating
discipline.

I am not simply advocating the writing of biography. Ellmann's *James
Joyce* is a monumental work, but one that in its brilliant inclusiveness
discourages the search for the mainspring of creativity. Certainly all
artistic careers are overdetermined. But the critic of careers will need to
sacrifice fidelity to the variety of a life so as to achieve a more limited
goal; the isolation of a career's governing paradigm. The major obstacle
to the study of a career is the abundance of contingencies that can
reasonably be assumed to operate upon it. Abstraction from the mass of
textual, biographical, and historical evidence must necessarily control the
act of interpretation. Every author acts out a number of competing or
parallel careers, and a book could well be written which treated his work
as a function of a host of variables. I have tried rather to trace one
variable—the wandering from and return to the source of authority
—through the first half of seven careers and the middle of an eighth. My
intention has been to sacrifice exhaustive depth so as to achieve suggestive
breadth.

Where do the paradigms come from? The search for some shaping
force in the lifework of the artist redounds back upon the critic, who
keeps being troubled into the awareness that to impose is not to discover.
Criticism seems always a compromise between these two modes of
definition. Looking at careers has the advantage of bringing this interplay
into the light. Something in the arc of the career answers something in the
experience of the critic, and the paradigm is born. There is no need to
apologize for this process; the challenge is to ask of oneself as much as
one asks of the artist—an inquest into one's reasons for writing. The
answers proposed may be no more than sufficient fictions, explanations
which temporarily arrest the curve of one's own trajectory in a meaningful
pattern. Such structures are made in order to be unbuilt; at least this
seems to be the lesson of these careers. One can specify turning points,
but only death has the privilege of defining ends. The truly fortunate
careers do not end; they are cut short. It is worth reminding ourselves
that from the perspective of an author a career is something evermore
about to be. The task is to keep moving on. Resolutions only clear the
way for new departures, and we can almost hear the still living artist say,
in his moment of hard-won survey,

I have walked through many lives,
some of them my own,
and I am not who I was,
though some principle of being
abides, from which I struggle
not to stray.

Notes

[Numerals at the left refer to pages in this book. The initial phrases of each note indicate the beginning and end of the passage in the text to which the note pertains.]

Introduction: The Moment of Return

xiii "I can . . . in tears."—*William Blake: The Critical Heritage*, ed. G. E. Bentley (London: Routledge & Kegan Paul, 1975), p. 32.

xv "meaning is . . . is important."—*All the King's Men* (New York: Harcourt, Brace, 1946), pp. 287-88.

xvi "precipitation."—*The Art of the Novel*, ed. Richard P. Blackmur (New York: Scribner's, 1934), p. 25.   "reflexion."—Ibid., p. 27.

xvii "revenge against time."—John T. Irwin, *Doubling and Incest: Repetition and Revenge* (Baltimore: Johns Hopkins University Press, 1975), p. 3.   "Writing seemed . . . dreaded maturity."—Geneviève Moreau, *The Restless Journey of James Agee* (New York: William Morrow, 1977), p. 271.

xviii "misdirects."—*Fifth Business* (1970; rpt. Middlesex, England: Penguin, 1977), p. 211.

xix "Perhaps,/The . . . most master."—*The Palm at the End of the Mind* (New York: Vintage-Knopf, 1971), p. 232.

1. Modernity and Paternity: James's The American

1 "How have . . . I made."—Milton, *Paradizse Lost*, 8, 408-9.   "uncanny brood." —Blackmur, *Art of the Novel*, p. 337.   "Actively believe . . . you'll see!"—Ibid., p. 341. "visitors."—Ibid., p. 337.   "the reappearance . . . drawing room."—Ibid.   "its maximum . . . 'The American.'"—Ibid., p. 344.   "the long-stored . . . garment misfitted."—Ibid. "A certain . . . soap-and-water."—Ibid., p. 337.   "literary manners."—Ibid., p. 344. "deputy or delegate."—Ibid., p. 327.   "a convenient . . . and disembodied."—Ibid.   "some more . . . less detached."—Ibid.
2 "the mere . . . irresponsible 'authorship'"—Ibid., p. 328.   "breathe and . . . great

game."—Ibid.   "it's not . . . of it."—Ibid.   "the point . . . answer for."—Ibid.   "We give . . . of choice."—Ibid., p. 348.   "leave us . . . such necessity."—Ibid.   "Our literary . . . we like."—Ibid., pp. 347-48.   "Our relation . . . is reconstituted."—Ibid., p. 348.

3 "creature."—F. O. Matthiessen, *The James Family* (New York: Knopf, 1947), p. 147. "abject want or destitution."—Ibid.   "how very . . . objective reconciliation."—Ibid., p. 148.   "The discovery . . . we exist."—Emerson, *The Complete Works* (1904), 3: 75. "the only . . . of spirit." Matthiessen, *The James Family*, p. 145.   *"vastation"*—Leon Edel, *Henry James* (New York: Lippincott, 1953), 1: 32.   "became a . . . quivering fear." —Matthiessen, *The James Family*, p. 217.   "spiritual sonship."—Ibid., p. 148.   "I should . . . own mind."—Ibid., p. 146.   "voice within him."—Ibid.   "obscure hurt." —Henry James, *Notes of a Son and Brother* (New York: Scribner's, 1914), p. 298.

4 "We ourselves . . . or living."—Matthiessen, *The James Family*, p. 149.   "Art *makes* life."—*The Letters of Henry James*, ed. Percy Lubbock (New York: Scribner's, 1920), p. 490. "The port . . . *my life."*—Edel, *Henry James* (1969), 4: 350.   "the tie . . . insulated family."—Matthiessen, *The James Family*, p. 55.   "I am . . . of pacification."—Ibid., p. 55.   "You know . . . of betrayal." Ibid., p. 56.   "discourage prodigality."—Edel, *Henry James*, 1: 20.   "property."—Matthiessen, *The James Family*, p. 52.   "every person . . . spontaneous affection."—Ibid., p. 57.

5 "The truth . . . the earth."—Ibid., p. 30.   "But it . . . spiritual mission."—Ibid. "did not . . . from unhappiness."—Ibid., p. 28.   "living superiority . . . of authority." —Ibid., p. 192.

6 "conscious victims . . . misplaced confidence."—*Henry James: The Critical Heritage*, ed. Roger Gard (London: Routledge & Kegan Paul, 1968), p. 48.   "unchallenged instinct." —Blackmur, *Art of the Novel*, p. 25.   "romantic."—Ibid., p. 30.   "effect . . . *after* the fact . . . conscious design."—Ibid.   "the cause . . . the other."—Ibid., pp. 30-31.

7 "I am . . . civilised man."—*The American*, ed. Roy Harvey Pearce and Matthew J. Bruccoli (1877; rpt. Boston: Houghton Mifflin, 1962), p. 32.   "I have . . . old civilisation."—*The American* (1907; rpt. New York: Scribner's, 1935), p. 45.   "modern."—Ibid., p. 229.   "history."—Ibid.   "Is she . . . in them."—*The American* (1877), p. 106.

8 "Newman wondered . . . a history."—*The American* (1907), p. 151.   "Besides, you . . . beyond you."—*The American* (1877), p. 160.   "Besides, you . . . reactionary enough." —*The American* (1907), p. 229.   "Time is money!"—*The American* (1877), p. 124. *"Combien?"*—Ibid., p. 4.   "He had . . . dry and sterile."—Ibid., p. 72.

9 "specialty . . . possible time."—Ibid., p. 134.   "He had . . . turned inward."—*The American* (1907), p. 102.   "You appear . . . for it."—*The American* (1877), p. 69.   "The fact . . . do them!"—Ibid., p. 31.   "resembling oneself."—Ibid., p. 177.   "doesn't have . . . a man."—Ibid., pp. 35-36.   "He doesn't . . . really *is*."—*The American* (1907), p. 50. "It is . . . the observer."—*The Letters of Ralph Waldo Emerson*, ed. Ralph L. Rusk (1939; rpt. New York: Columbia University Press, 1966), 1: 174.

10 "moments at . . . absolute forgetting."—*Blindness and Insight* (New York: Oxford University Press, 1971), p. 147.   "build the . . . the fathers."—*The Complete Works* (1903), 1: 3.   "parricidal imagery."—de Man, *Blindness and Insight*, p. 150.   "The historian . . . cannot coincide."—Ibid., p. 152.   "under too . . . for perspective." —Blackmur, *Art of the Novel*, p. 27.   "the critical . . . waked up."—Ibid., p. 25.

11 "Are you . . . a book?"—*The American* (1877), p. 22.   "One day . . . to ache."—Ibid. "new world."—Ibid., p. 23.   "all this . . . the theatre."—Ibid., p. 22.   "there are . . . little about."—Ibid., p. 23.   "I recall . . . enjoying it."—Blackmur, *Art of the Novel*, pp. 21-22.

12 "Up to . . . of Bellegarde."—Gard, *Henry James*, p. 47.   "to talk . . . extremely disagreeable."—*The American* (1877), p. 346.

13 "a passionate corrector."—*The Complete Tales of Henry James*, ed. Leon Edel (Philadelphia and New York: Lippincott, 1964), 9: 63.   "ideal would . . . a second."—Ibid., p. 63.   "constitutive affinity . . . no past."—de Man, *Blindness and Insight*, pp. 151-52. "fabulous antiquity."—*The American* (1877), p. 38.   "decent narrative."—Ibid., p. 304.

14 "Claire de Cintré . . . illegitimate birth."—'*The American*: A Reinterpretation," *PMLA* 74 (December 1959): 618.   "I see . . . my own."—*The American* (1877), p. 304. "I received . . . the world."—Ibid., p. 174.

15 "The old . . . Virginius did."—Ibid., p. 149.   "specie."—Ibid., p. 46.   "Remember what . . . less to-day!"—Ibid., p. 10.   "The result . . . sift it."—Ibid., p. 45.   "Her influence . . . than I."—Ibid., p. 51.

16 "You have . . . no *fiancée*."—Ibid., p. 56.   "stop her!"—Ibid., p. 355.   "rather disgusted . . . man's philosophy."—Ibid., p. 202.   "her father . . . married brother."—Ibid., p. 38.   "wild."—Ibid.   "especial . . . dear, no!"—Ibid., p. 129.   "Madame Bellegarde . . . eldest-born."—Ibid., p. 133.   "He is . . . second-hand."—Ibid.   "incarnation of . . . oneself seriously."—Ibid.   "with a . . . admirable mother."—Ibid., p. 95.   "You must . . . this one."—Ibid., p. 132.

17 "I have . . . tell you."—Ibid., p. 93.   "alone and palely loitering."—Ibid., p. 221. "Did you . . . sans Merci?"—Ibid., p. 220.   "statue which . . . as stone."—Ibid., p. 105. "He kissed . . . shining floor."—Ibid., p. 286.   "in observing . . . the moon."—Ibid., p. 102.   "very good friends."—Ibid., p. 105.   "we are . . . and Electra."—Ibid.   "honour of . . . other members."—Ibid., p. 95.

18 "I have . . . to know."—Ibid., p. 273.   "apologise for . . . my brother."—Ibid., p. 271.   "There's a . . . ask me."—Ibid., p. 283.   *"general . . . vulgar communities."* —Blackmur, *Art of the Novel*, p. 33.   "It is . . . your antecedents."—*The American* (1877), p. 252.   "hocus-pocus."—Blackmur, *Art of the Novel*, p. 34.   "greatest intensity . . . too rash."—Ibid., p. 33.   "elder brother."—*The American* (1877), p. 239.   "I ought . . . small boy."—Ibid., p. 267.

19 "With me . . . father's arms."—Ibid., p. 184.   "What we . . . no wrong."—Ibid., p. 340.   "great nonsense!"—Ibid.   "outrage."—Blackmur, *Art of the Novel*, p. 35. "I am . . . consoling themselves."—Edel, *Tales*, 2: 363.

20 "to invalidate . . . than fatherhood."—*The Greek Myths: 2* (1955; rpt. Baltimore: Penguin, 1968), p. 63.   "politico-religious allegory."—Philip Slater, *The Glory of Hera* (Boston: Beacon Press, 1968), p. 162.   "the oral-narcissistic . . . simultaneously violated." —Ibid., p. 88.

21 "the father . . . the family."—Ibid., p. 57.   "idealization."—Ibid., p. 53.   "capricious and irresponsible."—Ibid., p. 54.   "danger of . . . gobbled up."—Ibid., p. 189. "tragedies it . . . and destructive."—Ibid., p. 12.   "At some . . . their men."—Edel, *Henry James*, 1: 53-54.   "Before the . . . and contradictory."—Ibid., pp. 50-51.

22 "apparent ineffectuality."—Ibid., p: 52.   "duration."—James, *Notes of a Son*, p. 298.   "we wholesomely . . . drank contradictions."—Edel, *Henry James*, 1: 47.   "are creations . . . cultural treason."—"*The American*," in *The Air of Reality: New Essays on Henry James*, ed. John Goode (London: Methuen, 1972), p. 29.   "first assured . . . tenderest age."—*A Small Boy and Others* (London: Macmillan, 1913), p. 15.   "she was . . . *any* relation."—*Notes of a Son*, p. 179.

23 "How can . . . more so?"—Ibid., p. 180.   "To have . . . every penetration?"—Ibid., p. 177.   "role . . . the father."—Slater, *The Glory of Hera*, p. 179.

24 *"Soundless, selfless, sleepless."*—Edel, *Henry James,* 1: 41. *"idealist."*—*The American* (1877), p. 100. "mentally . . . not suspect."—Ibid. "Newman was . . . of women."—Ibid., p. 27.

25 "strong man."—Blackmur, *Art of the Novel,* p. 22. "a being . . . His creatures." —Matthiessen, *The James Family,* p. 168.

2. Yeats and Synge: The Cuchulain Complex

26 "Go to . . . Arran Islands."—David H. Greene and Edward M. Stephens, *J. M. Synge: 1871-1909* (New York: Macmillan, 1959), p. 61. "Did ever . . . be old?"—J. M. Synge, *Collected Works,* ed. Alan Price (London: Oxford University Press, 1966), 2: 57. "I gave . . . the answer."—Ibid. "But I . . . things plain."—*The Collected Plays of W. B. Yeats* (New York: Macmillan, 1952), p. 306.

27 "What if . . . that something?"—*A Vision* (New York: Macmillan, 1956), p. 29. "self-sacrifice . . . self-realization."—Yeats, *Autobiographies* (London: Macmillan, 1955), p. 465. "copy Christ."—Ibid., p. 330. "All my . . . complex forms."—Ibid. *"will-ful* failure."—Sigmund Freud, *Dora,* ed. Philip Rieff (New York: Macmillan, 1963), p. 13.

28 "new divinity."—*A Vision,* p. 27. "down soul . . . and body."—Ibid. "I— though . . . predestined part."—*The Collected Poems of W.B. Yeats* (New York: Macmillan, 1956), p. 247. "An abstract . . . stories run."—Ibid., p. 283.

29 "there is . . . and thought."—*Essays and Introductions* (New York: Macmillan, 1961), p. 107. "the Cuchulain . . . Irish sagas."—*Yeats and Anglo-Irish Literature* (Liverpool: Liverpool University Press, 1974), p. 75.

30 "best play."—*The Letters of W. B. Yeats,* ed. Allan Wade (London: Rupert Hart-Davis, 1968), p. 444. "old themes."—*Collected Poems,* p. 336. "And when . . . en-chanted me."—Ibid. "The first . . . my verses."—*In the Seven Woods* (1903; rpt. Dundrum: Dun Emer Press, 1970), p. 25. "compensating dream."—*Mythologies* (New York: Macmillan, 1959), p. 326. "There are . . . Judgment Day."—Ibid., p. 327.

31 "I think . . . not impossible."—Ibid., p. 336. "Man and . . . another's hearts." —Ibid., p. 335. "We meet . . . other Will."—Ibid., p. 337. "The doctors . . . chaos again."—Ibid., p. 341.

32 "Put up . . . my friend."—*Collected Plays,* p. 174. "We'll stand . . . this out."—Ibid., p. 177. *"First old . . . out, out!"*—Ibid.

33 "was written . . . own son."—Richard Ellmann, *Yeats: The Man and the Masks* (London: Macmillan, 1949), p. 169. "You've wives . . . you will."—*Collected Plays,* p. 171. "who was . . . intellectually dominating."—Ellmann, *Yeats,* p. 23.

34 "The poet . . . should not."—Joseph Hone, *W. B. Yeats: 1865-1939* (New York: Macmillan, 1943), p. 68. "It is . . . his friends."—William M. Murphy, *Prodigal Father: The Life of John Butler Yeats (1839-1922)* (Ithaca, N.Y.: Cornell University Press, 1978), p. 532. "a mere . . . real world."—Ibid., p. 529. "Every night . . . never exorcise." —Ibid., pp. 171-72.

35 "Boy,/If . . . the blood."—*Collected Plays,* p. 177. "[*Showing cloak . . . and* vanished."—Ibid., pp. 175-76. "It is . . . has slain"—Ibid., p. 180. "He was . . . my son."—S. B. Bushrui, *Yeats's Verse-Plays: The Revisions, 1900-1910* (Oxford: Clarendon Press, 1965), p. 60. "I cannot . . . a chicken."—Hone, *W. B. Yeats,* pp. 217-18.

36 "particularly impressive."—*Letters of W. B. Yeats,* p. 444. "In the . . . be old."

—*J. M. Synge: Collected Works* (London: Oxford University Press, 1968), 3: 13.   "I am
. . . the Sorrows."—Ibid., 4: 207.   "what is foretold."—Ibid., p. 209.

37 "Isn't it . . . the end?"—Ibid., p. 211.   "the choice of lives."—Ibid., pp. 267-68.
"aim of . . . seem impossible."—*The Playboy of the Western World: A Collection of Critical
Essays*, ed. Thomas R. Whitaker (Englewood Cliffs, N.J.: Prentice-Hall, 1969), p. 13.

38 "each of . . . in consequence."—Henri Bergson, *Laughter* (New York: Macmillan,
1913), p. 18.   "comic Oedipus."—Whitaker, *Playboy*, p. 57.   "Synge somehow . . .
apparent lightness."—Ibid., p. 76.   "two fine . . . of me."—*Collected Works*, 4: 93.   "I
won't . . . the world."—Ibid., p. 103.   "dirty deed."—Ibid., p. 169.

39 "stretch."—Ibid., p. 165.   "coming to . . . third time."—Ibid., p. 171.   "Them
that . . . lot surely."—Ibid., p. 99.   "I'm master . . . from now."—Ibid., p. 173.   *"with a
broad smile."*—Ibid.   "certain . . . and twenty."—*Autobiographies*, p. 343.

40 "But in . . . our life."—Ibid., pp. 345-46.   "He told . . . to America."—Ibid.,
pp. 343-44.   "subsequent visits . . . finally."—Hone, *W. B. Yeats*, p. 139.   "I did . . .
perhaps."—*Autobiographies*, p. 343.   "He first . . . Synge's death."—See *Essays and
Introductions*, pp. 337-38.   "man destroyed his da."—*Collected Works*, 4: 107.   "When
I . . . with him."—*Autobiographies*, p. 569.

41 "Incest and . . . possessed me."—*Collected Works*, 2: 11.   "He writes . . . utter
folly."—Greene and Stephens, *J. M. Synge*, p. 57.   "Poor Johnnie . . . tell him."—Ibid.,
p. 125.   "Your *Cuchulain* . . . daily bread."—Ibid., p. 305.   "I wrote . . . desired
dialect."—Ibid., p. 129.   "Neither I . . . from him."—*Autobiographies*, p. 511.   "I do
. . . not exist."—Ibid., p. 512.   "Synge has . . . never has."—Ibid.

42 "every now . . . Yeats' work."—*Letters to Molly: John Millington Synge to Maire
O'Neill, 1906-1909* (Cambridge, Mass.: Harvard University Press, 1971), p. 215.   "in-
clined to . . . great deal."—Ibid., p. 114.   "Lady Gregory . . . and kindness."—*Auto-
biographies*, p. 483.   "On the . . . John Synge."—Ibid., p. 380.   "where, but . . . of
Synge?"—Ibid., p. 381.

43 "The author . . . his father."—Hone, *W. B. Yeats*, p. 231.   "My father . . . thrown
back."—*Collected Poems*, p. 300.   "Kill the Author."—James Kilroy, *The 'Playboy'
Riots* (Dublin: Dolmen Press, 1971), p. 17.   "Isn't Mr. . . . a play?"—Hone, *W. B. Yeats*,
p. 230.   "It is . . . raving mad."—Kilroy, *The 'Playboy' Riots*, p. 19.   "No man . . .
forgot them."—*Autobiographies*, p. 483.   "Of course . . . pulled down."—*J. B. Yeats:
Letters to his son W. B. Yeats and others, 1869-1922*, ed. Joseph Hone (New York: E. P.
Dutton, 1946), p. 214.   "Yeats when . . . sore throat."—Greene and Stephens, *J. M.
Synge*, p. 249.

44 "Yeats took . . . his armory."—Hone, *W.B. Yeats*, pp. 231-32.   *"Old Man . . . of
Cuchulain."*—*Collected Plays*, p. 438.   "so old . . . and mother."—Ibid.   "an exchange
. . . remarkable tenderness."—Reg Skene, *The Cuchulain Plays of W. B. Yeats* (New York:
Columbia University Press, 1974), p. 233.   "nobody can . . . not guilt."—*Collected
Plays*, p. 349.

45 "of death and birth."—*Collected Poems*, p. 231.   "Re-live/Their . . . of God."—*Col-
lected Plays*, p. 431.   "Yeats thus . . . own plays."—James W. Flannery, *W. B. Yeats and
the Idea of a Theatre* (Toronto: Macmillan, 1976), p. 336.

46 "theatre business . . . of men."—*Collected Poems*, p. 91.   "sleepless nights . . .
from poetry."—*Autobiographies*, p. 491.   "It is . . . of it."—Hone, *W. B. Yeats*, p. 222.
"Yeats's drama . . . and action."—David R. Clark, *W. B. Yeats and the Theatre of Desolate
Reality* (Dublin: Dolmen Press, 1965), p. 105.   "My body . . . London shop."—*Collected
Poems*, p. 246.   "that his . . . than opponents."—Ellmann, *Yeats*, p. 211.   "your

letter . . . essential passage."—*Letters of W. B. Yeats*, p. 586.   "*old fathers.*"—*Collected Poems*, p. 99.

47 "fully evinced . . . particular man."—*W. B. Yeats: A Critical Anthology*, ed. William H. Pritchard (Middlesex, England: Penguin, 1972), p. 159.   "*Pardon that . . . and mine.*" —*Collected Poems*, p. 99.   "Receptive Man."—*A Vision*, p. 163.   "ready to . . . startling theme."—Ibid., p. 165.   "he is . . . other men."—Ibid., p. 164.   "the outcry . . . of seeing."—Whitaker, *Playboy*, p. 2.   "My mediaeval . . . beggar-man."—*Collected Poems*, pp. 317-18.

48 "Say my . . . such friends."—Ibid., p. 318.   "or . . . The Choice."—Ibid., p. 242 "what surrounds . . . its life."—Denis Donoghue, "The Hard Case of Yeats," *The New York Review of Books*, 26 May 1977, p. 3.   "Bid a . . . to nought."—*Collected Poems*, p. 209.

49 "there is . . . and primitive."—*Letters of John Butler Yeats*, p. 283.   "Though you . . . human love."—*Collected Poems*, pp. 209-10.

50 "Had you . . . ask her."—*Letters of John Butler Yeats*, pp. 280-281.

51 "I would . . . a father."—Ibid., p. 273.

3. Hemingway's Uncanny Beginnings

52 "I am . . . I die."—*For Whom the Bell Tolls* (New York: Scribner's, 1940), p. 16.

53 "At the . . . Nick asked."—*In Our Time* (1925; rpt. New York: Scribner's, 1970), p. 15. "uncanny . . . familiar."—Sigmund Freud, *On Creativity and the Unconscious*, ed. Benjamin Nelson (New York: Harper & Row, 1958), p. 124.

54 "mysterious and homelike."—*In Our Time*, p. 139.   "good place."—Ibid. "Where are . . . going, Dad?"—Ibid., p. 15.   "In the . . . never die."—Ibid., p. 19.   "Do ladies . . . having babies?"—Ibid.   "Is dying hard, Daddy?"—Ibid.   "Something." —Ibid., p. 31.   "He felt . . . ever lost."—Ibid., p. 48.   "He loved . . . near Sion."—Ibid., p. 82.   "the sails . . . a town."—Ibid., p. 31.   "Luz never . . . contracted gonorrhea." —Ibid., p. 66.

55 "*They hanged . . . the morning.*"—Ibid., p. 143.   "hell."—Ibid., p. 111.   "steady." —Ibid., p. 133.   "coffee according to Hopkins."—Ibid., p. 142.   "a good . . . the story."—Ibid.   "*No end . . . no beginning.*"—Ibid., p. 21.

56 "It would . . . like that."—Ibid., p. 155.   "clean and compact."—Ibid.   "This *unheimlich* . . . the beginning."—*On Creativity and the Unconscious*, pp. 152-53.   "He looked . . . days coming."—*In Our Time*, p. 156.   "Robert Cohn . . . Spider Kelly."—*The Sun Also Rises* (1926; rpt. New York: Scribner's, 1970), pp. 3-4.

57 "I was . . . was better."—Ibid., p. 31.   "You . . . have . . . your life."—Ibid.

58 "I walked . . . I walked."—Ibid., pp. 35-36.   "the feeling . . . through again."—Ibid., p. 64.   "I felt . . . all strange."—Ibid., p. 192.   "Rather it . . . the animal."—*Death in the Afternoon* (New York: Scribner's, 1932), p. 16.   "with a definite end."—*The Sun Also Rises*, p. 167.

59 "It's no . . . a steer."—Ibid., p. 141.   "people went . . . tragic sensations."—Ibid., p. 214.   "sure that . . . in flashes."—Ibid., p. 215.   "By the . . . our table."—Ibid., p. 153.   "Everything became . . . any consequences."—Ibid., p. 154.   "This hum . . . of it."—Ibid., p. 161.   "We could . . . to town."—Ibid., p. 164.   "Perhaps as . . . all about."—Ibid., p. 148.   "things that . . . disgusted afterward."—Ibid., p. 149.

60 "to get . . . of friends."—Ibid., p. 11.   "You'll lose . . . about it."—Ibid., p. 245. "In the . . . storm coming."—*A Farewell to Arms* (1929; rpt. New York: Scribner's, 1969), p. 3.

61 "I'm afraid . . . in it."—Ibid., p. 126.   "under their . . . with child."—Ibid., p. 4. "feel trapped biologically."—Ibid., p. 139.   "One day . . . was snow."—Ibid., p. 6.

62 "can be . . . is uncanny."—*On Creativity and the Unconscious*, p. 148.   "uncanny is . . . of repression."—Ibid.   "many people . . . to death."—Ibid., p. 149.   "An uncanny . . . hazy one."—Ibid., p. 157.   "The hay . . . what happened?"—*A Farewell to Arms*, p. 216.   "He had . . . killed you."—Ibid., p. 237.

63 "I could . . . only beginning."—Michael S. Reynolds, *Hemingway's First War: The Making of A Farewell to Arms* (Princeton, N.J.: Princeton University Press, 1976), p. 293. "I was . . . eating cheese."—*A Farewell to Arms*, p. 63.   "I do . . . you want."—Ibid., p. 106.   "splendid chance . . . a messiah."—Ibid., p. 328.   "mistake was . . . the beginning."—Soren Kierkegaard, *Repetition: An Essay in Experimental Psychology* (1941; rpt. New York: Harper & Row, 1964), p. 39.   "the man . . . into life."—Ibid., pp. 39-40.

64 "seeing it . . . chess game."—*A Farewell to Arms*, p. 26.   "They started . . . broken water."—*Across the River and into the Trees* (New York: Scribner's, 1950), p. 1.

65 "The world . . . broken places."—*A Farewell to Arms*, p. 249.   "heart broken." —*Across the River and into the Trees*, p. 114.   "why that . . . fail me."—Ibid., p. 118. "When it . . . the time."—Ibid., p. 138.   "merde, money, blood."—Ibid., p. 18.   "Every time . . . the last."—Ibid., p. 7.   "let us . . . of fun."—Ibid., p. 101.   "he swung . . . second duck."—Ibid., p. 5.   "They were . . . like this."—Ibid., p. 14.

66 "I know . . . is enough."—Ibid., p. 89.   "Death is . . . has entered."—Ibid., p. 219. "the static . . . in painting."—Ibid., p. 178.   "I made . . . And late."—Ibid., p. 94.   "The Colonel . . . reading, proceeded."—Ibid., p. 153.

67 "how close . . . is ecstasy."—Ibid., p. 219.   "a movement without hope."—Ibid., p. 297.   "All I . . . to kill."—*A Farewell to Arms*, p. 117.   "make up . . . in continuity." —*For Whom the Bell Tolls*, p. 168.   "He lay . . . his shoulder."—Ibid., p. 1.

68 "To blow . . . be done."—Ibid., p. 5.   "If you . . . left behind?"—Ibid., p. 21. "looking into . . . in English."—Ibid., p. 27.   "Now, *ahora* . . . your life."—Ibid., p. 166. "time waster."—Ibid., p. 28.   "That is . . . all finish."—Ibid., p. 14.   "That is . . . men end."—Ibid.   "best time."—Ibid., p. 84.   "notions about . . . of time."—Ibid., p. 168.

69 "She said . . . not accept."—Ibid., p. 73.   "Do you . . . to him?"—Ibid., p. 250. "evil visions . . . than that."—Ibid.   "death-to-come."—Ibid., p. 256.   ". . . it is . . . of man."—Ibid.   "in my work."—Ibid., p. 33.   "making believe."—Ibid., p. 346.   "a complete . . . not be."—Ibid., p. 348.

70 "*la gloria*."—Ibid., p. 379.   "nowhere."—Ibid., p. 159.   "dark passage."—Ibid. "now."—Ibid., p. 379.   "that nothing . . . all away."—Ibid., p. 73.   "I would . . . born here."—Ibid., p. 15.   "*I had . . . my father*."—Ibid., p. 59.   "to avoid being tortured." —Ibid., p. 67.   "maybe the . . . that one?"—Ibid., p. 338.   "embarrassed by . . . of it."—Ibid., p. 405.   "both he . . . his father."—Ibid., p. 338.

71 "coward . . . bully."—Ibid., p. 339.   "To understand . . . to forgive."—Ibid., p. 355.   "high plateau."—Ibid., p. 467.   "as true . . . all true."—Ibid.   "I go with thee."—Ibid., p. 463.   "I have . . . *right, have*."—Ibid., p. 467.   "He could . . . the forest."—Ibid., p. 471.   "I don't . . . father did."—Ibid., p. 469.   "I wish . . . more time."—Ibid., p. 380.

4. Faulkner and the Burdens of the Past

73 "Folks dont . . . changing names."—*The Sound and the Fury* (New York: Random House, 1929), p. 71.   "Calvin Burden . . . of Kentucky."—*Light in August* (New York: Random House, 1932), p. 228.   "by an . . . negro voting."—Ibid., p. 235.   "The only . . . grandpa's graves."—Ibid., p. 238.

73 "I didn't . . . forget it."—Ibid., pp. 238-39.   "Why your . . . name? Sartoris."—Ibid., p. 240.   "I think . . . French blood."—Ibid., p. 241.   "I guess . . . got religion."—Ibid. "those who . . . about it."—*The Unvanquished* (New York: Random House, 1938), p. 262. "when they . . . in words."—*Light in August*, p. 227.   "wild throes of nymphomania." —Ibid., p. 245.

74 "She began . . . or expiate."—Ibid., p. 248.   "frustrate and irrevocable years."—Ibid., p. 244.   "A full . . . Calvin's faces."—Ibid., p. 251.   "calm enormity . . . voice unfolded." —Ibid., p. 261.

75 "composed independently."—Regina K. Fadiman, *Faulkner's "Light in August": A Description and Interpretation of the Revisions* (Charlottesville: University Press of Virginia, 1975), p. 87.   "her father . . . a nose."—The manuscript of *Light in August*, in the William Faulkner Collections, University of Virginia Library, p. 93.   "older Calvin." —Ibid.

76 "Hightower has . . . (Faulkner's) consciousness."—*William Faulkner: Two Decades of Criticism*, ed. Frederick J. Hoffman and Olga W. Vickery (East Lansing: Michigan State College Press, 1951), p. 251.   "produces . . . without volition."—*Light in August*, p. 346. "skipped a generation."—Ibid., p. 452.   "only salvation . . . it began."—Ibid.   *"History shall . . . forget you!"*—Joseph Blotner, *Faulkner: A Biography* (New York: Random House, 1974), p. 22.   "Born in . . . in Mississippi."—*Selected Letters of William Faulkner*, ed. Joseph Blotner (New York: Random House, 1977), p. 7.   "It is . . . short space."—"The Falkners and the Fictional Families," *Georgia Review* 30 (Fall 1976): 576-77.

77 "William Faulkner . . . major author."—Ibid., p. 592.   "how close . . . to life."—Ibid., p. 573.

78 "Mother finally . . . days later."—John Faulkner, *My Brother Bill: An Affectionate Reminiscence* (New York: Trident Press, 1963), p. 11.   "he wasn't . . . of thing."—*William Faulkner: Three Decades of Criticism*, ed. Frederick J. Hoffman and Olga W. Vickery (East Lansing: Michigan State University Press, 1960), p. 56.   *"too much."*—*Absalom, Absalom!* (New York: Random House, 1936), p. 207.   "He built . . . Tippah County."—*Letters*, pp. 211-12.   "Suddenly . . . lost consciousness."—Blotner, *Faulkner*, p. 47.

79 "Tell your . . . Miss Fontaine."—Ibid., p. 53.   "A moment . . . his mouth."—Ibid., p. 54.   "If it . . . so much."—Ibid.

80 "Looking at . . . least twice."—Blotner, "The Falkners and the Fictional Families," p. 585.   "The bullet . . . Thurmond's bullet."—Donald Philip Duclos, *Son of Sorrow: The Life, Works, and Influence of Col. William C. Falkner, 1825-1889* (Ann Arbor: University Microfilms), p. 350.   "that an . . . his deeds."—Irwin, *Doubling and Incest*, p. 61.   "more or . . . great-grandfather."—Murry C. Falkner, *The Falkners of Mississippi: A Memoir* (Baton Rouge: Louisiana State University Press, 1967), p. 6.

81 "I would . . . (nameless) table."—*Letters*, p. 222.   "I will . . . the books."—Ibid., p. 282.   "it is . . . printed books."—Ibid., p. 285.   "no outsider . . . reading it."—Ibid., p. 212.   "Maybe when . . . for myself."—Ibid.   "I secretly . . . coat-tails."—Blotner, *Faulkner*, p. 1200.

82 "The analyst . . . psychic apparatus."—Irwin, *Doubling and Incest*, p. 3.   "an oblique . . . direct action."—Ibid.

83 "to use . . . narration's existence."—Ibid., p. 4.   "multidimensional imaginative . . . other element."—Ibid., p. 7.   "interstitial."—Ibid., p. 6.   "then he . . . it, himself." —*Go Down, Moses* (New York: Random House, 1942), p. 254.   "rhetoric of retellings." —Lawrance Thompson, "Afterword" in *Sartoris* (New York: Signet-Harcourt Brace, 1964), p. 310.   "personal."—"William Faulkner's Essay on the Composition of *Sartoris*," *Yale University Library Gazette* 47 (January 1973): 123.

84 "spirit of . . . dead man."—*Sartoris* (1929; rpt. New York: Random House, 1956), p. 1. "every time . . . damn story."—Ibid., p. 20.   "the bowl . . . enduring stone."—Ibid., p. 2. "(This transfer . . . was shot.)"—See Duclos, *Son of Sorrow*, pp. 352-53.   "Through the . . . very pipe."—*Sartoris* (1956), pp. 19-20.   "That 'us . . . wine, Bayard."—Ibid., pp. 22-23.

85 "Bayard . . . outen hit."—Ibid., p. 236.

86 "yellow fever . . . bullet wound."—Ibid., p. 90.   "John Sartoris' effigy."—Ibid., p. 304.   "melancholy excision . . . and son."—Blotner, "The Falkners and the Fictional Families," p. 583.   "The twins' . . . the family."—*Faulkner in the University*, ed. Frederick L. Gwynn and Joseph L. Blotner (1959; rpt. New York: Vintage, 1965), p. 251.

87 "revenge on perfection."—*Sartoris* (1956), p. 178.   "take our . . . get it."—Ibid., p. 56.   "the long . . . natural life."—Ibid., p. 160.   "For man's . . . remember death." —Ibid., p. 375.   "This inscription . . . Sept. 4, 1876."—*Ibid.*, pp. 375-76.

88 "Old Bayard's . . . for him."—Ibid., p. 374.   "It may . . . contradict it."—Cleanth Brooks, *William Faulkner: The Yoknapatawpha Country* (New Haven: Yale University Press, 1963), pp. 100-101.

89 "In defeating . . . one's masculinity."—Irwin, *Doubling and Incest*, p. 58.   "begin with . . . in it."—*Faulkner in the University*, p. 285.   "you have . . . in here."—"William Faulkner's Essay on the Composition of *Sartoris*," p. 124.   "I realized . . . invented me." —Ibid.

90 "The desire . . . for incest."—*Irwin, Doubling and Incest*, p. 43.   "psychological castration."—Ibid., p. 68.   "For Quentin . . . the latter."—Ibid., p. 69.

91 "prove that . . . better narrator."—Ibid., p. 119.   "that emotion . . . for release." —"An Introduction for *The Sound and the Fury*," ed. James B. Meriwether, *Southern Review* 8 (Autumn 1972): 709.

92 "When I . . . write it."—Ibid.   "I would . . . the other."—*As I Lay Dying* (1930; rpt. New York: Random House, 1964), p. 165.   "a shape . . . a lack."—Ibid., p. 164.   "One day . . . little girl."—"An Introduction for *The Sound and the Fury*," p. 710.

93 "What Faulkner . . . of repetition."—Irwin, *Doubling and Incest*, p. 170.   "Because suddenly . . . remembered, bragged."—*Requiem for a Nun* (New York: Random House, 1950), pp. 153-54.

94 *"Maybe nothing . . . is finished."—Absalom, Absalom!*, p. 261.   "The Civil . . . of Verbena."—*Letters*, p. 100.

95 "a prolonged . . . and doom."—*The Unvanquished*, p. 4.   "As I . . . of horses." —Ibid., pp. 292-93.   "I did . . . for revenge."—Ibid., p. 167.

96 "murdering scoundrel."—Ibid., p. 213.   "Ain't I . . . told you?"—Ibid.   "I was . . . The Sartoris."—Ibid., p. 247.   *"one more . . . a child."*—Ibid., p. 203.   "relinquished along . . . he fell."—Ibid., p. 252.   "dream."—Ibid., p. 255.   "I know . . . not afraid." —Ibid., p. 276.

97 "one still . . . for cowardice."—Ibid., p. 250.   "You ain't . . . it again."—Ibid., p. 289. *"Who lives . . . by it."*—Ibid., p. 246.   "you will . . . of God's."—Ibid., p. 273.   "Kiss me . . . was free."—Ibid., p. 262.

98 "I must tell Father."—Ibid., p. 263.   "You are . . . be unarmed."—Ibid., p. 266.

99 "the empty . . . for doing."—Ibid., p. 272.

100 *"fathered himself."*—*Go Down, Moses*, p. 118.   "durable, ancestryless."—Ibid., p. 104.   "magnum o."—*Letters*, p. 233.   "I will . . . my son."—*A Fable* (New York: Random House, 1954), p. 348.

5. Generating Voice in A Death in the Family

101 "choose a name."—James Agee, *A Death in the Family* (New York: McDowell Obolensky, 1957), p. 174.   "Oh, it's . . . beyond words!"—Ibid., p. 175.   "I want . . . a draft."—Ibid., p. 251.

102 "Rufus seldom . . . assured, here."—Ibid., p. 19.   "There were . . . boy child." Ibid., p. 20.   "silence was . . . more pleasurable."—Ibid.   *"Well."*—Ibid., p. 21. "voice is . . . self-confrontation."—Leslie Brisman, *Milton's Poetry of Choice and Its Romantic Heirs* (Ithaca, N.Y.: Cornell University Press, 1973), p. 220.   "father's burial."—*Letters of James Agee to Father Flye* (Boston: Houghton Mifflin, 1971), p. 171.

103 "Ever any more."—James Agee, *The Morning Watch* (Boston: Houghton Mifflin, 1950), p. 120.   "Agee is . . . essential otherness."—Alfred T. Barson, *A Way of Seeing* (Amherst: University of Massachusetts Press, 1972), p. 24.   "I've betrayed . . . those years."—"Dream Sequence," *Texas Quarterly* 11 (Spring 1968): 45.   *"A Death . . .* and participant."—J. Douglas Perry, "Thematic Counterpoint in *A Death in the Family*: The Function of the Six Extra Scenes," *Novel* 5 (Spring 1972): 241.

104 "all his . . . and mastery."—"Dream Sequence," p. 46.   And here . . . right too." —Ibid.   "If it . . . Every-Family."—Allen Shepherd, "'A Sort of Monstrous Grinding Beauty': Reflections on Character and Theme in James Agee's *A Death in the Family*," *Iowa English Yearbook* 14 (Fall 1969): 20.   "looked towards . . . word, *dead."*—*A Death in the Family*, p. 311.   *"see-oh . . . and another."*—Ibid., p. 105.

105 *"We are talking now."*—Ibid., p. 3.   "Agee's narrative . . . are bridged."—James Sonoski, "Craft and Intention in James Agee's *A Death in the Family*, *Journal of General Education* 20 (1968): 178.   *"voices gentle . . . sleeping birds."*—*A Death in the Family*, pp. 7-8.   *"ever tell . . . I am."*—Ibid., p. 8.   "If a . . . that anxiety."—Brisman, *Milton's Poetry of Choice*, pp. 264-65.   *"What's your name?"*—*A Death in the Family*, p. 215. "Don't you brag."—Ibid., p. 17.

106 "silence . . . to speak."—Ibid., pp. 195-96.   "thought transference."—Ibid., p. 188. *"presence."*—Ibid., p. 187.   "It just . . . about it."—Ibid., p. 190.   "driving him away." —Ibid.   "persistent insect."—Ibid., p. 23.   "the voice . . . great distance."—Ibid., p. 115. "he knew . . . his lips."—Ibid., p. 138.   "He's dead . . . isn't he."—Ibid., p. 146.   "sacrilege."—Ibid., p. 190.   "we can all hear."—Ibid., p. 159.   "grandmaphone."—Ibid., p. 300.

107 "Uncle Andrew . . . to try."—Ibid.   "It required . . . a fish."—Ibid., p. 171.   "I would . . . did originally."—*Letters*, p. 117.   "He wished . . . to say."—*A Death in the Family*, p. 144.   "He feels . . . he felt."—Ibid.   "I've always . . . *communicate—clearly."* —Ibid., pp. 176-77.   "She felt . . . beyond utterance."—Ibid., p. 145.

108 "nothing to say."—Ibid., p. 35.   "regret of . . . his noise."—Ibid., p. 47.   *"An auto . . . its incompetence."*—Ibid., p. 81.   "RHRHRH . . . rk."—Ibid., p. 41.

109 "Father Jackson . . . a brook."—Ibid., p. 297.   "fathered children."—Ibid., p. 69.

"every tone . . . on others."—Ibid., p. 68.   *"First an . . . any violin."*—Ibid., pp. 4-5.

110 "I want . . . *write symphonies."*—*Letters*, p. 47.   *"carry on . . . set bridge."*—*A Death in the Family*, pp. 5-6.   *"The noises . . . precocious grandchild."*—Ibid., p. 6. *"the faint . . . blue dew."*—Ibid., p. 7.   "furious and annihilating words."—Ibid., p. 166. "Andrew could . . . thee lie."—Ibid., p. 206.   *"How still . . . his mind."*—Ibid., p. 207.

111 *"To the . . . far away."*—Ibid., p. 93.   "Don't you . . . you fret."—Ibid., p. 94. *"she must . . . could remember."*—Ibid., p. 49.   "words cannot . . . only describe."—James Agee and Walker Evans, *Let Us Now Praise Famous Men* (Boston: Houghton Mifflin, 1939), p. 238.

6. Robert Penn Warren: The Critic as Artist

113 "participate more . . . and immediately."—*Selected Essays* (New York: Random House, 1958), p. 25.   "in an . . . argued form."—Ibid., p. 24.   "it is . . . do it."—*The Artist as Critic: The Critical Writings of Oscar Wilde*, ed. Richard Ellmann (New York: Random House, 1968), p. 359.   *"I am me."*—*The Cave* (New York: Random House, 1959), p. 388.

114 "Something is . . . proclaim this."—*A Place to Come To* (New York: Random House, 1977), p. 5.   "exploration of . . . of homesickness."—Leonard Casper, *Robert Penn Warren* (Seattle: University of Washington Press, 1960), p. 170.   "Return."—*Paradise Lost*, 4.481.   *"imperium intellectūs."*—*A Place to Come To*, p. 63.   "I wrote . . . my formulations."—Ibid., p. 9.

115 "the passion . . . big ideas."—Ibid., p. 234.   "Those who . . . about it."—*The Unvanquished* (New York: Random House, 1938), p. 262.   "the death . . . even possible." —*A Place to Come To*, p. 221.

116 "What had . . . sleeping face."—Ibid., p. 228.   "the relation . . . of Time."—Ibid., p. 256.   "after all . . . long lost."—Ibid., p. 390.   "in thir . . . in men."—*Paradise Lost*, 4. 291-95.   "I was . . . came back."—*All the King's Men* (New York: Harcourt, Brace, 1946), p. 123.

117 "he unobserved . . . house returned."—*Paradise Regained*, 4. 638-39.   "in a . . . own reconciliation."—*Brother to Dragons* (New York: Random House, 1953), pp. 27-28. "I reckon . . . his obligations."—*Selected Poems: 1923-1975* (New York: Random House, 1976), p. 69.   "Anchises' son."—Ibid., p. 51.

118 "He must . . . he was."—*All the King's Men*, pp. 368-69.   "kill."—Ibid., see p. 370.

119 "I'm Perk . . . his cheek."—*A Place to Come To*, pp. 389-90.   "All she . . . in vain."—Ibid., p. 394.   "no too . . . to Ma."—Ibid., p. 397.

120 *"exemplum."*—Casper, *Robert Penn Warren*, p. 104.   "The Cass . . . throw away."—Blotner, *Faulkner*, p. 1214.   " . . . The frozen . . . terrible thing."—*Robert Penn Warren: A Collection of Critical Essays*, ed. John Lewis Longley, Jr. (New York: New York University Press, 1965), p. 33.

121 "That we . . . say'st thou?"—*Paradise Lost*, 5. 853.   "Explanations can . . . the end."—*World Enough and Time* (New York: Random House, 1950), p. 116.   "There will . . . see it."—*Selected Poems: 1923-1975*, p. 273.   "Poems are . . . life record."—*Selected Poems, Old and New: 1923-1966* (New York: Random House, 1966), p. vii.   "Both fiction . . . of experience."—*New York Times Book Review*, 9 January 1977, p. 22.   "I started . . . more *you."*—*Sewanee Review* 85 (Summer 1977): 474.

122 "This/Is . . . Of joy."—*Selected Poems: 1923-1975*, p. 34.   "Borne in . . . these feet."—Ibid., p. 325.

123 "Gabriel, Gabriel . . . too late."—*Thirty-six Poems* (New York: Alcestis Press, 1935), p. 28.   "such a . . . ruined world."—Victor H. Strandberg, *The Poetic Vision of Robert Penn Warren* (Lexington, Kentucky: University of Kentucky Press, 1977), p. 48.   "Moonlight falls . . . *good night."—Selected Poems: 1923-1975*, p. 256.

124 "But no . . . his love."—Ibid., p. 203.   "There was . . . a poem."—*New York Times Book Review*, 9 January 1977, p. 23.   "Delight is . . . be trusted."—*Selected Poems: 1923-1975*, p. 188.   "delight."—Ibid., p. 100.   "When my . . . of death."—Ibid., pp. 77-78.

125 "The form . . . its rhythm."—Longley, *Critical Essays*, p. 246.   "Season late . . . fluent silver."—*Selected Poems: 1923-1975*, p. 78. This and the following quotations from "Birth of Love" are found on pp. 78-80.

126 "the Eye . . . Heart knows."—William Blake, *Visions of the Daughters of Albion*.

128 "The Birth of Love."—*The New Yorker* 22 July 1974, p. 36.

7. Davies and the Middle of the Journey

129 "My disunion . . . destroy it."—C. G. Jung, *Memories, Dreams, Reflections* (1961; rpt. New York: Random House, 1973), p. 21.   "this possession . . . talk about."—Ibid., p. 22.   "earliest dream."—Ibid., p. 11.   "first conscious trauma."—Ibid., p. 10.

130 "between three . . . years old."—Ibid., p. 11.   "Suddenly I . . . the ground."—Ibid. "rectangular chamber . . . feet long."—Ibid., p. 12.   "Something was . . . motionlessly upward."—Ibid.   "might at . . . toward me."—Ibid.   "Yes, just . . . to death."—Ibid. "At about . . . same time."—Ibid., p. 11.   "a figure . . . my father."—Ibid., pp. 10-11. "that the . . . Catholic priest."—Ibid., p. 11.   "lifelong friend and enemy."—*Fifth Business* (1970; rpt. Middlesex, England: Penguin, 1977), p. 9.   "the unforeseen."—Ibid., p. 10. "I had . . . the snowball."—Ibid.

131 "suddenly there . . . of propriety."—Ibid., p. 11.   "I was . . . for me."—Ibid. "the baby . . . too soon."—Ibid., p. 23.   "No I don't."—Ibid.   "Everything was . . . I could."—Ibid., p. 103.   "rattling on . . . of that."—Ibid., p. 217.   "But the . . . small egg."—Ibid., p. 252.

132 "The story . . . the snowball."—Ibid., p. 263.   "old paperweight . . . it forever!" —Ibid., p. 264.   "my paperweight was gone."—Ibid., p. 265.   "Who killed Boy Staunton?"—Ibid., p. 266.   "He was . . . the stone."—Ibid.   "Don't you . . . her bedroom."—Ibid., pp. 35-36.   "I know . . . the surface."—Ibid., p. 36.

133 "unchancy."—Ibid., p. 32.   "scrupulosity in money matters."—Ibid., p. 207. "repository of secrets."—Ibid., p. 215.   "grim-mouthed . . . and cruel."—Ibid., p. 217. "God sits . . . cathedral asunder."—*Memories*, p. 39.   "With the . . . shaming experience." —Ibid., p. 41.   "an overwhelming . . . to speak."—Ibid.   "It would . . . carved manikin."—Ibid.   "great achievement . . . with anyone."—Ibid.

134 "I was . . . imperishable stone."—Ibid., p. 42.   "Only much . . . ritual phallus." —Ibid., p. 12.   "Ultimately, the . . . in life."—Ibid., p. 23.   "it is . . . a *numinosum."* —Ibid., p. 356.   "When I . . . hewed stone."—Ibid., p. 175.   "fragment of . . . of satisfaction."—Ibid., p. 174.   "Christ."—Ibid., p. 210.   "a confession of faith."—Ibid., p. 223.   "incomprehensible to others."—Ibid., p. 228.   "a feeling . . . in stone."—Ibid., p. 225.   "I could . . . were identical."—Ibid., p. 12.

135 "dream is . . . lies hidden."—Ibid., p. 161.   "something that . . . get at"?—Ibid.,
p. 22.   "She always . . . my character."—Ibid., p. 25.   "might have communicated."
—Ibid., p. 48.   "consisted of . . . and frightening."—Ibid., pp. 48-49.   "lecture, spiced
. . . her before."—Ibid., p. 49.   "compassion."—Ibid., p. 24.   "pity."—Ibid., p. 55.
"fisher king."—Ibid., p. 215.

136 "I have . . . serious child."—Ibid., p. 31.   "I had . . . had vanished."—Ibid.,
pp. 32-33.   "this recovery . . . 'successfully' resolved."—Thomas Weiskel, *The Romantic
Sublime: Studies in the Structure and Psychology of Transcendence* (Baltimore: Johns
Hopkins University Press, 1976), p. 75.   "archaic and ruthless."—*Memories*, p. 50.
"Mother is . . . my secret."—*The Collected Works of C. G. Jung*, trans. R.F.C. Hull, vol. 9
(New York: Pantheon, 1954), p. 92.   "Freudians."—Robertson Davies, *The Manticore*
(1972; rpt. Middlesex, England: Penguin, 1976), p. 70.   "Freud has . . . about that."
—Robertson Davies, *World of Wonders* (1975; rpt. Middlesex, England: Penguin, 1977),
p. 34.   ("5:58 o'clock . . . December 1908.)"—*Fifth Business*, p. 9.

137 "My lifelong . . . Dempster began."—Ibid.   "one of . . . call synchronicities."
—Ibid., p. 126.   "The snowball . . . Dempster simple."—Ibid., p. 25.   "a world of
wonder."—Ibid., p. 43.   "when Percy . . . was vindictive."—Ibid., p. 9.   "guilty and
strange."—Ibid., p. 12.   "I was . . . a child."—Ibid., p. 24.   "I never . . . no pity."
—Ibid., p. 44.

138 "Joseph . . . celebrated cuckold."—Ibid., p. 172.   "the odd . . . other sex."—Ibid.,
p. 227.   "Every view . . . is *symbolic.*"—*The Basic Writings of C. G. Jung*, ed. Violet
Staub de Laszlo (New York: Random House, 1959), p. 275.

139 "the manifest . . . the myth."—Ernest Jones, *The Life and Work of Sigmund Freud*
(New York: Basic Books, 1955), 2: 452-53.   "an expression . . . yet unknown."—de
Laszlo, *The Basic Writings of C. G. Jung*, p. 275.   "From the . . . to *symbols.*"—Paul
Ricoeur, *Freud and Philosophy* (New Haven: Yale University Press, 1970), p. 27.

140 "Not a . . . conjurer's art."—*Fifth Business*, p. 211.   "frowzy rough-and-tumble."
—Ibid., p. 41.   "There are . . . a word."—*World of Wonders*, p. 212.

141 "giving things away."—Ibid., p. 16.   "What was . . . and cozy."—Ibid.   "en-
riching, but . . . seen."—Ibid.   "I have . . . to sleep."—Ibid., pp. 22-23.

142 "Agnes Day . . . Doe (libido)."—See Wilfred Cude, "Miracle and Art in *Fifth
Business* or Who the Devil is Liselotte Vitzlipützli?" *Journal of Canadian Studies* 9 (November
1974): 16. The names are found in *Fifth Business*, p. 118.   "I could . . . readily enough."
—*Fifth Business*, p. 124.   "to the . . . collective unconscious."—*Memories*, p. 158.   "idea
of . . . small potato."—Ibid., p. 37.   "I knew . . . eating me."—Ibid., p. 81.   "to eat."
—*World of Wonders*, p. 307.   "swallowed the pill."—Ibid., p. 304.   "to devour me "
—Ibid., p. 307.   "the least . . . the demons."—Ibid., 295.

143 "a hearty middle age."—*The Table Talk of Samuel Marchbanks* (Toronto: Clarke,
Irwin, 1949), pp. 247-48.   "for something . . . never happens."—*Autobiographies* (London:
Macmillan, 1955), p. 106.   "the quality . . . a death."—*Question Time* (Toronto:
Macmillan, 1975), p. 66.

144 "the major . . . Canadian Literature."—Claude Bissel, "The World of the Master,"
Canadian Forum 55 (December-January 1975/76): 31.   "final fascinating . . . Monica
Gall."—Geraldine Anthony, *Stage Voices* (Toronto: Doubleday, 1978), p. 58.   "for the
. . . action unfold."—Hugo McPherson, "The Mask of Satire," *Canadian Literature* 4
(Spring 1960): 28.   "A book . . . look out."—*A Voice from the Attic* (1960; rpt. New
York: Viking, 1972), p. v.   "was gathering . . . literary life."—Anthony, *Stage Voices*,
p. 58.

145 "it took . . . write it."—letter from Robertson Davies to David Wyatt, 4 May, 1978.

"What is . . . his hands."—*One Half of Robertson Davies* (New York: Viking, 1977), pp. 127-28.   "and I . . . to do."—Ibid., p. 131.   "rejected our . . . have foreseen."—*Fifth Business*, p. 262.   "the death . . . man's life."—*The Manticore*, p. 11.

146 "as my . . . father's death."—Jones, *Sigmund Freud*, 1: 324.   "the kind . . . it yourself."—*World of Wonders*, p. 312.   "sort of monkey,"—Ibid., p. 280.   "I am . . . Paul Dempster."—*The Manticore*, p. 287.   "educated."—*World of Wonders*, p. 20.

147 "But what's . . . the hero."—Ibid., p. 257.   "I suppose . . . have been."—Ibid., p. 20.   "He has . . . a villain."—Ibid., p. 138.   "that a . . . to death."—Ibid., p. 258. "name of . . . might do."—Ibid., p. 306.   "there must . . . of action."—Ibid., p. 287.   "understood time."—Ibid., p. 271.   "uncertainty whether . . . of uncanniness."—*Creativity and the Unconscious*, p. 136.

148 "We must . . . the self."—Ibid., pp. 140-41.   "Fetch."—*World of Wonders*, p. 188. "such ideas . . . the child."—*Creativity and the Unconscious*, p. 141.   invention of . . . against extinction."—Ibid.   "When your . . . your life."—*World of Wonders*, p. 90.

149 "eighty days in Paradise."—Ibid., p. 314.   "I was . . . of mine?"—Ibid.   "the elementary . . . a birth."—*Question Time*, p. 66.   "a Christ . . . old man."—*Fifth Business*, p. 176.   "The fathers . . . significant ones."—*The Manticore*, p. 289.   "A man . . . into being."—*The Collected Works of C. G. Jung*, 7: 45.   "Where there's . . . two ways." —*World of Wonders*, p. 316.

Epilogue: Career as Canon

152 "I have . . . to stray."—Stanley Kunitz, *The Poems of Stanley Kunitz* (Boston-Toronto: Little, Brown, 1979), p. 35.

Index

The Johns Hopkins University Press

This book was composed in Alphatype Palatino text and display type by David Lorton. It was printed and bound by Universal Lithographers Incorporated.

Library of Congress Cataloging in Publication Data

Wyatt, David
  Prodigal sons.

  Includes bibliographical references and index.
    1. American literature — 20th century — History and
criticism.   2. Fathers and sons in literature.
3. Psychoanalysis and literature.   4. English literature
— Irish authors — History and criticism.   I. Title.
PS228.F38W9   810'.9'3   79-22930
ISBN 0-8018-2325-0